Three Wise Men from the East

The Cappadocian Fathers and the Struggle for Orthodoxy

— PATRICK WHITWORTH —

Sacristy Press

Sacristy Press
PO Box 612, Durham, DH1 9HT

www.sacristy.co.uk

First published in 2015 by Sacristy Press, Durham

Copyright © Patrick Whitworth 2015
The moral rights of the author have been asserted

All rights reserved. No part of this publication may be reproduced or transmitted in any form or by any means, electronic, mechanical photocopying, documentary, film or in any other format without prior written permission of the publisher.

All scripture quotations, unless otherwise indicated, are taken from the Holy Bible, New International Version®, NIV®. Copyright © 1973, 1978, 1984, 2011 by Biblica, Inc.™ Used by permission of Zondervan. All rights reserved worldwide. www.zondervan.com The "NIV" and "New International Version" are trademarks registered in the United States Patent and Trademark Office by Biblica, Inc.™

Every reasonable effort has been made to trace the copyright holders of material reproduced in this book, but if any have been inadvertently overlooked the publisher would be glad to hear from them.

Sacristy Limited, registered in England & Wales, number 7565667

British Library Cataloguing-in-Publication Data
A catalogue record for the book is available from the British Library

ISBN 978-1-908381-17-0

*Dedicated to Henry Chadwick, Dean of
Christ Church, Oxford 1969–1979*

Black Sea
Constantinople
Thessalonica
Calchedon
Nicomedia
Nicaea
Sinope
Annisa
Neocaesarea
Nicopolis
Sebaste
Pergamum
Smyrna
Ephesus
Iconium
Nyssa
Nazianzus
Caesarea
Tyana
Athens
Miletus
Samosata
Antioch
CRETE
CYPRUS
Salamis
N
Mediterranean Sea
Damascus
Alexandria
Jerusalem

Foreword

For most students of theology and of early Christian history, the names of the three "Cappadocian Fathers"—Basil of Caesarea, Gregory Nazianzen and Gregory of Nyssa—are fairly familiar as defenders of what came to be recognised as orthodox teaching on the Trinity. But it is surprising how few books treat their thought and their lives overall. An enormous amount of excellent research on each of them as individuals and on specific aspects of their thinking has been done and continues to appear, with no sign of drying up, but there are few introductions that help us see them whole.

This is exactly what Patrick Whitworth has provided in this wonderfully comprehensive and clear survey. We are able to see the Cappadocians not as counters in the board game of controversy but as complex human figures wrestling with the challenges of internal and external crises for the Church, exploring how the Church can best serve the needs of a suffering and conflicted society, searching out the depths of contemplative experience to offer a path into the luminous darkness of God for those who are hungry for authentic encounter with the mystery that theology points to and never masters. Part of the fascination of the Cappadocians has always been the way they bring together theology, spiritual practice, biblical interpretation, and social witness, and this book does ample justice to all these aspects of their work. The figures who emerge here are definitely three-dimensional, not fodder for the textbook. And the context, in both political and intellectual history, is sketched in with a very sure hand.

This will be a really welcome tool for all students of early Christianity, and is excellent and accessible reading for anyone who wants to understand better the formative period of Christian teaching. Above all, it shows that there should be no gulf between reflection on the highest mysteries of the faith and the most practical details of pastoral and spiritual nurture: each feeds the other. It is a message that the Church of our own time should take very seriously.

Rowan Williams
Master of Magdalene College, Cambridge

Preface

Two and half years ago in May 2012 with two travelling companions, Paul Bright and Tom Peryer, I went on a pilgrimage to Cappadocia and then to Istanbul (Constantinople), where our wives joined us. Cappadocia is referred to in the New Testament and there is plenty of evidence of a thriving Christian Community there in Byzantine period. But "nothing beside remains" of it now, except for the tell-tale buildings of churches and monasteries. Practising Christian faith seems to have been long since swept away, but it was from this region that the Cappadocian Fathers came in the fourth century. One of them, Basil the Great, is still remembered in Kyaseri, and there is, apparently, an annual feast day for him still in a Muslim society.

Going to Cappadocia, together with previous reading, has helped to inspire this book, which I hope will be the middle volume in three books on the Early Church—from the Apostolic period to the Council of Chalcedon in AD 451, and its aftermath. Three hundred and fifty years of extraordinary change that formed our contemporary world, shaped the Church, the Middle East, Europe, and the world beyond. Orthodox understanding of the Christian faith was established then, and it has been foundational ever since. But for most people, and for most Christians, that period is a dim and distant past of which we have only a vague awareness. And today, in a culture not noted for its knowledge of the past, it may seem like an irrelevance where the ever-present dominates, whether through social media or current affairs.

Most travellers who travel by car today, before setting out on their journey, either Google their route or set their satnav; I prefer a bump of locality and a map! Indeed, ancient sailors and travellers alike, even certain Wise Men who arrived at a stable in Bethlehem after the birth of Christ, were guided by the stars.

The fourth century will seem like a very unfamiliar world with interminable wrangling over the meaning of Greek words, fierce conflicts and an equally fierce and ascetic spiritualties pursued in the wild fastness of the desert, where only burning heat could be easily found. As travellers in time, we might be tempted to turn back to the familiarity of the twenty-first century. So let me give you three stars to guide by.

The first star is <u>solitude</u>. Invariably the great leaders of the Church sought solitude, or the *philosophic life* as they called it. Together with solitude went a piety, which valued highly contemplation, prayer, renunciation of the world, virginity, and the stretching of the soul in pursuance of knowing God. This was true for the Cappadocians, Basil, Gregory and Gregory, whom we will meet and get to know. There in their chosen places of solitude, they could pray, fast, seek God, and encourage the ascent of their souls. It was their way or ordering and re-ordering their lives, both a re-orientating of their soul and a source of inspiration. Not only was this true for the Cappadocians but also for their great contemporaries: Athanasius and Anthony, Augustine, Jerome, Cassian, and many others. They were all given to solitude. It is a star for us to follow in understanding their lives

The second star is <u>struggle</u>. There was a struggle then for a true faith, for orthodoxy. The Greek mind was highly disciplined, speculative, and very analytical. It had been trained over eight centuries and more in philosophical enquiry, and, especially since Socrates and Plato in the fifth and fourth centuries BC, in using the finely tuned Greek language as its vehicle of understanding. Words were all important; reflection, rhetoric, and expression familiar tools. Latin and Roman writers had only added to this Greek base. And now in this context of historic enquiry the Christian faith was hammered out: how was the Son like the Father, how was the Spirit like the Son, how was the Trinity both distinct persons but of one substance? After the Nicene Creed and Council of Nicaea, these debates through which the Christian faith would be expressed in the future, turned on literally an *o* or an *i*, as we shall see. And these debates were hammered out in the teeth of Imperial power like Luther in the sixteenth century. The Cappadocians were at the forefront of this struggle, building on the bulwark of Athanasius' defence of the Son's full divinity, who was of the same substance with the Father. When confronting unfamiliar Greek terms, which seem arcane or abstruse, remember to look for the star of struggle. A struggle was needed to hold onto what was true, as expressed in the Scriptures.

Lastly there is the star of service. The Cappadocians were monk-bishops; at the heart of their discipleship was renunciation. They gave up to serve their fellow humans. They did this in their teaching and in their caring: in caring for the poor, in being advocates of their needs to Imperial officials and even the Emperor himself, and in founding institutions such as the *Basileiados* in Caesarea. Basil made sure the poor were at the heart of his ministry. The Cappadocians washed the feet of the poor and gave their inheritance to care for them. The star of service guided them.

If in immersing ourselves in the fourth century we are guided by these stars of solitude, struggle, and service we shall never be far from the heartbeat of their ministry and find points of contact between them and ourselves. These stars guided them and can also guide us: in reading, understanding, and living.

I would like to thank all those who have helped in the production of the book, and of conceiving of this project: Henry Chadwick, who was the Dean when I was at the House, Christ Church Oxford; Professor Mark Edwards, Student of the House and teacher of Patristics at the University of Oxford, who read my text and offered many helpful steers, and saved me from many pitfalls; the congregation of All Saints Weston for giving me time to write and travel; the team at Sacristy Press for their support; Gay Ridley for helping with the Bibliography; Ros Smallwood for the map; and my wife Olivia for her generous support and patience. It goes without saying that all the infelicities, mistakes, and oversights are entirely mine.

Patrick Whitworth
All Saints Day 2014 (especially remembering the Cappadocians)

Contents

Foreword v
Preface vii

Chapter 1: Tumultuous Times: The World of Church and Empire in the Fourth Century 1

Part I: The Struggle for Orthodoxy 17
Chapter 2: Through the Platonic Lens: The World of Hellenic Ideas . 19
Chapter 3: The Benchmark of Nicaea 36
Chapter 4: Contending for the Trinity: the Contribution of the Cappadocians 55
Chapter 5: The Cappadocians and the Spirit 85

Part II: The Orthopraxy of the Cappadocians 105
Chapter 6: Being Ourselves 107
Chapter 7: Social Justice and the Monastic Life 124
Chapter 8: The Ascent of the Soul 139
Chapter 9: The Work of a Bishop 166
Chapter 10: The Cappadocians and the Struggle for Orthodoxy ... 190

Conclusion 203

Brief chronologies of the Cappadocian Fathers 205
Glossary 207
Notes 209
Bibliography 224
Index 227

CHAPTER 1

Tumultuous Times: The World of Church and Empire in the Fourth Century

On Whitsunday in AD 337, the Imperial guard took the body of the dead Emperor and laid him in a golden coffin draped with a pall of imperial purple. They bore it from Nicomedia in the south-eastern corner of the Sea of Marmara to Constantinople, the newly founded eponymous capital. There Constantine lay in state in his palace, "surrounded by brightly burning candlesticks, guarded day and night by palace officials".[1]

Only weeks before, at Easter, Constantine had become ill. Sensing the imminence of his death, he felt "he should seek purification from sins of his past career, firmly believing that whatever errors he had committed as a mortal man, he would be purified from them through the efficacy of the mystical words and saving waters of Baptism".[2] Proceeding to Nicomedia, he summoned the Greek bishops and four bishops from the Latin West, led by Eusebius of Nicomedia, and told them, "The hour is come in which I too may have the blessing of the seal which confers immortality; the hour in which I may receive salvation".[3] Having relinquished wearing imperial purple for pure white, he was baptised and died soon afterwards; the "first of all sovereigns who was regenerated and perfected in a church dedicated to the martyrs of Christ".[4]

He was extravagantly and publicly mourned. Eusebius records that "[his death was] received with universal manifestations of grief, and his reign was regarded as continuing after his death . . . his funeral which took place in Constantinople was a magnificent spectacle".[5] With his second son Constantius at the head of the funeral procession, Constantine was

1

laid to rest in the splendour of his newly finished mausoleum next to the church of the Holy Apostles in Constantinople. Constantine's life ended amidst memorials to the Apostles, and in years to come, in the Eastern Church, Constantine was considered their equal.

The Roman Empire, both huge and vulnerable at the time of Constantines' death, began the process of decline which would see its break up in less than a hundred years. Following his accession as Emperor at York in 306, Constantine had proceeded to take the Western Empire at the Battle of Milvian Bridge outside Rome (312), after the famous dream in which he received a vision of Christ. Constantine then combined both Eastern and Western Empires after his defeat of Licinius, the ruler of the Eastern Empire, founding the new capital of the Roman Empire, sometimes called the new Rome. The sheer size of the Empire, together with the varied threats that surrounded it, made ruling both east and west together virtually impossible. The centralised political power of a Hadrian or even a Marcus Aurelius was no longer available, and the days of the Republic were as distant then as the Tudors are to us today. Constantine himself envisaged the splitting of the Empire into three. Each of his three sons, who had been made *Caesars* during their father's reign, were to rule different parts as *Augustii*; each inheriting a third of the Empire.

Constantine II, the eldest son, took Gaul, Spain and Britain; Constans the youngest would take Illyricum, Moesia, Italy and Africa; Constantius took the whole of the east. This state of affairs was only temporary. Constantine II was defeated and killed by his brother Constans' troops at Aquileia in 340, and some years later Constans fell victim to a usurper, Magnentius, who raised his rebellious standard at Autun in 350. Magnentius was a new breed of usurper; a man of barbarian origins whose family had settled on Roman lands.[6] Constantius, the only surviving son, focused on combating the Persian threat from the east, eventually turned his attention to Magnentius, whom he faced at Mursa on 28 September 351.[7] It was a battle of epic proportions: Magnentius lost two thirds of his men and Constantius half. It marked the start of a long drawn out campaign against Magnentius, who survived to fight again in Gaul, Italy, and North Africa. The end finally came on 10 August 353 when, fugitive and defeated, Magnentius committed suicide. Constantius took sole charge of the Empire for eight years. Like his eventual successor, Theodosius

(379–395), Constantius managed to keep the Empire temporarily unified. However, the process of disintegration both from civil war and external attack ultimately proved too hard to resist.

By the fourth century, the Empire of Caesar was unrecognisable. The centres of power had shifted from Rome itself to other emerging Roman cities like Milan, Trier, and Constantinople. Though still grand and bloated, Rome was far from the administrative or political hub it had once been. Power had dissipated, and retaining any unitary structure was nigh impossible. The size of Rome at its height—over a million inhabitants—made its life almost unsupportable: excavations in Carthage by UNESCO show the size of the docks needed to service the grain ships bound for Rome and its gargantuan appetite for bread.[8]

By the fourth century, the old Senatorial families, numbering some 900, had been weakened by their commitment to monogamous marriage and subsequent lack of heirs—statistics show that in monogamous marriage "20 per cent will produce no heirs and a further 20 per cent all girls".[9] Moreover, the refined Roman education as espoused by Symmachus *et al.*, concentrated on a narrow literary tradition which could not provide preparation for the changing world of the fourth and fifth centuries.[10] Focusing exclusively on the writings of Virgil, Cicero, Sallust, and Terence so as to express everyday occurrences in their style could not prepare young Romans for the complexities of ruling an Empire with new and unforeseen problems. There was a nostalgic sense amongst such conservative and traditional rulers of 'la recherche du temps perdu"!

The administration of the Empire had, unsurprisingly, changed greatly down the years. In 249 there were still only 250 senior bureaucratic functionaries in the whole Empire, but by 400 there were 6,000.[11] Most now operated in the key imperial headquarters from which the frontiers were managed, as the Empire's survival became increasingly dependent on the control and defence of its frontiers. As ever more tribes amassed on the Rhine or Danube to cross into the Empire to either destroy or settle or both, the Roman army found itself increasingly stretched and extended.

The decline, and eventual fall, of the Empire in the period which is covered by much of this book was far from inevitable given the residual strength of the army. Indeed some Emperors like Theodosius would show that, for a while at least, its internal contradictions and external pressures could be kept at bay; especially if they could raise armies of sufficient size and experience and lead them effectively. However, for most of the fourth century the Empire would face regular breaches of its frontiers on its north-eastern borders. At the same time, the prize of subjugating Persia made for some expensive and time consuming campaigns led by Theodosius, Julian, and Valens, designed to neutralise their threat and secure Armenia. But the incursions of the Goths, Sarmatians, Alamani, Quadi, and Vandals, and later the Huns, from across the Rhine and Danube, provided frequent warfare in most Emperors' reigns in the fourth and early fifth century.

The eventual sack of Rome in 410 had numerous precedents. According to the historian Ammianus Marcellinus, in the summer of 376 some 200,000 refugees arrived on the north bank of the Danube. These Goths—who in turn had been pushed eastwards by the new power in the region, the Huns, desperately sought new lands to settle, and these could only be found within the borders of the Roman Empire. Arriving as nomads from the Great Eurasian Steppe, a huge expanse of land stretching from the fringes of Europe to the borders of China, the Huns would soon come to dominate thanks to their fast horses, lightening cavalry charges, and their versatile and lethal bows and arrows, tipped with "sharp bone".[12] By moving further east, and so forcing the Goths to seek asylum within the Empire, they precipitated an inevitable conflict with Rome.

In the fourth century the empire's army totalled between 300,000 and 600,000 men: a formidable force.[13] It was taken from a population of some 70 million. The Goths, some of whose tribes numbered 200,000, could not realistically produce an army of more than 40,000. There could seemingly be only one winner. But circumstances, surprise, and ambition delivered a different result. Two Gothic tribes, the Tervingi and Greuthungi, who increasingly needed food, gathered in 376 on the Danube before moving across the river into present day southern Bulgaria. As they were not yet settled permanently they were unable to produce significant quantities of food and so were spurred on by hunger. The tension was increased when the Roman commander Lupicinus deceived some of their leaders, killing many of their commanders at a feast.[14]

In late winter 377, war began in earnest. Fritigern, the leader of the Goths, engaged the Romans, defeating Lupicinus. In response, the eastern emperor, Valens, left off his Persian campaign while the western emperor, Gratian, sent his field army to join with Valens, but the two armies remained uncoordinated. Valens marched into Thrace with some 15,000 troops in August 378 to engage the Goths. His exhausted troops, confined by the terrain and surprised by the more numerous Goths, were comprehensively defeated at Adrianople and the Emperor Valens was killed. Thereafter the Goths were seemingly intimidated by the walls and defences of Constantinople and never pressed home their advantage.[15] The Empire had suffered a great defeat, and it was a premonition of worse to come in the fifth century when Alaric's Goths would take Rome and the Vandals destroy Roman North Africa. Theodosius allowed the Goths to settle within the Empire with Goths agreeing to fight in the Roman army. The Empire was weakened, and after the death of Theodosius, who latterly ruled both east and west, it was more vulnerable to attack.

This period, from the death of Constantine to the start of Theodosius' reign following the defeat at Adrianople, coincides with a parallel struggle not between the Empire and the surrounding tribes, but between parties in the Church involved in a long lasting and sometimes bitter struggle between heresy and orthodoxy. This lasted from the Council of Nicaea in 325 to the Council of Constantinople in 381, the latter of which was overseen by Gregory of Nazianzus, who was, for a time, Bishop and Metropolitan of Constantinople. It is this struggle for the heart of the Christian faith that allowed the "three wise men" to make a significant contribution to the victory for orthodoxy, just when Roman armies were all but overwhelmed by foreign invaders.

The Church at the Start of the Fourth Century

In his farewell address to the Ephesian Elders on the beach of Miletus, the Apostle Paul warned that the Church would be attacked by "savage wolves" who "will come in among you, not sparing the flock. Some even from your own group will come distorting the truth in order to entice the disciples to follow them".[16] Like the Empire as a whole, the Church would be subject to violent and unremitting pressures both from without and within. From the outset the Church in Jerusalem was subject to persecution, first from the Sanhedrin objecting to the preaching of Christ as being both raised from the dead and the Son of God,[17] and then later from the Roman Empire itself which saw the Church either as a disturber of the religious *status quo* or as a disloyal part of the Empire unwilling to give full allegiance to the Emperor. However, both King Agrippa and Festus, the Roman Governor in Caesarea, found there was no charge they could bring against Paul, nor any punishment, whether imprisonment or death, of which he was deserving.[18] Nonetheless, because of his appeal to Caesar, Paul was sent to Rome for trial. In the persecution that broke out under Nero, according to tradition, both leading Apostles, Peter and Paul, were executed. Increasingly, the Church found itself the victim of persecution for its unusual characteristics: its pacifism, its dislike of the games or gladiatorial fights, its unwillingness to sacrifice to the Emperor, its eschewing of all pagan worship, its preaching of Christ as the *only* Lord.

This persecution of the Church came in waves. It was not uniform throughout the three hundred years in which Christianity was mostly proscribed in the Empire, neither in Judea nor later in the provinces of the Empire. There were peaks and troughs of persecution, notably in the late first century in the province of Asia, and then in a protracted period from the mid-second century to the mid-third century. These persecutions accounted for the death of several bishops: Polycarp of Smyrna, Ignatius of Antioch, Telesphorus of Rome. If a scapegoat was required for defeats, mishaps, or bad harvests alike then the Christians, with their apparently peaceful acquiescence to suffering which constituted a cardinal virtue in their faith, were never far from arrest. It was then that Tertullian said with his waspish humour, "If the Tiber rises too high or the Nile too low, the cry is 'The Christians to the lion'. All of them to a single lion?"[19] The persecution grew worse in North Africa in the mid-third century and throughout the Empire in the final years of the third century under Diocletian before the great reversal of the Church's political fortune under Constantine.

Persecution was rife in third-century North Africa under the Emperor Decius' rule, just as in the French Rhone valley nearly a century earlier during the reign of Marcus Aurelius. Decius demanded that everyone provide a certificate (*libellus*) that he had sacrificed to the gods. So great was the persecution that many lapsed. Cyprian of Carthage went into hiding and was later martyred under the Emperor Valerian in 258. But even before his death division had arisen on how to treat the *lapsed,* a division which has echoed through the Church ever since. The question of how far the Church can accommodate the demands of the state, or when it is right or warranted to resist it, continues to this day. Examples can be found in the modern era in Communist Russia and, indeed, currently in China. Whilst in the Church of the Eastern Empire the point of resistance revolved around the demand by provincial governors and magistrates that Christians sacrifice to the gods, in North Africa the issue was whether churches should hand over sacred texts to the authorities or agree not to meet publicly for worship. Mensurius, Bishop of Carthage, agreed not to meet and "he satisfied the friendly police with heretical volumes".[20] His compliance attracted bitter criticism. For others, including Cyprian, such compliance put a person outside the true Church and rendered their ministries ineffectual.

After Mensurius' death, rival bishops were consecrated. Caecilian, previously Archdeacon to Mensurius, was bitterly opposed by Majorinus and his successor Donatus for his compliance with the authorities. But Caecilian was reconciled to Rome by giving up Cyprian's sacramental theology that the ministry of the lapsed could never be authentic. A previous Bishop of Rome, Stephen, had strongly maintained that the authenticity of the sacraments depended not upon the orthodoxy or character of the minister using them but on the validity of the sacrament itself; a view which Augustine was later to endorse.

But lines of dispute with Rome were drawn up, with Constantine and the Catholic Church ranged on one side and the "purer" intransigent Donatist Church of North Africa on the other. This led to two separate Churches in North Africa which was a central issue of Church discipline for Augustine as Bishop of Hippo, near Carthage, and in 412 "a tariff of exceptionally heavy fines were applied to laymen of all classes who failed to join the Catholic Church."[21] The division of the Church in North Africa was a consequence of persecution and disagreement over the proper way to react. Such disputes weakened the Church and made it more susceptible to the apparent certainties and simple clarity of Islam.

Just as the Roman Empire was weakened by the civil war which followed the arrival of usurpers like Magnentius in the reign of Constantius and Magnus Maximus in reign of Theodosius, so too the Church spent much of the first four centuries contradicting and dealing with heresies, just as Paul had said on the beach of Miletus.

In this sense the history of the church paralleled that of the Empire. Heresy, or to put it more positively, the struggle for orthodoxy, is never far from the Church's life. The word heresy is derived from a transliteration of the Greek word for "choice", *hairesis*. The word came to mean "a school of thought" or philosophical tendency, but even in the New Testament it had a more pejorative overtone for a sect, part, or faction.[22] As Chadwick observes, "The term, especially after Justin in the mid-second century, could indicate both a doctrine and the group asserting it".[23]

From the era of the New Testament we can see the existence, both within Judaism and Christianity, of different factions or parties holding to different doctrinal or ethical assertions within the broad tradition of their own faith. In Judaism there existed the Pharisees—with its own differing parties represented by Gamaliel and Hillel—and the Sadducees, the community at Qumran, and the Essenes. In the early Church the main fault lines were between the tectonic plates of Judaism and the followers of the Way, with their new found freedom from the Law or Torah.[24] The extent to which Judaism was to be part of the practice of the Christian faith and in particular its observance of the Sabbath, its practise of circumcision, and its observance of the Law, was a matter of critical importance, as we can see from Paul's Letters to the Galatians. They were in danger of overturning their new found freedom in Christ and going back to a slavish observance of the Law in the hope of finding salvation thereby.[25] This issue was settled formally for the Church by the Council of Jerusalem in *c.* AD 49, but undoubtedly it was not so easily or finally resolved.

With this early dispute a pattern was set which would often be repeated. A doctrine or practice was advocated by a group seeking either to re-interpret the faith or impose a practise upon it followed by a controversy, long or short, then settled by a council of the Church. Opposing such "heresies" was critical to the well-being and mission of the Church but it absorbed enormous energy: intellectual, moral, and spiritual. The greatest of these struggles was the Arian controversy over the doctrine of the Trinity whose settlement would take nearly a hundred years.

Before the Arian controversy broke fully at the beginning of the fourth century, the Church had already been thrown into a number of vehement disputes with various heresies over the previous two centuries. These disputes with the Gnostics, the Marcionites, and the Montanists of North Africa, as well as with those holding different views of the Father and Son expressed in the so called Monarchian controversy of the third century, were doctrinal skirmishes in the main campaign and battle caused by the Arian controversy which spanned most of the fourth century.

Towards the end of the apostolic era, the Gnostic heresy was well underway. John found himself writing squarely against its anti-material stance by insisting in the prologue of the gospel that the Word took on flesh[26] and that those who say that Jesus only *seemed* to come in the flesh were of the evil one.[27] Gnosticsm to Irenaeus of Lyons was "a ragbag of heathen speculations with bits taken from different philosophers to dress out a bogus and antirational mythology".[28] Gnostics looked for a spark of knowledge (*gnosis*) which explained how evil had entered the world through some grand and highly speculative scheme and how deliverance might be gained from it. The content of the Gnostic gospel was an attempt to rouse the soul from its sleep-walking condition and to make it aware of the high destiny to which it was called.[29]

The corollary of this was to seek freedom from the body by saying that what was done in it was unimportant, or conversely, to so loath the flesh that stringent ascetic rules were made to govern all its desires so that, for instance, marriage was despised as simply a concession to sexual desire, itself suspect. Furthermore, Gnostics sought freedom from all obligations to civic and human institutions which were regarded with deep scepticism. Such a collection of beliefs could lead either to irresponsibility because of a false notion of freedom or to an asceticism that robbed adherents of natural God-given pleasure. Its main opponents from within the Church were Irenaeus and Justin.

Justin was well versed in Platonic understanding from his philosophical studies in Ephesus c.AD 135, and he equated the transcendent God of Plato, beyond human comprehension, with the God of the Bible. The Father for Justin is God transcendent; the *logos* is God immanent. The divine *logos* both inspired the prophets of the Old Testament and was in some way present where true wisdom and reason were to be found in the world. Unlike the Gnostics, Justin affirmed the goodness of creation as the work of the supreme Creator. Human salvation for Justin did not consist in the deliverance of an immortal soul from a physical frame but rather through the *logos* assuming a complete human entity: body, soul, and mind. Such teaching, which was affirmative of much of Platonic teaching and the Greek philosophical tradition while contrary to the Gnostics, was influential in Alexandria, particularly on Clement, and later in Cappadocian theology. Justin was a graceful and elegant defender of orthodoxy who, in the end, suffered martyrdom.

Irenaeus also opposed Gnosticism in a remarkably fair minded way. His work *Against Heresies* (one of only two extant works by Irenaeus, the other being *Presentation of the Apostolic Teaching*) was entitled by its author, *The Refutation and Overthrowing of the So-called "Knowledge"*. In it Irenaeus presented a remarkably coherent structure to his theology, seeing the new covenant and the coming of Christ as a "recapitulation" of the original creation, so what was lost in the fall was restored by redemption. "In Christ the divine Word assumed the humanity such as Adam possessed before the fall . . . by faith in Christ mankind may recover the lost likeness".[30] Just as Irenaeus saw this divine plan clearly in redemption he also saw it in revelation. The dissociation put forward by Marcion between the God of the Old Testament and the God of the New held little interest for him. Instead, Irenaeus saw the steady revelation of God through the Old Testament and the New as both unitary and progressive. Once again Irenaeus' love of coherence and over-arching thesis opposed the fragmentary views of the Gnostics and Marcion alike. His thought was highly influential, providing a cathedral-like theology which was all embracing and strengthening of the whole edifice of the faith.

One further controversy should be mentioned: the *monarchian* controversy, so named because those advocating this position sought to defend the supremacy and singularity of God. "The orthodox had insisted that there is no first principle other than God the Creator, no coequal devil. No coeternal devil, no coeternal matter, but a single *monarchia*".[31] This position was a reaction to Justin's theology which stressed the distinctiveness of the divine *logos* in a way which would be captured later by Origen's use of the term *hypostasis* for the separate members of the Trinity. This reaction sprang from Rome and the separate teachings of two men, Callistus and Hyppolytus, who came to represent the two positions held in Rome at the beginning of the third century. Sabellius represented the view that would become so familiar at Nicaea: that Father and Son are one and the same with the consequence that Father suffers along with the Son in redemption. Such *Patripassianism* was a totemic and polemical principle rather in the same way as the notion of *Theotokos* (bearer of God) was to become the polemical or totemic word which stressed the single divine nature of Christ. While Sabellius in Rome stressed the singularity of the divine nature, Hyppolytus stressed the distinctiveness of the Father and Son as two *prosopa*. A compromise position was put forward by deacon Callistus which tried to say that the Father and Son were distinct but "the difference was that the Father was the name of the divine Spirit indwelling the Son who is the human body of Jesus".[32]

The controversy spread to North Africa where Tertullian expressed his view of the Trinity with admirable clarity and brevity saying that God was one substance consisting in three persons. Tertullian was one of the first theologians to write in Latin, giving the Western Church a vocabulary with which to debate the Trinity, using words like *substantia* and *persona*—the Latin equivalent of the Greek *ousia* and *hypostasis*. But Tertullian was partly the prisoner of his own character: "brilliant, exasperating, sarcastic, and intolerant, yet intensely vigorous and incisive in argument, delighting in logical tricks and with an advocate's love of clever sophistry and a powerful writer of splendid, torrential prose."[33] Tertullian was attracted to the charismatic, rather puritanical and prophetic group called the Montanists, who were high on the Spirit and impatient of any form of compromise with impurity in the Church.

By the mid-third century the elements of further theological controversy had been established without conclusive resolution of the issues previously raised. When Constantine recognised the Christian Church as the religion of the Empire with the Edict of Milan in AD 313, a new ingredient was added. Previously there could be theological disputes which were purely a matter for the Church and not the state, but when a new, articulate, and widely received heresy was advanced by Arius in Alexandria which struck at the heart of the faith by denying the oneness of the Father and the Son, it now concerned not only the local Christian communities but the good order of the Empire itself. In other words, it became a matter for the Emperor too, and the Emperor would intervene, as he did at Nicaea, decisively.

Although theological centres had existed in Alexandria, Antioch, Caesarea (in Palestine), Rome, and latterly in Constantinople, a broad consensus remained elusive. The different theological schools of these cities, each with its own theological trajectory together with the added twist of competition between the different sees for pre-eminence and the interplay of imperial power, made for a complex struggle for orthodoxy in the fourth century. Apart from Hilary of Poitiers in the West and Athanasius in the East, some of the staunchest pro-Nicene theologians were the so-called Cappadocian Fathers, our three wise men from the East: Basil of Caesarea, Gregory of Nazianzus, and Basil's younger brother, Gregory of Nyssa. Although they were far from homogeneous as theologians, they adopted a common cause in refuting "Arianism". At the same time they advanced many other doctrinal ideas and an ascetic spirituality which would have a lasting influence.

The Cappadocian Fathers

The name that unifies these three Church leaders is Cappadocia. Cappadocia lies in a mountainous region north-eastern Turkey now well-known for its cave churches in curiously formed mountains. The main river is the Halys—the modern Kizil Irmak which runs to the north of present day Kayseri (Caesarea). It had been a Roman dependency from 191 BC, and, later a province from AD 17 after its inclusion by Tiberias.[34] Although briefly united with Galatia in AD 72, it regained its independence soon after. It was a border province of the Empire with several stationed legions, and along its roads Emperors Constantius, Juilian, and Valens, among others, would pass with armies to fight the Persians. But in 371 the Emperor Valens, no friend of Basil's, divided the province in two, creating separate capitals at Caesarea and Tyana. This may well have been done to reduce the influence of Basil of Caesaera, who in turn created two new dioceses at Sasima and Nyssa to which he appointed his friend Gregory and his brother respectively.

There had been a Christian community in Cappadocia since the earliest of times. Among other pilgrims recorded as being present on the day of Pentecost were "Parthians, Medes and Ealmites; residents of Mesopotamia, Judea and Cappadocia, Pontus and Asia, Phrygia".[35] Surely some returned to Cappadocia and founded the first Christian churches amongst the Jewish communities. Nor was Paul far away on both his missionary visits to Galatia, in particular when at Pisidian, Antoch, and Iconium (present day Konya).[36] It is not hard to think that Christians from the neighbouring province came over the provincial border with the "good news". The Apostle Peter wrote to the Christians of Cappadocia around AD 65 calling them to steadfastness as a pilgrim people in the face of growing opposition and persecution.[37] However, a major missionary thrust occurred in the third century when Gregory Thaumaturgus (Gregory "the Wonderworker", c.210–275) came to Cappadocia. A man on whom both Basil and his brother Gregory of Nyssa laid so much emphasis, and who was a pupil of the great Origen when he was in Caesarea in Palestine, this Gregory was to be called "the Apostle of Cappadocia".

Basil and Gregory of Nyssa's family were the spiritual beneficiaries of the Wonderworker's ministry. Basil's and Gregory's maternal grandmother, Macrina, was brought to the faith by Gregory Thauamturgos so, not unsurprisingly, both Basil and his friend Gregory of Nazianzus pay him tribute.[38] Basil was one of ten children, born around AD 330 during the reign of Constantine, five years after the Council of Nicaea. There were five brothers and five sisters. His brothers, besides his younger brother Gregory, were Peter (later Bishop of Sebastse in Armenia), Naucratias (a talented and gentle soul who lived in community looking after a group of the elderly but who was mysteriously killed while out hunting),[39] and a further unknown brother.[40] Of his sisters, Macrina, named after his grandmother, was the most influential, inspiring both a *Life* of rare beauty, written by her brother Gregory in 379 shortly after Basil's own death, and also a Platonic dialogue, *On the Soul and Resurrection*, in which the role of Socrates—who asks the questions in Plato's *Pheado*—is taken by Macrina.

The family was well to do. Whilst there is uncertainty as to the exact occupation of their father (the older Basil), he appears to have played a teaching role as a rhetor and a minor administrative one in the local community. Gregory of Nazianzus says that Pontus, Basil the Elder's province, "put him forward at that time as its common teacher of virtue".[41] The family owned estates at Annisa, a plateau near the Black Sea, to which Basil would retire in 357 after his tour of ascetic communities in Syria, Palestine, and Egypt in his early quest for the philosophic or ascetic life. This community would contain his mother, sister, and his friend, Gregory of Nazianzus.[42] "The distinguishing characteristic of both his mother's family and his father's family was piety".[43] It was a family life which nurtured the twin emphases of piety and education, the Christian and the Hellenic combined together, and which also valued the ascetic goals of virginity and withdrawal for study, prayer, and the nurture of a like-minded community. These values were to be demonstrated in many ways throughout the lives of the Cappadocian Fathers. It seems they were present in the soil of Christian discipleship from the third century onwards.

If Basil and Gregory's background was one of serious Christian discipleship in the context of a reasonably wealthy and well educated family with connections to the ruling classes in the Eastern Empire, Gregory of Nazianzus, the third of our Cappadocian spiritual triumvirate, was not dissimilar. Gregory was born into a family of landed gentry on a country estate called Karbala, near Arianzus, a village in the hilly centre of Cappadocia, some time between 326 and 330. His father, also called Gregory, was a member of a Judeo-Christian sect called *Hypsistarii*, the servants of the Most High God, which he later left.[44] His mother, Nonna, came from a wealthy local Christian family and was the sister of Amphilochius the Elder. His son, also named Amphilochius, was to become a close associate and correspondent of Basil and the Bishop of Iconium. Gregory the Elder, who became a Christian through the strong encouragement of his wife, was chosen, when still a layman and aged 50, to be the Bishop of Nazianzus, a small town some eight miles to the northwest of the family villa at Karbala. He took this responsibility seriously, building a church for the faithful in Nazianzus and defending Nicene orthodoxy although with no great knowledge. Gregory and Nonna had three children, Gorgonia—their devout eldest daughter—and then two boys, Gregory and Caesarius. "Gregory tells us that before his birth, his mother prayed earnestly to have a son, like several mothers of Old Testament prophets; having been shown in a dream that her prayers would be answered, she dedicated Gregory to God's service as soon as he was born, a promise he regarded as the origin of his vocation".[45]

Gregory was close to his siblings. His sister, Gorgonia, married a senior military officer, Alypius, who became a Christian shortly before his death and lived in Iconium where there were family connections on his mother's side. His brother, Caesarius, became a court doctor taking a post at the Imperial Court and then, after the Emperor Julian's brief reign (361–363), became a senior financial officer in Bithynia in 368. Soon after the disastrous earthquake in Bithynia of that year, Caesarius died in his mid-thirties. The sudden death of his brother had an enormous effect on Gregory, who wrote, "I died to the world and the world to me, and I have become a living corpse, as devoid of strength as a dreamer. Since that day my life is elsewhere."[46] A year later his sister, Gorgonia, died in 369/370 and Gregory gave the funeral oration, praising her pursuit of "virtue", her ardent desire for the philosophic life, her well-ordering of a large and well-regulated household, and her general rather austere demeanour: "The only rouge she valued was the blush of modesty; her only white powder was the pallor of self-denial".[47]

Gregory, then, like his two associates, Basil and Gregory, shared many of the same characteristics in terms of culture and background. All came from strongly Christian families in which their fathers were involved in community affairs either teaching, as Basil the Elder, or with the Church, as with the older Gregory. Both mothers were strongly Christian, with daughters in Macrina and Gorgonia who were unusually pious and devoted. They were landed families with influential relatives and links with both the Imperial household and the Imperial civil service. It made them potential leaders but alongside these natural advantages was the tension of their education. All four—Basil, Gregory (Nyssa), Gregory (Nazianzus), and Caesaruis—went through a Hellenic education but from a strongly, especially maternal, Christian background. They were "expected to take their place as members of educated Christian elite in the Empire of Constantine's descendants, education necessarily meant both absorbing the heritage of Greek literary and philosophical culture and deepening their own intellectual identification with the Church's tradition of faith: a hybridisation of humanism and theology",[48] which was to be a central dynamic and preoccupation in each of their lives. For Gregory of Nyssa it would develop into a love of speculative theology; for Basil, a groundwork for defending the Nicene faith in different stages of development; and, for Gregory of Nazianzus, this hybrid education led to an unresolved tension between advocating with great elegance the Nicene faith and fleeing to follow an uninterrupted philosophic life far from the intrusions of pastoral responsibilities and ecclesiastical dispute. The formation of each of them was, in the first instance, the prayers and example of parents, and grandparents but also the Hellenic schools of the Mediterranean, and especially the influence of Plato.

Part I: The Struggle for Orthodoxy

CHAPTER 2

Through the Platonic Lens: The World of Hellenic Ideas

All of us view the world through one philosophic or religious lens or another, and what is true of us was just as true of those contending for orthodoxy in the fourth century. We have seen the forces at work during this period: the disintegrating pressures at work in the Roman Empire and the pressures of persecution and of heresy upon the Church, as well as the tension inherent in a culture which sought to merge Greek intellectual culture with a biblical understanding.[49] In fourth-century provincial Christian culture there was a self-conscious attempt to combine a pious Christian life with the academic standards of a classical education. Our *Three Wise Men* were themselves educated in classical thought either directly in the schools, as in the case of Basil and Gregory of Nazianzus, or, in the case of Gregory of Nyssa, by proxy—since he was largely educated by his older brother, Basil. It is important to appreciate that the only education to be had was, by definition, a classical one, and the greatest influence on classical learning, especially in philosophy, was Plato. The Cappadocians were no exception. The extent of their education was considerable even by modern standards; indeed, in length even surpassing ours. Gregory of Nazianzus, admittedly from a well to do family, was away being educated for ten years!

Gregory of Nazianzus was clear about the merits of education. Writing in his fourth Oration he states: "I take it all intelligent men agree that among human advantages education holds first place. I refer not only to our nobler form of it which disdains all the ambitious ornaments of

19

rhetoric and attaches itself only to salvation and the beauty of what is accessible to the mind, but also that external culture which many Christians by an error of judgement scorn as treacherous and dangerous and as turning away from God". He goes on to say, "And from such material (i.e. principles of enquiry and speculation) we have drawn profit for piety, by learning to distinguish the better from the worse, and from its weakness we have made our doctrine strong."[50] Gregory's belief in the benefits of a classical education was in line with Justin Martyr and Clement of Alexandria, theologians who were not intimidated by the schools whether in Rome or Alexandria. His own education, together with that of his younger brother Caesarius, was extensive. After the usual elementary studies at Nazianzus and then several months of instruction from his uncle Amphilochius at Iconium, Gregory and his brother were sent in c.346 to Caesarea in Cappadocia.[51] After a brief stay in Caesarea Maritima in Palestine, latterly the home of Origen, the brothers moved on to Alexandria in Egypt, the chief intellectual centre in the Empire where both scientific and philosophical studies flourished. In Alexandria Gregory learnt more rhetoric from the graceful stylist Thespesios, for whom he wrote an Epitaph,[52] and there he may have encountered the lay scholar Didymus the Blind. It is also possible that they may have met Athanasius, the central force for Nicene orthodoxy in the Empire who may well have been in the city after his second exile in the West in 346. Whomever they met and whatever lectures they attended, Gregory began that blend of humanism and theology "that was only in its beginning stages but that was to be a central pre-occupation, in a variety of ways of Gregory's future life".[53]

Toward the end of 348 Gregory left his brother in Alexandria and went to Athens. Although Athens was no longer the political power it once was, it was still an important centre of learning. There Gregory would pursue his literary studies, the better to express himself and persuade others (the object of classical education). But, during a severe Mediterranean storm while crossing from Alexandria, Gregory made a promise to serve God: "If I escape a double danger, I shall serve you."[54] His response to a tight spot, like many others before and since, was to bargain with God or at least to make a *volte face* spiritually should he be delivered from death. This marked the beginning of a more serious spiritual quest. In Athens he was to meet a fellow Cappadocian who had recently arrived, Basil, who was himself to stay in the city for nearly five years following a period of education in Constantinople under the famous teacher Libanius.

From Gregory's later *Oratio* on Basil we know a good deal about their time in Athens. Teaching in Athens created fierce rivalries, with students of different teachers eager to virtually kidnap new pupils for their preferred master.[55] For this reason much of the teaching occurred in private homes where there was less disruption. Basil's own chief teachers were Himerius and the elderly Christian teacher Prohaeresius, then in his eighties. Both are described at length in Eunapius's *Life* of the teaching in Athens.[56] The teaching they received was generally neo-platonic in content, along the lines of Plotinus. The general focus of their training was of an advanced rhetorical kind, meaning the study of the classical authors with a view to felicity of expression, ease of allusion to classical literature, and the ability to persuade. "A cultured gentleman of the time was expected to have a smattering of knowledge on a great many subjects—geography, history, natural science and above all, the tradition of Greek philosophy—most of them learned from handbooks compressing a great deal of information into schematic form".[57] Julian, the future apostate Emperor who was also brought up on Imperial estates in Cappadocia, was a student in Athens for a few months while Basil and Gregory were there, but it is unclear as to whether they met. For Julian, later known as the Apostate for his reversion to paganism, it was a time of mentally overthrowing the Christian understanding of life in favour of classical learning, secret mysteries, and pagan or occult practices.[58]

For Gregory and Basil it was an opportunity to use classical learning in order to explore more deeply the Christian doctrines of creation and salvation, and to pursue a life of *virtue* based on the Scriptures. But while for Gregory the experience was largely positive, Basil has little good to say about Athens, calling it later in his homilies and letters a "school of impurity"[59] which in turn could all too easily lead to the pursuit of intellectual novelty and the origins of heresy.[60] Basil's complaint was not unlike that of Luke's in reporting the Apostle Paul's visit to Athens three hundred years previously, when it was said of the city, "All the Athenians and the foreigners who lived there spent their time doing nothing but talking about and listening to the latest ideas".[61] Later, in a letter to the

Bishops of the West, Basil makes clear the connection between error and traditional education, "The teachings of the Fathers are scorned; the apostolic traditions are set at naught; the fabrications of innovators are in force in the churches; these men, moreover, train themselves in rhetorical quibbling and not in theology; the wisdom of the world takes first place to itself, having thrust aside the glory of the Cross".[62]

The varied responses of Basil and Gregory to a classical education in Athens, both of whom spent over five years there, was indicative of their on-going general conclusions about learning. Basil would use classical allusion in his writings[63] but mostly sparingly, and only rarely by way of explaining theology. In contrast, Gregory of Nazianzus would more consciously employ the rhetorical arts of his classical education to formulate, promote, and proclaim Christian doctrine, as in his Orations. Basil would describe classical learning in his pamphlet *Ad adulescentes* as a spur to a philosophic or contemplative life and virtue in the broadest terms but it would be no more than that.[64] The years in Athens taught Basil to eschew worldly wisdom, to beware the arguments of men, and to be wary of those who sought to impress only with the classical arts. A further negative effect of classical learning was that it propelled him into a life of self-knowledge to seek for greater inner purity, to eschew the enslavement of property or fame, and to make both contemplation and the pursuit of virtue his goal: to reach out for the philosophic life. This was Basil's aim and would never leave him. It also formed that hybrid spirituality of a Platonic Christian tradition which would over time and place morph into a more pronounced Christian ascetic spirituality. Finally, it would be the focus of his life in the years immediately after leaving Athens (356–364) before he was more systematically pressed into the service of the church as a priest.

On the other hand, Gregory of Nazianzus lingered a little longer in Athens, feeling somewhat betrayed by Basil who had left Athens before him. However, he would follow his close friend, returning to the relative Cappadocian backwater of Nazianzus—no doubt to help his father with his pastoral ministry. Gregory's return only served to highlight a tension that would continue for the rest of his life: "the tension between contemplation and pastoral action, between the quiet scholarly life of an ascetical but comfortable Christian gentleman and the assumption of responsibility for leadership in the turbulent Church of Asia Minor in the mid-fourth century—a level of responsibility commensurate with his education and family connections".[65] Examples of this tension can be found later in his life in his flight to Pontus following his ordination as a priest, overwhelmed by the responsibility. So too in his flight from Constantinople in 380 when he was Archbishop and Metropolitan in the face of ecclesiastical wrangling brought on by a rival candidate for Bishop of Constantinople, Maximus, presented by Egyptian bishops to the Emperor and city of Constantinople. But his own philosophic bent was set both by nature and inclination, by education and by aspiration. Well aware of Stoic speculations on the inherent order of the world, admiring of the detachment inculcated by the Cynics and their freedom from material attachments, and deeply influenced by the neo-Platonists, Gregory was ever-affected by his classical studies in the way he expressed Christian truth.[66] His philosophy was divided between the Platonic tradition of the contemplative and the Greek concept of a wisdom which was practical; between what could be conceived intellectually and what could also work pastorally. This dialectic of the contemplative and the virtuous, pure philosophising and the goal of pastoral formation never left him. His theological writing, which was principally contained in the Orations, would "philosophise about God", extolling his being but, at the same time, would encourage the pursuit of personal virtue, making his readers stretch forward to *know* him. This is well-indicated by this passage from the Orations:

> God always was and is and will be—or better, God always "is". For "was" and "will be" are the divisions of the time we experience, of a nature that flows away; but he *is* always, and gives himself this name when he identifies himself to Moses on the mountain. For he contains the whole of being in himself, without beginning or end, like an endless, boundless ocean of reality; he extends beyond all our notions of time and nature, and is sketchily grasped by the mind alone, but only very dimly and in a limited way; he is known not indirectly, as one image is derived from another to form a single representation of the truth: fleeing before it is grasped, escaping before it is fully known, shining on our guiding reason—provided we have been purified—as a swift, fleeting flash

of lightning shines in our eyes. And he does this, it seems to me so that so that, insofar as it can be comprehended, the Divine might draw us to himself.[67]

Here is philosophising about God, or we might say theologising, which in turn leads to the mystical pursuit of God in heart and spirit.

Furthermore, this philosophy should give self-mastery and self-control. He expected as much from Basil when the division of his diocese by the Emperor occurred. "I consider," he wrote to Basil, "this moment, in fact to be really the time when my Basil will show his true colours, and when the philosophy you have been putting together for yourself all this time will be fully revealed".[68] Similarly, Gregory praised his sister Gorgonia's life, in his funeral oration for her. Speaking of her complete self-mastery he says, "she was so outstanding in self-control . . . she mingled the beauty of celibacy with marriage, and showed that neither of them binds us completely to God or to the world".[69]

Lastly, Gregory's grammar and style of expression was itself formed by his studies in Athens. The *Forty-Four Orations*, Gregory's theological legacy, were themselves imitative of the classical arts. The revival of rhetoric associated with Flavius Philostratus, who died c.AD 250, profoundly influenced the schools of oratory in Athens and elsewhere. Members of this newly founded so-called *second sophistic* period, from the third century onwards, celebrated the fact that "traditional Greek ideals of virtue and heroism was now transplanted from the culture of small cities to that of a highly bureaucratic and centralised Empire".[70] Gregory, in his writing, employed "highly structured sentences built on the foundation of symmetrically arranged *cola* or phrases; sheer verbal abundance; clever plays on words and tricks of sound; abrupt changes of rhythm and reference; dramatic metaphors; and the constant presence of scriptural and classical allusion. Providing his entire train of thought with a parallel world of remembered significance, evoked in a kind of running semiotic counterpoint—all these features turn Gregory's lectures and sermons into exquisitely self-conscious works of art".[71] Theology in classical literary art is the legacy that Gregory preserved for the modern Christian world, principally through his Orations.

If Gregory of Nazianzus was immersed in classical learning through ten years of educational travel, in the midst of which he had a profound spiritual experience through a storm, and formed a lifelong friendship with a man who deeply influenced him from Athens onwards (of whom he wrote: "For God had given me yet one priceless gift, uniting me with Wisdom's wisest son, Himself alone above all life and word: who this could be, ye soon shall know full well; Basil his name our age's great support"),[72] then his great friend's younger brother, Gregory of Nyssa, had none of these educational advantages or academic exposure.

Gregory of Nyssa attended none of the great universities of his day, whether Caesarea in Palestine, Alexandria, Athens, or Constantinople. He was, it seems, entirely dependent on his older brother Basil for his education and philosophical learning. But he had a natural aptitude for it and, whereas his brother remained cautious of its influence, for Gregory there was no such restraint. It seems he had a subtler, more enquiring mind, not given to easy solutions to the great dilemmas of faith and life. He must have had ready access to a local library of books. At some point between 362 and 371 he became a teacher of public speaking (rhetor). "You had rather be thought of as a Rhetor than a Christian", chides Gregory Nazianzus,[73] and like most contemporaries he was deeply influenced by Plato and neo-Platonism.

Through the Platonic Lens

It is hard to gauge the influence of Plato on the outworking of Christian theology. He appears to have had some influence on the very expression of Christian truth in the scriptures themselves. For instance the Jewish Apostle Paul in his use of a term like "immortality"[74] and also the Apostle John's very Hellenic way of expressing the divinity of the Son by colonising another Greek word *logos*[75] (meaning controlling intellect or reason)—to describe both the divinity and pre-existence of the Son—show two leading Apostles using terms which had been readily used by Hellenic philosophers but which were now pressed into service to describe either the destiny of humanity or the Godhead. If Greek philosophical influence is present even in the foundation documents of Christianity then it is hardly surprising that Greek ideas, and especially Platonic and neo-Platonic ones, are influential in the theology of the early Fathers.

Soon after the time of the rebuilding of the Temple in Jerusalem by Nehemiah after the traumatic Babylonian Exile of the Jewish people, Plato was born probably in Athens between 428–427 BC. He was a pupil of Socrates whose death he tried to prevent and for whom he had a profound affection and respect. Plato went on to found an Academy of Philosophy which lasted off and on until Justinian closed it in the sixth century AD. The main influences on Plato were the Greek philosophers and mathematicians: Pythagoras, Parmenides, Heraclitus, and Socrates. From Pythagoras he gained "the religious trend, the belief in immortality, the other worldliness, the priestly tone and all that is involved in the simile of the cave".[76] From Parmenides he learnt the notion that "reality is eternal and timeless and that, on logical grounds, all change must be illusory".[77] From Heraclitus he derived the negative doctrine that there is nothing permanent in the sensible world. From this doctrine, together with what he learnt from Parmenides, came the conclusion that knowledge is not to be gathered by the senses, but is only to be gained by the intellect. From Socrates he learnt preoccupation with ethical problems and with understanding and pursuing the Good. And if a man is to be a good statesman he must know the Good.[78]

What concerns us most of all here is not Plato's conception of statesmanship, or the perfect state Utopia. After the death of Socrates (399 BC) when Plato was about thirty, he sought a structure for the state which would deliver both security and permanence. He sought to experiment with the ideas in Syracuse through the dictator Dionysius but himself came dangerously close to losing his life. It was around then that Plato came up with the political theory of Utopia, a state based on the Spartan model in which the practise of eugenics in breeding, the removal of children from parents at birth, and marriages arranged by the state makes look twentieth totalitarian states in Europe look mild. So a powerful state—in fact unsupportable in its rigidity, totalitarian in nature which may have provided power for a few but in reality was inhuman—was envisaged. The model of a philosopher king at the helm was more sympathetic, but what kind of philosophy would be beneficial to the citizens? If these ideas are scarcely known or mentioned amongst the Cappadocians, others formed the background to much of their studies and thinking even if several were clearly rejected.

The Platonic ideas which were influential either negatively or positively on the Cappodocian Fathers were these: the idea of universal knowledge or form, the idea of the immortality of the soul, Plato's ideas about development and personal growth or the pursuit of virtue (more a Stoic concept), his understanding of creation, and, finally, his theory of knowledge.

Plato's theory about ideas or the theory of *universal forms* is still widely known, if not precisely then in a general way. The theory emanates from the existence of a final Universal Form or Being. In the *Republic* it is called the Good; in *Parmenides*, the One; in *Timaeus*, the Being; in the *Symposium*, Beauty. This supreme Good was held responsible for the character rather than the existence of time and space conditioned reality.[79] Alongside this existence of ultimate reality or god, there is uncreated substance which this Supreme Being takes and fashions into perfect Form. In this way every article or being is created in its perfect form whether cat or bed or table. "Of this one bed, made by God, there can be *knowledge*, but in respect of the many beds made by carpenters there can be only *opinion*".[80] This distinction of opinion and knowledge, so important to Plato and predicated on this theory of creation being related to the idea of Universal Forms, has important consequences for Plato's dependent theory of knowledge and perception.

If every thing or being has a perfect Universal Form then the perfect human Form which is the essence of our being is the soul. If man is a composite of soul and body then the soul is both our nobler part and the pure vision of humanity to which we must aspire. So Socrates, unafraid of death, sought fellowship with other souls who had preceded him and who were better than those he would be leaving in dying. In so describing man, Plato commits human life to a binding dualism consisting of "reality and appearance; ideas and sensible objects, reason and sense-perception, soul and body".[81] If the soul was the nobler part and the final Form of humanity, by contrast the body was a kind of prison. It was a hindrance to the acquisition of knowledge, its lusts needed to be tamed, its pleasures laid aside, its senses not dependable in the ascent of understanding. For Plato:

> The body is the source of endless trouble to us by reason of the mere requirement of food . . . it is full of loves, and lusts, and, fears and fancies of all kinds, and endless foolery. Whence come wars, and fighting and factions? Whence, but from the body and the lusts of the body.[82]

Platonic dualism predicated on the superior nature of the soul and innate suspicion of the body was to bind the development of Christianity for the best part of twelve centuries until the Aristotelian paradigm took hold through the writings of Thomas Aquinas. The ideas were deeply influential in the ascetic movement amongst the Cappadocians as in Egypt, Syria, Palestine and later in western monasticism through Benedict.

It is not surprising therefore that, with both the idea of Universal Forms and the idea of the immortality of the soul, Plato should develop a theory of knowledge and self-improvement. The taming of the body by the aspirations of the soul was a natural corollary. From this dynamic we get the idea of idea of the activation of the desire in man which will lead the soul to regain its heavenly home, its greater conformity to its own final Form:

> The natural desire for the good and beautiful needs to be released and reactivated by a moral and spiritual training or *askesis,* which helps it to regain the primal vision by growing once again the "wings of the soul" which had been lost by the fall of the soul at the beginning of time. [83]

The force of *eros* would enable this upward movement and would be the principle force of motivation. Replace *eros* with *agape,* or indeed mingle the two together as in the dynamic of the Song of Songs, then are we are not far from the aspirations of the Christian mystic. If we add to the mixture the idea that knowledge for Plato was gained by use of recollection, reflection, or reminiscence, rather than through the bodily senses, then a way is made for the importance of contemplation and solitude. Likewise, in the famous description of the cave in which humans are imprisoned, seeing only shadows on the wall, and need to be released by the instruction of philosophy then Plato makes the case that instruction in the context of a search for sunlight in which the eye of the soul is turned towards the outward illumination of the sun will bring enlightenment and transformation. If this dynamic is familiar to the Christian the power and reality is absent from the Platonic vision. Yet it provides a powerful model of ascent or transformation that would be quickly harnessed by any Christian mystic.

However, Plato's cosmogony, or understanding of creation and the physical universe, was not to be so readily accepted by the Cappadocians. Plato's cosmogony is set forth in *Timaeus*, which was translated into Latin by Cicero and later Calcidius. Calcidius' incomplete translation (part one, up to 53 c) was widely known in the Middle Ages. Timaeus, the subject of this Platonic dialogue, is a Pythagorian astronomer who proceeds to tell the story of the creation and history of the world down to the creation of man. Plato's god's creative act was to bring order out of chaos, to take already existing matter and shape it into form and being. So, unlike the Judeo/Christian doctrine of creation, god did not create *ex nihilo*. As Timaeus was Pythagorian, the creative process was governed by numbers, each of the elements—fire, air, water, and earth—having a special number that governed their relations to the other elements. Creation was given both soul and body but being sensible was not eternal. The theory of creation contained three parts: unchangeable essence which is the soul of something; changing substance which is the body of the essence; and free space which is eternal and provides space for all created beings whether planets, stars, fish, birds, or land animals to live and develop. The space is itself composed of different forms of right angle triangles.[84] Man when created was composed of both a mortal and immortal soul; one part (the mortal) was driven by desire, the other (the immortal) was driven by the quest to know the good so that it can rise up the ladder of knowledge by contemplation, philosophy, and the practise of virtue.

Although attractive in some of its parts and highly influential in scientific thinking until Galileo's revolution and Newtonian physics, this cosmogony was never fully accepted either by the Cappadocians or by Christians in general. For them God created *ex nihilo* and a complete distinction was drawn between the Creator and the created order; this absolute division was of enormous importance in rejecting Arianism which made the *logos* part of the created order. But the temptation of placing the Son in some kind of "chain of being" between the Creator God and all of his creation was made much more plausible by the highly influential neo-Platonist Plotinus.

Plato lived some seven hundred years before the Cappadocians and so, although still hugely influential in the Greek schools and upon the early Christian writers especially Justin Martyr[85] and Clement of Alexandria, it was through the writings of Plotinus in the mid-third century that Platonic thought was revived and once again given centre stage. Plotinus took up philosophic study at the age of twenty-seven and travelled to Alexandria, then a leading centre of academic study in the Empire, where he attached himself to the teacher Ammonius Saccas. After eleven years he joined an ill-fated expeditionary force to Persia where he hoped to investigate the teachings of the Persian and Indian philosophers, but after the failure of the expedition, the death of its commander Gordian III, he made his way back to Antioch with difficulty, eventually going to Rome where he gathered pupils around him—including his eventual biographer Porphyry.

Plotinus' contribution, made through a succession of essays written over seventeen years called the *Enneads*, to the development of Christian theology was twofold, one negative and the other positive in its effect. Plotinus' theory of substance or being seems an amalgam of Platonic and semi-Christian thought. His metaphysical system originates with a trinity, in the form of the One, Spirit, and Soul. The One is the transcendent one, also "the is" as in Parmenides, or indeed in the revelation of God in the Hebrew scriptures as at the burning bush: "I am who I am".[86] The Spirit or the Intellectual principle[87] was described by Plotinus as the *nous*. The *nous* is the image of the One; "it is engendered because the one, in its self-quest, has vision; this seeing is *nous*".[88] As with Plato, the One is both the sun and the light, the giver by which the sun knows itself. With Plotinus the *nous* is that light or illumination by which the One knows himself—that is the expression of the One through whom knowledge comes. Furthermore when humans are most god-like, the body and its futile senses may be put aside and the residual divine mage by which the Soul is given light discovered.[89]

The response of Christian teachers was complex, on the one hand the chain of being predicated in Plotinus in which the whole of the universe was organised in a descending order of being (*hypostases*), including this trinity of One, Spirit (*nous*), and Soul, was mostly rejected. However, it provided a contemporary philosophical framework present in Alexandria, and then Rome, that would give rise to the thinking of Arius. On the other hand, the general idea of the ascent of the soul to a heavenly experience, so present in Platonic thinking, was further affirmed by Plotinus, albeit in a structure which was thought to be wrong. However, to fully understand the trajectory of thought and theology, especially in Alexandria, at the time of the Cappodocian Fathers the influence of Origen must be discussed.

Plato Mediated through Origen

Origen (184–249) bestrode early Christian theology, biblical studies, and spirituality like no other until the coming of Augustine of Hippo. He stood in the tradition of Alexandrian philosophical schools and like Plotinus was taught by Ammonius Saccas. Plotinus himself held him in high esteem as a fellow student and Porphyry praised him as the author of three, now lost, philosophical treatises.[90] Origen was also heir to the writings of Clement who, like him, was well acquainted with the classics, but Origen gave none of the easy allusions in which Clement so revelled. But "throughout Clement's works there is a note of cheerfulness and open-eyed enjoyment of the Creator's mercies. In Origen there is a sterner austerity, a steely determination of the will to renounce not merely all that is evil but also natural goods if they were an obstacle to the attainments of higher ends".[91] His Father, Leonides, died a martyr when Origen was 18 during one of the purges of Emperor Septimus Severus, and so Origen was always conscious of his noble heritage having a "martyrdom in the family". In fact Origen, together with many others in Alexandria, made martyrdom and virginity important goals of their spirituality.

Origen's study of the scriptures and the philosophical classics, to which he made little outright allusion but which nevertheless shaped his thought, arguably more than Clement, was rigorous. He devoted many hours to prayer and studying the scriptures each day. He forced himself in unending toil, ate little, and may even have castrated or mutilated himself so as not to fall into sexual temptation.[92]

Despite, or maybe because, of Origen's way of life and personality, his views were both influential and controversial. There are several areas of theology where his influence was considerable, although at times potentially or actually misleading. His more controversial views sprang from a worldview influenced by a strong sub-current of Platonism and from his handling of the Bible—both prodigious and at times highly speculative, looking for an interior or spiritual meaning in the text—and from his own advocacy of a spirituality which was both exacting and, at times, ill-advised.

His doctrinal teaching was summed up in the text *Peri Archon* written in Alexandria when he was in his forties and by then a mature theologian. *Peri Archon*, meaning fundamental or first principles, was a kind of handbook of Origen's thinking about doctrine and—for the purposes of his influence on the Cappadocians—there are several areas of his thought which are found there which are very influential on them, particularly about the status of the *logos*, the immaterial creation that pre-existed material creation, and the dynamic of salvation which stressed the growth of the soul rather than its outright redemption.

Origen makes clear the complete distinction between the Creator and the material world he created (adopting here the non-platonic view that creation was made *ex nihilo*), and so emphasising the Father's simplicity, sovereignty, and otherness in respect of material creation. However, his description of the Trinity as being co-equal in being and substance is not so sure-footed. Despite his huge knowledge of scripture and being able to quote almost any text at will, he still took a platonic view of the Godhead. This surely comes from a world-view deeply affected by the neo-Platonists informed no doubt by his early studies in Alexandria. Thus "Origen found useful the Platonic concept of hypostasis as a way of speaking about the Son and the Holy Spirit as having a separate existence from the Father in the unity if the Trinity".[93] From the fourth century onwards, Origen was criticised for Platonic ideas and interpretations of scripture which relegated the Son and the Spirit to being inferior in some ways to the Father. This remains an on-going debate in academic circles as to the degree to which Origen envisaged a Trinitarian godhead in which the unity of the Godhead, Father, Son, and Spirit, allowed for a more independent existence of the Son and Spirit from the Father. However, what may have been an exploration in Origen later became a threat with Arius. While his views, at the time of their expression, were not considered so controversial, with the advent of Arius and the re-assessment of theologians in the light of the Arian controversy, Origen's description of the Trinity became more suspect.

Furthermore, Origen's understanding of the fall, the immortality of the soul, and final consummation of all things are important background to the controversies of the fourth century in which the Cappadocians were engaged. Origen's idea of the fall was distinctly Platonic. He believed that there was a former spiritual creation prior to the present material one in which three types of being first existed and then fell: the first group being angels did not fall very far and so were easily restored; the second group, the demons, were actively aggressive and sought to prevent the return of others; and the third group, invested with the image of God, the *psuchai* (humans), were capable of restoration. In fact, for Origen, the material creation, about which we know far more now than Origen ever could, was the middle part of a creative sandwich in which, prior to creation, there were immaterial souls, and following the end of the material creation there would be a reconciliation of all things to the Creator. The function of the *logos*—as the one pre-existent heavenly soul that did not fall—was to redeem those who had and were amenable to reconciliation.

This whole complex scheme—part biblical, part Platonic—was integral to Origen's *oikonomia* (God's plan) in which humans had responsibility for their response and each had a set capacity to respond to revelation. Rather than there being a sudden justification of the sinner, redemption was a gradual process: "atonement is going on all the time and, since it is God's way not to use force but to respect freedom, the work of restoration to a correspondence with the divine intention is a slow and painful ascent".[94] So the emphasis of the ministry of the *logos* in Origen's scheme was more as a teacher than a sacrificial redeemer. He developed much more vividly than Justin the idea of the Incarnation as the means by which God enables humankind to receive "knowledge that calls men to lead a good and blessed life from no other source but the very words and teaching of Christ".[95] For Origen, the advent of knowledge, gained from Christ in scripture mingled with love (e.g. his commentary on the Song of Songs), was the path to salvation, hence his unrelenting emphasis on scripture as demonstrated by his prodigious work *Hexalpa*, an immense six-column biblical commentary in which Origen painstakingly compares the Septuagint with the Hebrew bible and four other Greek translations. Only fragments of this mammoth production remain.

Finally, Origen's *oikonomia* or dispensation concludes with the idea that, in the afterlife, a final purging of failure, misunderstanding, or inadequacy takes place, so "souls who have departed this life will pass through 'a lecture hall or school' where they learn to understand mysteries" until eventually they are ready to see God".[96] For Origen, his eschatological expectation was that "the end is always like the beginning"[97] meaning that all that God has created will be reconciled to him. This has come to be known as a universalist position in which all are reconciled regardless of their response to him in this life and there is no final separation of created beings from God in the end: thus "the end is always like the beginning".

Origen remained a lay teacher in Alexandria until 215 when a dispute with the Bishop of Alexandria, Demetrius, over Origen's unwillingness to be under his authority led him to leave the city. He first went to Rome where he received new patronage from the wealthy Ambrosius who published and circulated Origen's writings. A little later, being asked by the mother of the young Emperor Alexander Severus to go to Antioch, he returned East, in this case to Caesarea in Palestine where, at the invitation of the Bishop Theoctistus, Origen was ordained presbyter. This worsened the rift with Demetrius who was horrified that he had accepted another bishop's authority, and likewise that Theoctistus had ordained someone whom he had no right to do so. Origen was to remain at Caesarea for the rest of his life, where, geographically, he was closer to Cappadocia.

The theological influence of Origen, in the principal centres of learning especially in the eastern part of the Empire and for the remaining part of the century, was substantial. Like Calvin in Geneva more than a millennium later,[98] Origen embarked on a verse by verse exposition of the text for three years of daily expository preaching, in which much of the Old Testament was covered: 250 homilies are extant in Latin, translated by Rufinus or

Jerome. He believed in the transformative study of scripture.[99] It was here too that he wrote to a lady, Tatiana, his famous treatise *On Prayer*, which was not so concerned with the philosophical mechanics of praying as the thought that its main benefit was not so much the answering of our petitions as being the chief means by which we become more like God. To this period also belong his famous commentary on the Song of Songs, probably written during a break in Athens,[100] his work *Contra Celsum* (a defence of Christian thought against Celsus who advocated the persecution of Christianity for its subversive and unclassical ways), and his commentary on the Pauline Epistles of which only his commentary on Romans survives. It was here too that his famous pupil Gregory Thaumaturgus wrote his memory of Origen entitled *Address to Origen*, the same Gregory the Wonderworker who would have such an influence on Basil and Gregory of Nyssa's grandmother.

Origen died in Palestine after a renewed outbreak of persecution led by the new Emperor Decius who succeeded Philip the Arab. Many were martyred. He was imprisoned and tortured but released and died soon afterwards, his health broken, in 249. He had been in Palestine for 15 years; his influence had spread. And so it is not the least surprising that Basil and Gregory of Nazianzus, in one of the first spiritual and intellectual actions together, published excerpts from Origen's work in their *Philocalia* in 358, a work designed to show, from drawing extensively on *Contra Celsum* and *Peri Archon*, that, by becoming a Christian, you were not committing intellectual suicide. (One might be tempted to say, bearing in mind the strictures of Dawkins and Hitchens, *plus ça change, plus c'est la même chose*.) By the middle of the fourth century and until the coming of Augustine, Origen could never be ignored nor his contribution to theology disregarded. His theology was an important ingredient to the background which formed the intellectual and spiritual climate in Alexandria which in turn led to the rise of Arius and the struggle for orthodoxy which ensued for nearly a hundred years. To understand the Cappadocians, this trajectory of thought coming from Alexandria and Antioch must be understood as well as those spiritual events which occurred in Alexandria which had at first nurtured Origen and reflected the schools from which Origen emerged.

CHAPTER 3

The Benchmark of Nicaea

Alexandria became the eye of the theological storm that enveloped the Empire from around AD 320 to 380—and particularly until 370 and death of Athanasius—until the arrival of the orthodox Emperor Theodosius after the defeat of imperial forces at Adrianople. Alexandria was founded by Alexander the Great through the inspiration of a dream, as legend has it, in which "a venerable old man with a look of Homer himself is said to have appeared in his (Alexander's) sleep and recited lines from the Odyssey which advised him where to site his city."[101] Alexander established the city after a cruise down the Nile from Memphis to the delta and before he consulted the oracle of Ammon at Siwah in the Western Desert, near the border with Libya, about his forthcoming expedition to the east to destroy the Persian Empire. Callisthenes tells us that Alexander thought, "the place was most beautiful for founding a city and that the city would be highly favoured".[102] Built around an Old Persian fort, it comprised Macedonian veterans, Greeks, prisoners of war, a contingent of Jews, and native Egyptians. The boundaries of the city, designed by Cleomones, were marked out by barley meal and in the shape of a Macedonian military cloak.

Taken over by the Ptolemies, who requisitioned Alexander's body and carried it off to his eponymous capital, to give the city greater status and Alexander a fitting mausoleum, it soon became a cultural, intellectual, and political centre only rivalled in the Empire by Rome and Constantinople. The Ptolomies founded the famed library initially around the Museum and the Serapeum, and it was in Alexandria that the 70 Jewish Scholars translated the Hebrew Scriptures into the Septuagint. Yet it was the final days of the Roman Republic, played out on its shores and in its colonnades, which forever marked out the political fortunes of the place.

In September 48 BC the great Pompey, foe of Caesar, already defeated at Pharsalus came in his ship to the port of Alexandria. After several days of waiting on board, he boarded a small landing craft to be taken to King Ptolemy XIII who was waiting on the shore. The crew turned on him with swords, and "Pompey, drawing his toga over his face with both hands, endured them all, nor did he say anything unworthy only gave a faint groan"[103] and died. Caesar was to follow Pompey and also fatefully to meet Cleopatra who made her dramatic entrance into the palace in a rolled carpet to evade her brother's forces, in place to prevent his ever headstrong sister from making contact with Caesar. In less than a year, and after a cruise on the Nile, Cleopatra bore Caesar's child, Caesarion. But, after Julius Caesar's assassination, Mark Antony became likewise besotted by the fascinating Egyptian Queen of whom Shakespeare wrote "and Anthony enthron'd in the market-place, did sit alone, whistling to the air; which, but for vacancy, had gone to gaze on Cleopatra too, and made a gap in nature". [104]

Like Pompey before him, Mark Antony was more than half defeated—at the naval battle of Actium by Octavian's forces—before he reached Alexandria in pursuance of Cleopatra and the scant protection that she could afford him. Mark Antony and she were tracked down by Octavian (Caesar's adopted heir—later styled Augustus) until both died, taking their own lives, in 30 BC. Not far away, and some years later, in another part of Augustus' Empire, a decree went out in Palestine in *c*.4 BC "that a census should be taken of the entire Roman World . . . and everyone (including Joseph and Mary) went to his own town to register".[105] A further forty years after that, the Apostle Mark is reputed to have founded the church in Alexandria. The church flourished and grew, but its inter-face with both Judaism and Greek philosophy was eventually to give birth to a heresy which dominated the Church, so recently endorsed by Constantine in the Empire, for sixty years.

Alexandria at the Start of the Fourth Century

Alexandria's history is one of intellectual strength. Eusebius reports that Philo (*c.* 20 BC—*c.*AD 50) "welcomed with whole-hearted approval the apostolic men of his day, who it seems were of Hebrew stock and therefore, in the Jewish manner, still retained most of their ancient customs".[106] It is highly probable that among the large Jewish Diaspora of the city, which was as much as a third of its population, a Christian community sprang up. Philo was anxious to prove a strong connection between the Greek philosophers, especially Plato, and Moses and the Jewish scriptures. He proceeded by way of arguing that Greek philosophy owed a good deal of its integrity and inspiration to the Jewish scriptures, and invited a synthesis between the two. Indeed it could be said that there appeared to be two conflicting movements in Alexandrian intellectual life in the third and early fourth centuries. One was to merge or synthesise the differing intellectual traditions as far as possible; this was true of the philosophical Jew Philo seeking to merge Greek philosophy with Jewish teaching but equally of Clement (*c.*150–*c.*215), a very sophisticated and urbane Christian theologian and lay teacher who "was concerned to show that his religion was both true, moral, and intellectually defensible in terms familiar to contemporary well educated students of philosophy".[107] The age-old issue of interpreting Christianity in the light of the chief intellectual movements of the day is what drove these teachers. What Philo and Clement sought to do in Alexandria, Justin Martyr was doing in second century Rome. Likewise, Origen, studying at around the same time as the neo-Platonist Plotinus, under Ammonius Saccas, was interpreting Christianity in part within the model of neo-Platonism as we have seen, but nevertheless the fusion of neo-Platonism in his thinking, especially his *oikonomia* (i.e. the dispensation or economy of God), in his *First Principles* is marked. The schools in Alexandria and the relative independence of some churches and their leaders enabled such a development to take place.

But at the very time of the emergence of Arius another movement was taking place, the growth of the power of the bishop and his teaching office. The teaching authority of the Bishop of Alexandria was already present in a man like Bishop Demetrius (who was shocked by Origen's independence) but became much more marked through three successive bishops: Alexander, Athanasius, and Cyril. Each seemed more dogmatic than the last. This process of strengthening the power of the bishop in part came about through the so called Melitian schism when Bishop Melitius of Lycopolis aroused the anger of fellow bishops, who had been imprisoned for their faith, through meddling in their dioceses and ordaining priests without consulting with their official visitors who were appointed while their own bishop was in prison to run the affairs the diocese. Furthermore Melitius criticised Peter, Bishop of Alexandria, for the leniency of his regulations for readmission of Christians to the Church who had compromised their faith in some way in the face of persecution. Melitius went further and set up an alternative hierarchy of bishops. Peter was in fact martyred for his faith but not, ironically, before ordaining Arius deacon, who was to become the eye of the storm of the Arian controversy, and who confronted Peter's successor Alexander of Alexandria. "The episcopacy of Alexander occurred during a time when the church in Alexander was still moving towards acceptance of a monarchical vision of episcopacy in which the bishop's authority over matters of faith and practice was unique and exceeded all authorities in the diocese".[108] So in Alexandria twin processes were at work which, given the spark of Arius himself, would create the highly combustible controversy which would dominate the Church for the rest of the century. On the one hand, there was free-thinking Alexandria, used to its philosophical schools, and, on the other hand, there was a newly strengthened teaching ministry of the Bishop recently tested and proven in several controversies. The emergence of Arius, and the heresy he expressed, was not just the work of a single man. Rather it reflected a trajectory or trend of thought present in the Church and wider intellectual community in Alexandria and beyond, which had swirled around for some time but which Arius dared to express more openly, more confrontationally, and more attractively than others. He represented free-thinking Alexandrians emanating from the schools with their neo-Platonism and tradition of independent thinking. The origin of this aspect of Alexandrian life reached back to Philo, Clement, and Origen who themselves sought to fuse either Judaism, in the case of Philo, or Christianity, in the case of Clement and Origen, with Greek Platonic and neo-Platonic thinking. This created the intellectual conditions which Arius focussed with a magnifying glass on the issue of the divinity of Christ.

Indeed, you might say that, from its foundation, the spirit of Alexandria was to challenge the Empire and it was proud of its independence; what it had done in the days of Cleopatra and the Ptolomies, merging Pharonic deities and Greek thought and paganism in a new deity, it would seek to do again. What others may have toyed with, Arius expressed: but his was not a single cloud coming out of a clear blue sky but a storm which had been brewing for years.

It would be too simple to say that Arius made explicit what was already implicit in others, especially Origen. Since the late fourth century and the strictures of Epiphanius, historians have pointed to *Origen* as the source of Arianism which fundamentally denied the divinity of the Son. But such a view is too simple. In Nicene studies the debate ebbs to and fro: Basil Studer talks about "The Origenist controversy at the start of the fourth century"[109]; Simonetti in *La Crisi* likewise, as if Arius is simply an extension of Origenist thought. Alternatively, the controversy is cast as between those who stand in the tradition of Origen and those like Marcellus of Ancyra who stressed the unity of the Godhead and were little influenced by Origen. But the question remains, did Origen pave the way for Arius, did the neo-Platonism of Plotinus shape both Origen and Arius in their teaching about the Trinity?

Again the answer is complex: when it comes to Origen's doctrine of creation he appears deeply influenced by neo-Platonism, especially in his positing of a pre-material world in which souls existed. But when it came to teaching about the Trinity, and in particular the relationship of Father and Son, could he be charged with "subordinationism"? That is, the concept beloved of neo-Platonists that different hierarchies of being were involved in creation as well as in the revelation of knowledge about the divine. First, Origen was far too much of an exegete of the Bible to fall into that crude statement,[110] but he did search for a vocabulary to express what he found in the Bible in describing the relationship of Father and Son. For Origen, the Son was eternally generated from the Father (i.e. there was never a time when the Son was not, to answer the Arian ditty that there was a time when the Son was not). Indeed, the Father was eternally the Father because the Son was eternally the Son; there was never a time that Father was not the Father because there was never a time in which the Son did not exist. Origen argues that Father and Son are co-relative terms. Likewise "For Origen, he who is God's Wisdom and Power must have always been with the Father".[111] The Son reveals, or is the image of, the Father as light from light, or brightness from the Sun,[112] and what was a new metaphor for Origen becomes accepted both in the creeds of Nicaea in 325 and in Constantinople in 381. Indeed the reception of vocabulary and metaphor in the description of the Trinity is itself a fascinating study of *sifting* by the Church and also one of adopting some words or metaphors as being both orthodox and biblical while discarding others as being misleading and heretical.

Two words which are important in the controversy which were used by Origen are *ousia* and *hypostasis*. The Greek word *ousia* or substance was used in the Trinitarian disputes to describe the mode of unity between Father, Son, and Spirit, while *hypostasis* was used mostly to describe the distinctiveness or individuality of the each person of the Trinity. The fact that these terms had been previously used as vocabulary in the second century disputes with the Gnostics made fixing their precise meaning in a different dispute about the unity of the three persons of the godhead as well as their separateness all the more difficult. Indeed the process by which terms at the centre of the fourth century Trinitarian dispute gained an exact and widely held meaning is hard to follow, and, at a distance of nearly two thousand years, such forensic philology is hard to undertake. The meaning of the words at the heart of this dispute is very much part of the struggle for orthodoxy. For Origen, *ousia* was too material a concept so he denies that the Son came from the Father's *ousia*",[113] but this was a throwback to earlier Gnostic disputes. "Thus *ousia* language in most forms seemed to Origen unsuitable for application to the divine essence"[114]. Nevertheless, *ousia* language was to be at the heart of the struggle for orthodoxy.

Equally *hypostasis* was a Platonic concept. It was used by Origen as a philosophical term which spoke of the Son and the Spirit, having a separate existence from the Father, although he used it in a distinctively biblical way of distinguishing their complete separation from creation.[115] In *Contra Celsum* Origen speaks of the Father and Son as two big things (*pragmata*) in *hypostasis*.[116] Origen is searching for a way of saying that the Father and the Son have a distinct existence.[117] In his commentary on John 2:27 Origen writes: "We are here persuaded that that there are three *hypostases*, The Father, the Son, and the Holy Spirit, and we believe that only the Father is unbegotten".[118] The sharing of substance (*ousia*) and the separateness of identity (*hypostasis*) would be central to the controversy of the following eighty years which first took hold with the emergence of Arius and his self-consciously heterodox views that he expressed to Alexander, Bishop of Alexandria.

Arius and Alexander

The eye of the heretical storm which blew from Alexandria across the Empire was centred on Arius. Arius came from Libya, possibly from Ptolemais, the chief city of Upper Libya, the old Cyrenacia from whose five cities—the Pentapolis—and their bishops Arius was given consistent support. Given the claims the Alexandrian see made over its western neighbour, it is not surprising that when one of their own should be in dispute with the Bishop of Alexandria, Arius should be given support by the Bishops of the Pentapolis, the five coastal settlements of Upper Libya.[119]

Knowledge of Arius' early life and education is sketchy at best. In a letter to Eusebius of Nicomedia, a supporter, he describes himself as a *sulloukianista* which is generally taken to mean a fellow-Lucianist.[120] This implies Arius to be a pupil or follower of Lucian of Antioch. Lucian was an influential "subordinationist" (i.e. believing that the Son is not equal but subordinate to the Father) theologian and martyr who died in 312 in Nicomedia. Arius was not included in the list of Lucian's pupils drawn up by Philostorgius, but Philostorgius is not always regarded as a reliable source.[121] Nevertheless, there is some overlap between the views of Arius and Lucian. This may imply a time of convergence with Lucian's theological thought, before a later divergence. Equally, Arius' philosophical education is uncertain. A shadowy Christian Aristotelian teacher in Alexandria noted by Eusebius of Nicomedia called Anatolis, who later became Bishop of Laodicaea in *c*.270, may have been his teacher, but if this was the case the resulting dating would mean that Arius's birth would have to be in the early 250s creating other difficulties. Alternatively, Arius may have been taught by Iamblichus, a neo-Platonist teaching in Antioch around 300 and a pupil himself of Anatolius. Both ideas are possible, even tempting, but neither are certain. The clearest description of Arius is by Epihanius, the puritan and orthodox Bishop of Salamis, which is worth quoting in full:

> He was very tall in stature, with downcast countenance—counterfeited like a guileful serpent, and well able to deceive any unsuspecting heart through its cleverly devised appearance. For he was always garbed in a short cloak (*hemiphoron*) and sleeveless tunic (*kolobion*); he spoke gently, and people found him persuasive and flattering.[122]

Arius was ordained by Bishop Peter in 312 who later excommunicated him for his role in the Melitian controversy in which the ascetic Arius demanded more rigorous treatment of Christians seeking re-admission to the Church following their acquiescence to the authorities. However, after being reconciled to the Bishop, Arius was subsequently ordained as a priest by Peter's successor Achillas (312–313), with whom he had an alliance, and was appointed to the important Alexandrian city centre church of Baucalis. He was a popular preacher and teacher, liked by the dockers of Alexandria for whom he wrote theological sea shanties, and he was also popular among a large following of young women.[123]

In c.321 he threw down, quite self-consciously, his theological gauntlet in a credal letter to Bishop Alexander which was to stir the world: "The Son who is tempted, suffers, and dies, however exalted he may be, is not to be equal to the immutable Father beyond pain and death: if he is other than the Father, he is inferior".[124] By the time Arius wrote this provocative credal letter to Bishop Alexander in c.321, he may well have been a relatively old man, probably in his sixties. As Rowan Williams concludes: "it seems safe to assume that he was not a young man when the crisis broke".[125] But its effect was to precipitate the Church into its greatest controversy to date. From that moment events were to move quickly.

The precise order of events from Arius' initial credal letter to Alexander (c.321) which precipitated the controversy to the calling of Nicaea (325) is hard to fix.[126] What is clear is that a mix of statements, synods, encyclical correspondence by bishops, on both sides of the dispute, and imperial interaction with the protagonists fuelled the controversy.

The extant documents at the root of the controversy that can be ascribed to Arius are four in number: the confession of faith presented by Arius to Alexander, signed by Arius and eleven supporters; Arius' letter to Eusebius of Nicomedia; the confession submitted by Arius to Constantine after Nicaea in 327 as a further statement of faith; and lastly the *Thalia* (probably written earlier in 321 after the initial storm), of which only fragments remain. The theology which comes from these documents is, in general, that the Son is said to be "produced by the Father before all ages".[127] God pre-exists the Son, giving rise to the familiar Arian slogan "There was when He was not". God the Father alone is supreme, is a single, simple, spiritual reality and the Son is like the created order made out of nothing.[128] "The Word who is subject in the experiences of Jesus of Nazareth is a passible being and therefore distinct from God".[129] As a distinct individual, *hypostasis* or *ousia*, he is not part of God, and could never have been "within" the life of God; he is dependent and subordinate. The *Thalia*, of which only a fragment remains and which is quoted by Athanasius in his later rebuttal of Arian heresy, takes traditional concepts found in Alexandrian theology, especially Origen, Clement, and Philo, and pushes them to an extreme. It is conservative in the sense that there is almost nothing that could not be found in earlier writers; it is radical and individual in the way it combines and reorganises traditional ideas and presses them to logical conclusions—God is free, the world need not exist, the Word is other than God, the Word is part of the world, so the word is freely formed *ex nihilo*. Arius therefore took Origen's ideas about the relationship of Father and Son to an extreme; unhinging them from the restraining exegetical work which was so much part of Origen's ministry. Arius allowed neo-Platonism, as expressed in Plotinus, and in particular the notion of there being a hierarchy of several distinct hypostases, to lead him to the conclusion that the Word did not exist before the divine decision to create the world. God the Father is an absolute unity and cannot be fully understood or conceptualised by the Son, and the defining attributes of one subject cannot be shared with another.[130] Understandably, this set of ideas shook the Church to its roots, and its most sustained opponents were to come originally and most resolutely from Alexandria, firstly Alexander and then his secretary at Nicaea and before, Athanasius.

The response of Alexander to Arius was clear. He wrote an encyclical letter to Bishop of Alexander of Byzantium in c.321–2 (the city had not yet been re-founded as Constantinople). The letter, which is called *Hē philarchos*, strongly condemned Arianism, saying that, "by their hypothesis that he [Christ] was created out of nothing", and that, "they overthrow the testimony of Divine Scriptures, which declares the unchangeable nature of the Word and the Divinity and Wisdom of the Word, which Word and Wisdom is Christ".[131] It went on to denounce the Arians: "O what wicked arrogance! O What excessive folly! What false boasting, joined with madness and Satanic pride, has hardened their impious hearts!"[132] Consequently Arius and Achillas, his chief episcopal associate in Alexandria, were expelled from the church, but, like others before them, they left Alexandria and found refuge in Caesarea in Palestine.

In Palestine Arius appears to have set up congregations under the patronage of two powerful bishops: Eusebius of Caesarea, the early Church historian, and Eusebius, bishop of Nicomedia. Nicomedia was the eastern imperial capital whose bishop therefore was a powerful voice at court. A further synod at Alexandria condemned Arius, although another synod in Bithynia supported him. At this point, Constantine, hearing of the increasing ferment and division in the church, and following his victory over Licinius (the eastern Emperor whom he deposed militarily) and failing to heal the rift by sending a legate, Bishop Ossius, with a letter begging both sides in Alexandria to settle their doctrinal differences, called a Council of all the Bishops to settle the questions in dispute once and for all. So the Council of Nicaea was called under the patronage of the now sole Emperor and under the chairmanship of Ossius to hammer out an orthodox creed for the Church. It met under the watchful eye of an Emperor resolved to create a united Church in his refreshing summer residence on the shores of a delightful lake.

Nicaea, Its Aftermath, and Athanasius

Some 270 bishops, mostly drawn from the East, were gathered at Nicaea (present day Iznic) not far from Constantinople or Byzantium for the first great Ecumenical Council of the Church. There had been other councils but none so self-consciously important or far reaching; there had been other creeds which were local and baptismal in scope but none so intentionally binding and canonical for the whole Church, even though the West was more poorly represented. The exact nature of the proceedings or how people participated is not known, but it is known that Ossius of Cordoba, the Emperor's episcopal legate, presided, and Constantine himself was there for at least part of the time. The key participants were Alexander of Alexandria (with his young secretary Athanasius), Eustathius of Antioch (who had not yet fallen from Imperial grace for criticising Contantine's mother Helen), Marcellus of Ancyra, and the two prominent Eusebians, Eusebius of Nicomedia and Eusebius of Caesarea. Their object, as defined by Constantine, was to bring unity and consensus to the Church by agreeing a creed to which they could subscribe and dealing with the issues concerning the Son's divinity raised so provocatively by Arius. The Eusebians of Caesarea and of Nicomedia both presented creeds:[133] the former's was very mild or non-committal on key issues such as the Son's generation and was, in his words wholeheartedly accepted, whilst the latter's was badly received. The object of the Alexandrian bishops and their supporters was to secure the outright rejection of Arius and the condemnation of his views. They therefore used a key word which he and his supporters had previously rejected to describe the relation of Son to Father, and this was *homoousios*—meaning of the same substance or from the essence of the Father.

The creed which was hammered out was as follows:[134]

> We believe in one God, the Father almighty, maker of all things, visible and invisible;
> And in one Lord Jesus Christ, the Son of God, begotten from the Father, only-begotten, that is, from the substance of the father, God from God, light from light, true God from true God, begotten not made, of one substance with the Father, through Whom all

things came into being, things in heaven and things on earth, Who because of us men and because of our salvation came down and became incarnate, becoming man, suffered and rose again on the third day, ascended to the heavens, and will come to judge the living and the dead;

And in the Holy Spirit.

But as for those who say, There was when he was not, and, Before being born He was not, and that he came into existence out of nothing, or who assert that the Son of God is from a different hypostasis or substance, or is created, or is subject to alteration or change—these the catholic Church anathematizes.[135]

The creed therefore both proclaims in its first part and denounces in its second: "Anyone who affirms that the Father pre-existed the Son, or that the Son is a creature produced out of nothingness, or is subject to moral change or development, is formally declared a heretic".[136] But it was not quite so plain sailing for, like any document, it was open to interpretation in two ways: firstly, what its words actually meant and secondly, how it was to be interpreted as a whole.

The two most important words are "*ousia*" and "*hypostasis*"; both of which are taken from Greek thought and philosophy, and both had been wielded in former theological controversies, and both were seminal to the meaning of the creed. The issue with words is what do they mean and is their meaning unmistakeable.

> Any attempt to define fourth-century theological terminologies by reference solely to their philological origins or to a history of non-Christian philosophical development runs the constant danger of resulting in an artificial clarity that is not reflected in actual theological usage. Rather, we need to be attentive to the histories of theological use of these terms prior to Nicaea.[137]

The usage of each term is seminal to the meaning of the creed.

Ousia (substance) occurs three times in the creed. Firstly when the Son is described as being "of the *ousia* of the Father"; secondly, as a probable gloss on that original statement, in which the creed goes on to say that

Father and Son are *homoousios* (of the same substance); and lastly it says that those people are anathematised who say that the Son is of "another *hypostasis* or *ousia*". The fact that the controversy continued for at least another fifty-five years until the Council of Constantinople shows that the word *ousia* was clearly liable to different understandings.[138]

Previous uses of *ousia*, prior to Nicaea, show a variety of meanings. The term had been used by the Gnostics in the second century to indicate either different semi-divine beings (*ousias*) which were made out of pre-existing substances, or to describe a substance (or ontological links) capable of being shared with hierarchies of higher or lower deities and enlightened humans. The term for some Christians was "irredeemably materialist", and, by the fourth century, Manichees taught that deities were made through the sub-division of other divine beings with whom they shared an ontological status. Although we do not know if the Manichees actually used the word *homoousios*, we do know that pro-Nicene theologians were being accused of being Manichaeist even before the council met.[139] In addition, Paul of Samosata, a third century bishop of Antioch whose Christology was likewise condemned by at least three church councils, also used the word *homoousios*. And Dionysius of Rome criticised some local Sabellians—who had a modalist[140] view of the Trinity—and claimed that Father and Son were of the same substance (*homoousios*). In other words, the term already had a history of use which made it suspect to some whilst others were content to deploy it. The term *hypostasis*, on the other hand, was less significant in the creed, for the intention of the creed was to ensure that Father and Son were regarded as sharing the same being; *hypostasis* was, rather, a term which was used by Origen to emphasise a "circumscribed individual reality".[141] This was not the main focus of the creed but would be an important building block for later Cappadocian Trinitarian theology.

If the creed was at pains to stress that Father and Son were of identical substance, does that mean to say that the idea of "numerical identity of substance"[142] was the true function of the creed? In other words, was the Creed stressing the unity of the godhead and not simply that Father and Son were of the same substance, and that therefore the Son was fully God? The answer must be that the great issue of the Council "was not the unity of the Godhead as such; it was the Son's co-eternity with the

Father, which the Arians denied".[143] The creed did not attempt to tackle the closely related issue of the relationship of the divine unity, but it did bring that issue forward as well as the relationship of the Spirit to the Father and the Son.

When the Council of Nicaea was over the matter was far from resolved. Although Constantine stood by the settlement at Nicaea for the rest of his life until May 337, a further twelve years, there was a kind of rowing back from its clarity and three parties seemed to emerge. The Eusebians, who more or less sided with Arius (though by no means could be called Arians, although Athanasius would have them known as such), the Nicene party, led principally by Athanasius (Alexander, Bishop of Alexandria's young and fearless secretary), and the party which sought to defend the unity of the Godhead. This group was led by Marcellus of Ancyra and argued that the *hypostases* of the Son and the Spirit only truly existed during the time of their respective engagement with redemption and creation respectively, and then were resumed and subsumed into the divine unity.

The Eusebians consisted principally of Eusebius of Caesarea, the Church historian, and Eusebius of Nicomedia. Although they had signed up to the Nicene Creed they in fact supported other more local creeds in which the word *homoousios* had been omitted. Eusebius of Nicomedia was critical of the phrase "from the *ousia* of the Father" as suggesting a materialistic view of the Son's generation and stating that nothing could in fact share the Father's *ousia* since he was unbegotten. Likewise Eusebius of Caesarea, writing before Nicaea, demonstrates similar worries saying that the phrase, "from the *ousia* of the Father," implies a materialistic diminution of the Father's being in the generation of the Son.[144] Despite their hesitations they were able to engineer the exile of their principal opponents: Athanasius who, from 328 was patriarch of Alexandria, Eustathius of Antioch, and Marcellus of Ancyra. Arius and most of his supporters were, at Constantine's request, readmitted to communion within two or three years of the Council, exiled bishops returned to their sees, and even Arius appeared before the Emperor and a council of bishops at Jerusalem in September 335. Constantine and then the Bishops at a subsequent council accepted Arius, writing to Athanasius in Alexandria to inform him of their decision. A year later, following an appeal from Athanasius, Arius' case was reheard in Constantinople in 336 at another synod. Arius swore to a statement of belief which indicated some acceptance of Nicaea, "but Athanasius reports that Arius read a statement of his belief but kept concealed about his person a fuller more unequivocally Arian confession; this enabled him to swear solemnly that he held *ex animo* 'to what he had written'".[145] At this point the Emperor ordered Alexander, presumably also in Constantinople, to admit Arius to fellowship again. "Faced with this ultimatum, Alexander in dramatic fashion (accompanied by Athanasius' friend, the presbyter Macarius) withdrew to the episcopal church (*Hagia Eirene*) and prayed that either he or Arius might die before morning. Arius meanwhile, smitten 'by the necessities of nature', retired to a public lavatory, and died, apparently from some kind of internal haemorrhage or rupture. The Emperor and the city were duly shocked and edified".[146] Although Arius had died, the battle with the teaching he had espoused and other teachings like it raged for another forty-four years.

The Rise of Athanasius

Three years after Nicaea, Bishop Alexander of Alexandria died and, after a rather "managed" election, Athanasius succeeded him. He was just thirty and had been Alexander's secretary for a number of years, attending him at Nicaea and writing some of the refutations of Arius for Alexander prior to that. Athanasius was born between AD 295–299, and one source suggests that his parents were not Christians and "that he was the son of an eminent woman who was a worshipper of idols and very rich".[147] The same text says that that both Athanasius and his mother were baptised and taken under the tutelage of Alexander. Athanasius "memorised the gospels and read the divine scriptures and when he was mature, Alexander ordained him a deacon and, made him his scribe and he became like an interpreter of the Father and a minister of the word which he wished to speak." Such was Athanasius' familiarity with the scriptures that Gregory of Nazianzus says of Athanasius in his funeral oration that "he meditated on every book of the Old and New Testament with a depth which no one has reached with even one of them".[148] His education had given him familiarity with the Stoic cosmology "which is employed to speak of the Word as the principle of harmony in the cosmos, and a Middle Platonic ontology in which God is characterised as true being, to which creature being is linked in participation."[149] It may be that this familiarity with Greek philosophy gave him the spur to write *"Against the Greeks—On the Incarnation".*

Between 328 and 335, the start date of Athanasius' first exile, he faced a stormy time in Alexandria. Athanasius was accused by the Melitian party of rigging his own election to the see when he was below canonical age, encouraging the breaking of a chalice by his close associate Macarius over the head of a Melitian priest, Isychras, and the murder of a bishop! Summoned by the Emperor to a council at Tyre in 335, he was found guilty of some of the charges, was opposed by Eusebius of Nicomedia, and sent into exile at Trier. Two years later Constantine died and one of his sons, Constantinus, accepted Athanasius' account of the Council of Tyre, and then persuaded his brothers to accept an amnesty for all exiled bishops which enabled Athanasius' return to Alexandria. His first of many exiles was over.

But it was short lived. Despite being met by cheering crowds, and having personally consolidated monastic support, particularly that of St Anthony, calling a council in Egypt in 338 which gave him support, and having the support of Pope Julius, his case was heard by another council convened at Antioch in 339 and he was again deposed. From the outset it was clear that the aim was to exile him once more. The same charges were brought against him as at Tyre, only now others were added, such as that he had returned illegitimately to Egypt and that he was stealing funds from the sale of grain meant for the Empire.[150] Athanasius was once again exiled and this time Gregory of Cappadocia (not one of the Cappadocian Fathers) was made bishop in his place. Nonetheless, Athanasius remained typically unmoved. Writing in his Festal Letter (XI:12) he said, "let us consider as nothing the afflictions or tribulations which the party of Eusebius has caused us because of their jealousy".[151] If anything Athanasius grew stronger by being opposed. For this second exile he went to Rome where, for the most part, he stayed until 346.

While in Rome Athanasius was able to deepen his defence of Nicaea. It was here that he wrote *Orations against the Arians* in which he largely eschewed the language of *homoousios* as being not sufficiently biblical and chose to defend Nicene orthodoxy from scripture.[152] Here too he met Marcellus and for a time made common cause with him, rejecting the idea of God being three distinct *hypostases*[153] and so calling into question the creeds of the Council—especially the Dedication creed—in which there is no mention of *ousia* and God is described as existing in three *hypostases*.[154] Here too he rejected the *Thalia* by Arius, and began his successful polemic against what he termed a conspiracy of Arianism, calling his opponents Arian madmen (Festal letter for 338) or Ariomaniacs which he most probably drew from Marcellan and Eustathian (of Antioch) circles.[155]

The theology Ahthanasius developed during this period was most maturely expressed in his three *Orations against the Arians*. In his *First Oration* he concentrates on issues relating to the generation of the Son, that is, how did the son come to exist. Athanasius refutes the Arian question, "did God make him who was not, from nothing or from something pre-existing?".[156] Arians expected the answer that God made the Son from nothing, but Athanasius rebuts this as a human way of thinking, as God's "making" is not like our own. Although some analogies may be useful, others do not accurately reflect scripture and so are misleading. Athanasius also appeals to unity of action between Father and Son especially in the Son's redemptive activity and in his Deifying activity.

"Athanasius' argument speaks not of two realities engaged in a common activity, but develops his most basic sense that the Son is intrinsic to the Father's being".[157] It is also (and here is one if his chief arguments) that because the Word and Son is *proper* to the father's essence that redemption is possible in Christ. Only the "natural and true" Word could draw us into the Father's presence. Lastly, Athanasius is seeking a new vocabulary to describe the closeness of Father and Son, so in his First Oration he writes "For the Son is in the Father, as is it is allowed us to know, because the whole being of the Son is *proper* to the Father's essence, as radiance from the light and stream from the fountain; so that whoever sees the Son sees the Father, and knows that the Son's being, because from the Father is therefore in the Father" using the term *proper* (*idios*) to describe the identity and closeness of Father and Son. There are strong foretastes of Gregory of Nyssa's description of the Trinity in Basil's Letter 37, normally now ascribed to Gregory. In 346, following the failure of another council summoned by both Constantantius and Constans at Serdica (Sophia, Bulgaria) where the Eastern bishops and Western bishops would not meet in the same room, and Athanasius and Marcellus were *personae non gratae* to the Eastern group, a meeting between Athanasius and Constantius was eventually engineered. Unexpectedly cordial, with Constantius seeking rapprochement so as to unite the Empire more effectively in a campaign against the Persians, Athanasius was re-instituted as Bishop of Alexandria, Gregory of Cappadocia having died. Athanasius returned in great pomp in 346. One modern writer observes "his triumphant progress into Alexandria resembled less the return of an exiled bishop than the adventures of a Roman Emperor".[158] A flavour of Athanasius reading of his return is caught in this passage from *History of the Arians*:

> I hardly need to speak of the Bishops of Egypt and Libya and of the people of these lands and of Alexandria. They all assembled together and their joy was unspeakable, for not only had they received their friends back alive, which was beyond all their hope, but they delivered from the heretics, who were like tyrants and raging dogs. Great was the delight of the people as they gathered in worship and incited each other to virtue ... There was deep and wonderful peace among the churches, as the bishops wrote from everywhere to Athanasius and received from him the customary letters of peace.

Although Athanasius enjoyed his see for ten years, the longest continuous period of office in his forty-six years as a bishop, this peace did not last beyond 356 when his third exile began. In 350 Constans, the Emperor in the West, was killed by his general and usurper Magnentius. Eventually Constantius, after years of campaigning, repressed Magnentius' insurrection, who committed suicide; Constantius became sole Emperor of East and West until his death in 361. Constantius was determined to exert his will upon the Church. The First Council of Sirmium virtually declared invalid the Nicene creed in which it interpreted the Son as being the extension of the Father's being, prompting Jerome's famous remark "that the whole world groaned to find itself Arian". Further pressure was exerted upon the Western and Eastern bishops by Constantius in a more aggressive policy of doctrinal enforcement at the Councils of Arles 353 and Milan 355. Then on 8 February 356, just after midnight, troops were sent into the church of Theonas in Alexandria to arrest Athanasius.

Under the Imperial commander Syrianus, 5,000 troops surrounded and invaded the church. Athanasius sat on his episcopal throne; "So I sat upon the throne and urged that first the deacon should read the psalm [Psalm 36] and people respond, 'For his mercy is forever' and then everyone should leave and go away to their homes. But the general then entered by force and the soldiers surrounded the altar in order to arrest us".[159] Somehow Athanasius escaped, avoiding the fate of Thomas Becket almost a millennium later, and went into hiding in the Egyptian desert.

Athanasius in Egypt and Hilary in the West were undoubtedly the chief protagonists for orthodox Trinitarian theology, but in Cappadocia a further development in orthodoxy was emerging in the lives and writings of the Cappadocian Fathers. In 360, after some years of community life following his return from Athens and a tour of monastic communities with his friend Eustathius of Sebaste, Basil was ordained deacon. It signalled the start of his and other's engagement with the struggle for orthodoxy; Alexandria would give way for a while to Cappadocia as the region which took forward a more mature theology of the Trinity.

CHAPTER 4

Contending for the Trinity: the Contribution of the Cappadocians

The years from 351 and the First Council of Sirmium, following the accession of Constantius as sole Emperor in 350, until the Emperor's death in 361 saw further complicating developments in the Trinitarian or Arian controversy. After his dramatic escape from arrest in 356, Athanasius went into exile until 362 for a third time, this time to the Egyptian desert where he was not idle: on the one hand espousing more clearly than ever the life of an ascetic, in keeping with the tradition of Anthony, but on the other hand honing his polemic against the Arians and defending the *ousia* language of Nicaea as being completely necessary.[160] At the same time the doctrinal controversy surrounding the relationship of the Father and the Son in the 350s became considerably more complicated as the decade continued, splintering the opposition to the Nicene *homoousios* orthodoxy into three parties.

Despite the resistance of the new Pope Liberius, the Emperor Constantius sought to gain the condemnation of Athanasius at two councils in the West, at Arles in 353 and Milan in 355, and also to uphold the Arian creed of the first council of Sirmium in 351. By the end of the decade, in the East, the twin Councils of Seleukia and Ariminium gave rise to what Jerome called a state in which "the whole world groaned, amazed to find itself Arian". Twenty years later the Church had more or less returned to orthodoxy.

Ousia Battles, Aetius, and Eunomius

Following Nicaea the main theological fault line ran along the question of whether the Son was of the same substance as the Father *(homoousios)*. Athanasius himself tried to demonstrate the unity of Father and Son with a different vocabulary, either explaining the relationship of Father and Son with clearly scriptural language, especially from St John, or using a new phrase like "the whole being of the Son is *proper* to the Father's essence".[161] He did this principally in his three Orations against the Arians written during his second exile in Rome. He looked for a new vocabulary with the hope of drawing together those who found agreement about *homoousios* difficult because of its Gnostic and material associations.

Nevertheless, different parties decided to interpret *homoousios* in whatever way they chose. Eusebius of Caesarea had said in a letter to his diocese shortly after Nicaea that the word *homoousios* did not imply any material division of God and that it was still possible to read Nicaea as implying a certain subordinationism.[162] With such variant interpretations of a single word it is not surprising that other related but more nuanced words emerged which more accurately reflected the theologies of different parties. When this happened it was not surprising that Athanasius in his third exile in Egypt reverted to a more outright defence of *homoousios*.[163]

From the 350s onwards three main groupings emerged in opposition to Nicaea, for the most part grouped around different *ousia* words. These were the *homoiousios* party, the *homoian* party, and finally the *heterousian* (or *Anomians*) party, each of which needs to be explained.

If *homoousios* meant of the same essence and substance then the first and most finessed difference from that position was the *homoiousios* party, meaning *like* in substance or essence. This word-party represented the most moderate dissenters from the full Nicene orthodoxy, but for the likes of Epiphanius they were still semi-Arian.[164] Unlike the Sirmium Creed of 357, which seemed to banish all *ousia* language and drew on the earlier fourth Antioch creed of 341, this party held to the middle ground, on the one hand not supporting *homoousios,* but equally not going for more radical alternatives.

The most influential people to emerge in association with this Trinitarian theology were Basil of Ancyra and Cyril of Jerusalem. Although there is no absolute clarity over Basil's position "he offers an argument parallel to that offered by Athanasius in his Orations, Basil argues a number of times that the Son is like the Father in both activity and essence and that likeness in certain activities indicates likeness in essence".[165] Father and Son both have a likeness in wisdom and essence, and the Son was the revealer of the Father. He argued that, as God's essence is incomprehensible to us, we cannot speculate on the generation of the Son, which seems eminently sensible. Basil's position was in fact cautiously welcomed in later years by Athanasius in his *De Synodis* where he says, "But since they [e.g. Basil of Ancyra and others] say that he [the Son] is "of the essence" and "like in essence", what do they signify by these but *homoousios*". [166]

Cyril was bishop of Jerusalem from 348 until his death in 386 or 387 and although the legitimacy of his episcopal election was challenged (and he was briefly deposed for selling church furniture to feed the poor!), he left a lasting legacy in his famous catechetical lectures. Cyril stressed the monarchy of God, his singleness, his incomprehensibility, and, like Basil, he emphasised the incomprehensible generation of the Son which occurs "in the context of the Father's immateriality and immutability".[167] In his eleventh lecture Cyril wrote, "He was begotten Son from the beginning, Son of the Father, like in all things to his Genitor, begotten Life of Life, Light of Light, Truth of Truth, Wisdom of Wisdom, King of King, God of God, Power and Power".[168] Cyril's generous use of the X from X (e.g. Light from Light) language was to show that Father and Son were one; but it seems that oneness was still like-substance rather than being the same substance.

The second word-party which existed around this time was the *homoian*-party, a party which held that the Son was like the Father (not like in substance thereby dropping the *ousia* concept). It was one further step away from the unity of the Father and Son as expressed in *homoiousios*. The leadership of this party or alliance was never entirely clear but Acacius, Bishop of Caesarea—who succeeded Eusebius—and Eudoxius, Bishop of Antioch from 357 and who later became Bishop of Constantinople, were seemingly the front runners. Theirs was a reaction to Marcellus of Ancyra who, although supporting the *homoousios* statement of Nicaea, did so from the position of stressing the singleness or unity of the Godhead to the detriment of their separate *hypostases*. The *homoian* party ensured the Son's distinctiveness from the Father by saying that the Son was like the Father, and there appears to be a greater degree of subordination in this description than in the earlier *homoiousios* description.

In 359 Constantius decided to emulate his father by calling a general council. In the end two councils were convened for East and West. The Eastern group met at Sirmium and drew up what was later called the Dated Creed because the prologue had a date in it, and its opponents came to ridicule the idea that a creed could have a date, and not be true for all time! In this creed all *ousia* language was omitted, the power of Acacius at court became evident, and Basil of Ancyra only signed it by adding the phrase that there was a likeness of *being* between Father and Son. Basil of Ancyra, seems to have been upstaged, and despite letters of revision by George of Laodicea following the Council its tenets held. Thus the *homoian* party appears to have swept the theological field. George of Laodicea's pithy summary of the *homioans* was that they believed Father and Son were "like in will, unlike in essence". But Basil wanted to know how that could be the case if in the creed leaders signed up to the statement the Son "is like the Father in all respects". However, even for George—"there seems to be a sense in which although the Son shares the Father's attributes derivatively the Father remains ontologically superior".[169]

The Western Council, which met at Ariminum (northern Italy), refused the Dated Creed and Valens and Ursacius, leaders of the Arians in the West, were excommunicated. Nevertheless, a minority of bishops went from the Council of Ariminum to the Emperor at Nike in Thrace where they were persuaded to accept the Dated Creed. Such a *volte face* was in part due to imperial pressure and the fear of exile. The Eastern council then met in September 359 at Seleukia at which Acacius produced a creed very similar to the Dated Creed which was rejected, and at the same time the ejection of Acacius as bishop of Caesarea was engineered.

However, delegations were sent to the Emperor at Constantinople, and a further creed which was a variation of the Dated Creed was drawn up which gained the support of the *homoian* and *homoiousian* parties on the final night of 359, but, in some kind of ecclesiastical coup, Basil of Ancyra and others of his persuasion were deposed. Acacius was made Bishop of Constantinople, the creed of the same name was published, and "the world groaned to find itself Arian".

Essentially, it was a *homoian* creed and it would remain on the credal statute book for twenty years until a new Creed from Constantinople was promulgated by Theodosius supported by Gregory of Nazianzus and Gregory of Nyssa (by then Bishop of Sebaste) in the imperial capital. This creed was the result of a long struggle for orthodoxy fought by the Cappadocian Fathers building on the earlier struggles of Athanasius in the East and Hilary and others in the West.

The third word-party which existed during this period was the *anomians* or *heterousian* party. In a word they believed that Father and Son were *unlike* in substance or essence. Clearly this was the most extreme reaction to *homoousios* or Nicene theology, and although strongly advocated by Aetius and Eunomius it never gained the support of the Emperor Constantius and was roundly condemned by the Cappadocians and others. Heterousians stressed the differences between Father and Son and the unlikeness according to essence of the Father and the Son. They were not necessarily a neo-Arian party, for they restricted the *unlikeness-of-Father-and-Son* to essence rather than other characteristics which they admitted Father and Son shared. Their virtually contemporary historian Philostorgius cast Aetius and Eunomius as true heroes, preserving the Antiochene theology which came from Lucian of Antioch.[170]

Aetius was educated in his theology by several supporters of Arius during the 320s and "even in these circles he gained a reputation for pushing a strong subordinationism".[171] He came from the hotspot of Alexandria to Antioch in 357 when Eudoxius was made bishop. The main building block of his Trintarian theology was that the essence of God lay in his *ingeneracy*—that is his eternal existence which distinguished Father from Son, for in some sense he believed the Son was generated in or by the Father. His was, therefore, a neo-Platonic view of God expressed with very logical or syllogistic argument, only a small portion of which remains in his work the *Syntagmation* (little book). His logic was that "all that is generated and all that generates from its own substance must be compound. God, not being compound, cannot generate in this way, but only by God's will or authority".[172] The Son, being the product of God's will, must be subordinate. This argument is dependent on a Greek philosophical paradigm which seeks to explain the existence of God in its own Hellenistic terms and therefore makes this construct or premise superior to the thing which it is describing—or at the very least makes the subject fit the philosophical framework rather than vice versa.

This is a methodological weakness but it must be recognised that every age uses its own philosophical constructs to explain God and these will be limiting, but another methodology needed to be found and this was part of the Cappadocian contribution.

Eunomius was some twenty-five years younger than Aetius and from about 355 was his secretary. He was made Bishop of Cyzicus in 360, probably through the influence of Eudoxius, and was to die in 394 or 395 in Dakora near Cappadocian Caesarea.[173] For Eunomius, the very fact of the Son being begotten makes him unable to share the Father's simplicity or essence. Furthermore, the characteristic of ingeneracy distinguishes the Father from the Son, who also admitted in scripture that the Father is "greater" than him[174] and was also ignorant of certain things (e.g. the time of his Second Coming; see Mark 13:32). Eunomius makes the same distinction in his *Apology* as Aetius, that since the Father alone was ingenerate the Son could not share his essence, and therefore the Son was begotten by the Father's will; hence, in some way, the Son is inferior, or at least unlike, the Father. Although Eunomius does describe the Son as created, he implies that the Son is nevertheless distinct from all other creation and remains maker of all things. The Spirit likewise does not share the Father's essence but is a product of the Father's will through the Son, and is therefore inferior to both.

These views seem to be the final logical extension of the *homoian* position, but in the end they were never fully taken up by the court.[175] Following a Sirmium Council in 358,[176] Basil of Ancrya petitioned the Emperor to discipline Eunomius and his associates. Eudoxius, Aetius, and Eunomius were all exiled, and it seems that Constantius was persuaded by Basil of Ancyra to uphold the earlier Dedication creed from Antioch (*c*.340). But such were the vagaries and twists and turns of the controversy that either creeds or the promulgations of Synods or Councils did not seem to stick for long. Two years later all was reversed. Eudoxius was made Bishop of Constantinople in succession to Macedonius (who was associated with a party which questioned the full divinity of the Spirit), Eunomius, Bishop of Cyzicus, and the *Homoian* creeds of Armininium and Seleukia triumphed. In the meantime, a Eunomian church with alternative episcopal oversight was set up which lasted into the next century. It was against this backdrop that the Cappadocians set to work to restore orthodoxy.

Basil's Call to the Struggle

To date, Basil's pious but privileged background, his lengthy education from the great rhetorician Libanius in Constantinople (with whom he kept up a correspondence) to his time in Athens, his enjoyment of study and seclusion were all preparation for a man of his abilities and gifts to take his place in Christian society in Cappadocia. By AD 360 he was thirty and that year was something of a turning point for him in many respects. The Council at Constantinople ratified the semi-Arian Creed, or *Homoian* creeds, of Ariminium and Seleukia. Constantius the Emperor, who in a real sense patronised these creeds, died in c.360–361. He was succeeded briefly by the Apostate Julian, one of the children of Constantine's stepmother Theodora (most of whom were massacred after Contantine's death),[177] and whom Basil may have met whilst both were at university in Athens. It may have been these events that prompted Basil to leave the seclusion of his community in Pontus near his family estates at Annisa and accept ordination, having been baptised a little earlier, in 360,[178] by the Arian Bishop of Caesarea, Dianius.

There is little doubt that he valued the solitary and contemplative life, which would figure strongly in his correspondence to his friend Gregory of Nazianzus who had visited him at Annisa after several appeals. Basil praised the solitary life. A little before his ordination in 362 he says:

> For just as animals are easily subdued by caresses; so desire, anger, fear and grief, the venomous evils which beset the soul, if they are lulled to sleep by solitude and are not exasperated by constant irritations, are more easily subdued by the influence of reason. The very beginning of the soul's purgation is tranquillity, in which the tongue is not given to discussing the affairs of men,

nor the eyes to contemplating rosy cheeks or comely bodies, nor the ears to lowering the tone of the soul by listening to songs whose sole object is to amuse, or to words spoken by wits and buffoons—a practice which above all things tends to relax the tone of the soul. For when the mind is not dissipated upon extraneous things, nor diffused over the world about us through the senses, it withdraws within itself, and of its own accord ascends to the contemplation of God".[179]

It is probable that during this time of seclusion Gregory and Basil wrote the *Philocalia*, a kind of anthology of Origen's work which they had both encountered on their educative travels in Palestinian Caesarea, Alexandria, and Athens, as well as in Basil's more recent tour of early monastic communities in Egypt and Syria with his later-to-be controversial companion, Eustathius of Sebaste.

At some point following his ordination as deacon by the Arian Dianius he left Caesarea and stayed with Gregory of Nazianzus, writing from there to the community of monks in Caesarea as to why he had left the city. He wrote:

But do you, O dear ones divine and best beloved of all, beware of the shepherds of the Philistines, lest they secretly obstruct your wells and pollute the purity of the knowledge of faith. For their aim is ever this, not to instruct the more stainless souls through the teaching of divine scriptures, but through extraneous wisdom to set the truth to one side. For he who introduces "unbegotten" and "begotten" into our faith, and declares that He who always was, at one time was not,[180] and that he who naturally and always was Father became Father, and that the Holy Spirit is not eternal is he not an out-and-out Philistine? . . . And so draw down upon themselves the words of the Prophet (Jeremiah 2:13) "They have forsaken me, the fountain of living water, and have digged to themselves cisterns, broken cisterns, that can hold no water".[181]

Despite Dianius' own theological leanings, Basil was ordained priest by him in 362,[182] but by 364, following Dianius' death, Basil became more influential under his rather ineffective successor Eusebius. In 364 Basil published his work *Against Eunomius* which sets out his response to the Arian controversy; by 370 Basil would become Bishop of Caesarea.

Basil's Response to Eunomius

Eunomius, the pupil of Aetius, was initially given support by the new Bishop of Constantinople, Eudoxius, who himself had briefly been Bishop of Antioch until he was deposed by Constantius for his Anomean views, on the request of Basil of Ancyra. Eunomius was made Bishop of Cyzicus in Mysia in 360 by Eudoxius but was soon banished for his views. He was gradually estranged from Eudoxius, who refused to restore Aetius to his teaching post at Antioch. Such shifting appointments were far from uncommon in what was a turbulent time. In 360 Eunomius published his *Apologetikos*, and it was this work which sparked Basil to make his reply *Against Eunomius* in 364. This reply, more than anything else he had written, catapulted Basil into prominence in Cappadocian Caesarea. Basil would not now leave the care of the churches and the defence of orthodoxy, either as presbyter or bishop, for the rest of his life.

The controversy was to continue to the very end of his life so that in 376, two years before he died, Basil, in a letter to the Westerners, recounts the trials of faithful orthodox laity ejected from their churches by the ceremonies, liturgy, and teaching of the Arians. He writes, "But a summary of the evil is as follows: the laity have abandoned the house of prayer and are congregating in desert places a pitiable sight—women, and children, and old men, and the otherwise infirm, in the most furious rains, and in snowstorms, and in winds and frost of winter, and likewise also in summer suffering under the heat of the sun. And this they suffer for not consenting to become a part of the wicked leaven of Arius."[183] In 378, just a year before Basil's death, Eunomius issued a rejoinder called An "Apology of Apologies" to which Gregory of Nyssa would extensively reply in his *Contra Eunomius*.

Eunomius' theology of the Godhead was essentially based on philosophy and logic, stemming from a Platonic view of God. His theology was the prisoner of his philosophy and it proceeded along logical lines, no doubt admired in the schools and attractive to a purely Hellenic way of thinking, but uninformed biblically and therefore in error and heretical. He held to a single supreme substance whose simplicity is opposed to all. The essence or defining characteristic of this substance compared to all other was that he was ungenerate or unbegotten (*agennetos*). Contrastingly, the Son was begotten, and not from within the substance of the godhead but produced or generated by the power of the Father from whom in turn the Son received creative power so that he both resembled the Father and acted creatively and redemptively. The first creative act of the Son was to generate the Spirit so that, in neo-Platonic terms, both Son and Spirit were emanations of the godhead but did not share the Father's substance. The spirit was the sanctifying power of the Son, and growth in sanctification depended on exact knowledge of doctrine rather than experiential knowledge of the Trinity. In some ways this thinking was the last throes of Arianism; its most fruitful result was to shape the Cappadocian Father's response and thereby give lasting shape to a more mature understanding of the Trinity.

Basil's response to the various currents and eddies of Arianism, from *homoiousian* to *homoian* to *anomian* (as described above), resembled a ship navigating in heavy seas which, having sailed close to the sandbanks of *homoiousian* theology, gave an increasingly wide berth to the certain danger of the rocks of *homoian* and *anomian* theology. In other words, Basil's writings gave ample evidence of a theologian in constant development.[184] In early correspondence with Apollinarius (who was an early opponent of Arianism, and who defended the divinity of Jesus at the expense of his humanity, by claiming that Jesus did not have a human spirit as it was replaced by the divine *logos*), Basil stressed that the term *homoiousios* needed to be qualified by the phrase "invariably like according to essence".[185] So for Basil to say Jesus was like in substance to the Father was insufficient; to say that he was like according to substance was also not enough; Basil insisted on the adverb "invariably" being added too. As such, in order for Basil to use the word *homoiousios*, it must always be carefully hedged about by a qualifying clause. Basil's initial caution with the Nicene word *homoousios* was in case it did not do justice to the separate hypostasis of Father and Son and played into the hands of Marcellus of Ancyra who stressed the undivided nature (monad) of the Trinity at the expense of the separate hypostasis or entity.

Thus, when we speak of the Son being "light of light", we must be sure that we are speaking of one substance but also of two hypostases. Here was the beginning of the distinctive Cappadocain theology which worked the theological space between the overemphases of either an Apollinarian (a Christological over-emphasis on Jesus' divinity at the expense of his humanity) or a Marcellian view (an over-emphasis on the singularity of the Godhead at the expense of the Son and the Spirit), and the overemphasis of Arianism which likewise defended the divinity of the Father but at the expense of Son and Spirit, neither of whom, for him and his followers, fully shared the Father's essence (*ousia*). Basil by virtue of navigating around these various positions, which presented themselves in this second stage of Arianism after 360, defined the space between them, marking out new theological territory shaped both by an identity of substance between Father, Son, and Spirit, but equally a separateness of hypostasis or person of each member of the Trinity. (Nor is it surprising that, following the settlement of the Trinitarian controversy—in theory at least—with the Council of Constantinople in 381, the spotlight should next focus on the Christological controversy of how Jesus was both God and man).

It is easy to see at a distance how the theological trajectories of Eunomius and Basil were opposed: they started from different places. Eunomius, more in the tradition of Alexandrian neo-Platonic philosophy, began with a concept of God's existence which was so singular as to baulk no similarity with any other being, however closely identified with him. He took concepts which were philosophic and built up an impeccable logical argument on the notion of the *agennetos* or the ingenerate nature of God. So, since the Son was begotten, and presumably the Spirit likewise, they could not fully share the godhead which was more than anything else defined by being *aggenetos*. From such immovable philosophic building blocks taught in the schools of Alexandria and Caesarea in Palestine, not to mention Antioch, and following in part the tradition of Origen and some of his writings, Eunomius' trajectory ended up a great distance from the orthodox Nicene faith. In this period from 360 to 380 the Cappadocians provided another way.

Basil mapped out in his reply to Eunomius in c.364 a different methodology.[186] In short, his method was a meditation on scripture in a particular philosophical context in order to hew out a faithful doctrine of the Trinity. He appeared to use a working model of Stoic and Aristotelian logic in which he accepted the Stoic understanding of a universal and undifferentiated substrate (i.e. *ousia*) as the basis for individuated existence which in turn is expressed then in individual qualities. Thus we may not know *what* God is but *how* he is.[187]

The word he used for this process of knowing was *epinoia* which could be described as "the activity of reflecting on and identifying the distinct properties of something".[188] *Epinoia* had a long history of use both in Stoic philosophy as well as in Origen's work, especially, and not surprisingly, in his commentary on John.[189] In using this method, Basil was saying that we know God by the engagement of the mind and soul with scripture guided by the Spirit, and not by the logical development of philosophic concepts based on words like *agennetos*, which were not themselves scriptural. His explanation of *epinoia*, expressed in *Contra Eunomium*, 1.6 suggests that realities first seen as "simple and undifferentiated"[190] can, through this process, be understood as a complexity of attributes and qualities. So the reality of Christ is grasped by understanding the metaphors used by him in scripture in which he describes himself as "the door, way, bread and light". These in fact are his properties (*idiomata*), and it is through understanding these, as well as the activity of God, that anyone may come to know the reality of his being. We may not be able to grasp his essence or *ousia* since this will be beyond knowing, but we may grasp those properties which he has revealed to us and by which he may be known. These are the *idiomata* open to our knowing, but the essence (*ousia*) and energy (*energia*) of God may *not* be known and remains dark or hidden from us. And now we are on the brink of apophatic theology

For Eunomius, the *energia* of the Father produced the Son by his own will, though in a passionless kind of way, but, for Basil, both the *ousia* and *energia* of the Godhead were fully shared by Father and Son so that the one generated fully shares both substance and power but nevertheless could not be fully known except in individuated properties. This too introduces the strong seam of apophatic theology running through the Cappadocians (as is also present in Athanasius and Basil of Ancyra) which stressed the unknowable and incomprehensible qualities of God.[191]

In summary, Basil offers a different way or method of doing theology to Eunomius: whereas Eunomius began with neo-Platonic philosophy as his way of understanding, Basil began with the Bible—using philosophy as a tool of expression and a way of presenting his thinking; whereas Eunomius proceeded by logic, only working from premises presented by philosophy, Basil used the method of contemplation on the text to understand what in the end is a mystery; whereas Eunomius imprisoned the freedom of God in the straightjacket of human thought, Basil recognised that God's ways were greater than ours and was prepared to live with the inexpressibility of apophatic theology. If we cannot understand what is around us like the ant, "how can you boast the incomprehensible power of God is apparent to you?"[192] It was a clash of theology, a clash of culture, and clash of how to use the available tools of human thought. It was the second stage of the struggle for orthodoxy which followed the initial fierce battles between Arius and Athanasius, but it was as important to establishing orthodoxy as in the initial onslaught.

Although at first Basil was tempted to consider the merits of the case for saying Father and Son were *homoiousios,* like in substance, as time went on he preferred the original Nicene declaration that Father and Son were *homoousios,* of the same substance. He became wary of any different word capable of misconstruing the truth. Increasingly his contribution, especially with the writing of *On the Holy Spirit* in 374 and his letters after 370, was to show that, although that Father, Son, and Spirit shared the same substance, they were also distinct *hypostases.* To do this Basil was content to use analogy from human life: just as Peter and Paul were quite distinct characters yet the shared common humanity so likewise Father and Son, and just as only the spirit of a person knows the thoughts of a person so also the Son is the fullest expression of the Father's mind and only the Spirit can fully search them out.[193]

Here then is the distinctive blend of Basil's theology, a unity of substance in the Godhead but a distinctiveness of person within the unity. If anything, his fellow Cappadocians share these convictions more strongly, coming to them with less equivocation.

Gregory of Nyssa answered Eunomius's reply to Basil at yet greater length and stressed the apophatic theology still more, while Gregory of Nazianzus formulated a theology of the Trinity with unsurpassed theological flourish, untarnished boldness, and rhetoric in his Orations. The Arian controversy was finally settled, at least formally, at the Council of Constantinople, the successor to Nicaea, which was called by the new Emperor Theodosius in 381.

Gregory of Nyssa

Gregory was one of five brothers. Basil was the third eldest, and Gregory the youngest, born in *c*.335. Unlike Gregory of Nazianzus and Basil, Gregory did not travel for his education. For the most part he appears to have been dependent on his older, well-travelled, and well-taught brother Basil for education; and in that role of tutor Basil seems to have succeeded well. Gregory married, perhaps unhappily, Theosebeia, and this, he seems to complain, excluded him from a monastic life.[194]

His learning may have been more restricted than his elder brother's but his mind was naturally more speculative and wide ranging. In particular he was more sympathetic to culture and more innately interested in philosophy, especially Plato.[195] Whereas Basil was more Aristotelian in his approach to nature, showing this in his commentary on Genesis 1 in which he displays great knowledge of abstruse theories of the origin of the world, Gregory is "far more interested in the inner connection of events, the *akolouthia* or the connectivity of life."[196] Gregory's writing was more occasional, not burdened or constrained by the responsibilities of high ecclesiastical office, although he was made a bishop by his brother of the relatively unimportant town of Nyssa after the Emperor Valens had split Basil's diocese in 372 to reduce Basil's influence. In making both Gregorys bishops, he sought to gain support in his diocese but neither were enamoured of the sees, especially Gregory of Nazianzus.

Gregory's attitude to his elder brother was at once both respectful and at times strained, sometimes because of his own naivety and sometimes purely because of his elder brother's slightly censorious attitude. For instance, in Letter 58, Basil writes to Gregory angrily rebuking him, understandably, for forging letters to him on behalf of an uncle, also Gregory, from whom Basil, had become estranged. These forged letters were received with relief and joy by Basil, but when later repudiated by Uncle Gregory himself it brought humiliation. The culprit Gregory, his brother, was not unjustifiably blamed. The purpose of the letters was laudable; to bring about reconciliation, but the means was deceptive, and Basil had a right to be annoyed.

After this had occurred three times Basil wrote, "I write these words to upbraid you for your fatuity—which I consider at no time befitting a Christian, and entirely out of place at the present moment—in order that in the future, at any rate, you may guard yourself, and spare me; because—for I must speak to you frankly—you are no trustworthy agent in such matters."[197] Such, not unreasonable, strictures on his younger brother's rather irresponsible behaviour would have only cooled their friendship. But by 379, when Basil died, Gregory had earned his respect, for by then Gregory had proved himself a stalwart defender of Nicaea against Eunomius and both an effective polemical and spiritual writer.

Gregory was to live for a further sixteen years after his brother Basil's death and so he lived well into the period when orthodoxy was re-established. He attended the Council of Constantinople in 381, and by then he was Bishop of Sebaste, when the Nicene Creed was confirmed and developed. For the years following the Council he was much in demand as a preacher, teacher, and church leader in the East.

Although he wrote polemically, as we shall see against Eunomius and for a certain Ablabius, it was for his speculative and spiritual works on humankind as well as the spiritual life that he is especially well known. He developed the apophatic spirituality of God's incomprehensibility as both a foundation stone in his polemical works against the neo-Arians as well as making it a pillar of his spiritual writing. The darkness of God was to be a watchword for him, and also the distinguishing feature of much of his teaching. In order to place his works in the context of the struggle against the neo-Arians his polemical works must be appraised, in relation to the struggle for the doctrine of the Trinity. His important works in this respect are the earlier work, *On Not Three Gods* or *Ad*

Ablabium, written around 375,[198] his *Contra Eunomius*, 382-4, and his *Catechetical Orations* of 385.

The context of his first short defence of the Unity of the Godhead was his reply to Ablabius who had requested help from Gregory in defending the Trinity from the accusations of some "Macedonians" who denied the divinity of the Spirit. They took the line that to speak of God, as the Cappadocians did, as being like three men (e.g. Peter, James, and John) who are separate in existence (*hypostasis*) yet sharing one substance (*ousia*) divided the unity of the Godhead. Gregory's reply was that, linguistically, in describing three men they should more properly be described as not "three men" but rather three expressions of a single humanity. So of these three men he says "their nature is one, at union with in itself, and an absolutely indivisible unit, not capable of increase by addition or of diminution by subtraction, but in its essence or being continually remaining one, inseparable even though it appear in plurality, continuous, complete, and not divided with individuals who participate in it".[199] Gregory argues that, in describing the Trinity, people naturally choose to express the plural rather than the singular nature they represent, as it is normal to describe a person by what distinguishes them rather than by what unites them in common with others.[200]

The Macedonians said that to describe God as Father, Son, and Holy Spirit was tantamount to saying there were three gods, a charge which Gregory also refuted in his *Contra Eunomius*.[201] Gregory's argument against the idea of there being three gods is not only the linguistic one of people generally choosing to identify what distinguishes someone rather than what unites—since that is the only easy method of identification—but that God is known by his activity and not in his substance. And this is an important part of Gregory's argument. The distinction which is common to all Cappadocian theology of the Trinity, but which is especially present here in *Ad Ablabium*, is that we know God in his power and activity, and not in his substance. The names of God do not describe his nature or substance directly, but each one describes the action of God, with divine nature remaining unknown. In fact his substance is incomprehensible and this is the entrance to apophatic theology which, in Gregory of Nyssa, is the unknowable darkness (or mystery) or the otherness of God.

Another point that Gregory makes in *Ad Ablabium* is that what each member of the Trinity does all do: that far from acting separately they act together, and in knowing the action of one you know the character of all.

> In the case of the divine nature we do not similarly learn that the Father does anything by Himself in which the Son does not work conjointly or again that the Son has any special operation apart from the Holy Spirit. For this reason the name derived from the operation is not divided with regard to the number of those who fulfil it, because the action of each concerning anything is not separate and peculiar, but whatever comes to pass in reference either to the acts of his providence for us, or the government and constitution of the universe, comes to pass by the action of the Three, yet what comes to pass is not three things.[202]

What one does all do, and what all do each does. All may be known in the action of the one, and each known through the action of all; and yet each in their substance is unknown, and all are only known in their activity. This seems to be the upshot of Gregory's theology. Gregory concludes, "For we believe the divine nature to be unlimited and incomprehensible, conceive no comprehension of it in all respects as infinite: and that which is absolutely infinite is not limited in one respect while it is left unlimited in another, but infinity is free from limitation altogether."[203]

Once again it is because of the incomprehensible substance or nature of God that he may only be known by a combination of *epinoia* and *askesis*.[204] "Thus Gregory understands the good practice of *epinoia* (the activity of reflection and contemplation) to be part of a spiritual *askesis* (stretching) of heart and mind through which 'we may guide ourselves by the aid of such terms towards the comprehension of things which are hidden'".[205] But, for Gregory, theological terms themselves and naming them may take us only to the extremities of the divine nature, where we can only wonder at the sense of that which is beyond. He rebuts the "three gods" charge with his own questioning which demands to know: what is divine nature and how is it possible to speak of it?[206]

If Gregory's short defence or apology against the charge of advocating three gods was his *Ad Ablabium*, then by far and away his longest polemical work in defence of orthodoxy was *Contra Eunomius*. Eunomius, who was a fellow Cappadocian, pupil of Aetius, and briefly Bishop of Cyzicus, was regarded by Gregory as of low origin and a social climber, but nevertheless he had great dialectical and reasoning gifts; maybe for all these things he excited the animus of Gregory.[207] He had strong logical powers but based his arguments upon philosophical ideas which bear little relation to scripture. Eunomius wrote two works, the first of which survives,[208] written in 363 and to which Basil replied, but his second work, *Apology for the Apology*, written after Basil's death in 379, is only to be found in fragmentary form in Gregory's own response of *Contra Eunomius*, written between 382 and 384.[209] It was extremely long and begins with a strong personal attack on Eunomius himself. Eunomius' thesis, that only the Father is ingenerate (*agennetos*), having no beginning and no end, and who is therefore superior to the Son, and the Spirit is attacked throughout. Gregory takes issue with Eunomius's method, about which he writes, "He [Eunomius] did wrong, when mentioning the doctrines of salvation, in adopting *terms of his own choosing* instead of the traditional terms, Father, Son, and Holy Spirit".[210]

In place of describing God in the biblical terms of Father, Son, and Spirit, Eunomius preferred to describe God as "both un-begotten and without beginning, admitting of no being prior to himself (for nothing can exist prior to the Unbegotten) nor with himself (for the Unbegotten is one and only he is God) nor in himself (for he is simple and un-compounded)."[211] Gregory's main lines of attack were firstly that, "the idea of God should not be unreservedly connected to the first person of the Trinity—it belongs to all three as the biblical witness of Father, Son, and Spirit",[212] and secondly that "the divine nature cannot be defined, and any attempt to do so is ill advised".[213] Gregory's stress on the mysteriousness, infinity, and un-knowability of God, together with his appeal to scripture, was a metaphysical and scriptural response to the claims of Eunomius.

It could be argued that the greatest effect of the neo-Arians, especially Eunomius, on the Cappadocian Fathers was to provide the irritant which formed the pearl of their Trinitarian theology, and none was more polished in their response to neo-Arianism than the third of our wise men, Gregory of Nazianzus. He was to provide an eloquent statement of their theology in the form of his Trinitarian Orations, if forged in rather different circumstances to Basil's and Gregory of Nyssa's: at once more digestible than the long refutation of Gregory of Nyssa's which is *Contra Eunomius*, more memorable and vivid in their succinct and elegant expression, and more dramatic in the circumstances that led to their publication.

Gregory of Nazianzus

Gregory of Nazianzus was left in Chapter 2 in the wilds of Pontus where he fled to after his almost forced ordination by his father, Gregory, in 362. Susceptible to either panic or severe reluctance to take on responsibility, and always frightened of his father's anger at his unwillingness to serve as a priest, he nevertheless had fled to Basil's estate at Annisa, Pontus; it was a habit he would repeat when faced with the struggles and conflict of public office. In his autobiographical poem, he writes:

> Like an ox stricken by a gadfly, I made for Pontus, anxious to have the most godly friends as medicine for my agitation. For there, hidden in the cloud, like one of the sages of old, practising union with God, was Basil, who is now with the angels. With him I soothed my agony of Spirit.[214]

Just as an Englishman might joke about the wild, remote, and wet scenery of the Western Highlands of Scotland, so Gregory loved to joke about the damp and cloudy climate of Basil's estate. But, stricken by conscience, he soon returned from this now familiar place of retreat to take up his duties at Nazianzus under his father's supervision. Little is known of his work there during the years 362–372, but then Basil made him Bishop of Sasima, an inconsequential town in the now administratively divided province and diocese of Cappadocia, of which he scathingly wrote about as follows:

> Midway along the high road through Cappadocia, where the road divides into three, there's a stopping place. It's without water

> or vegetation, nor quite civilised, a thoroughly deplorable and cramped little village. There's dust all around the place, the din of wagons, laments, groans, tax officials, implements of torture, and public stocks. The population consists of casuals and vagrants. Such was my church at Sasima. He [Basil] who was surrounded by fifty *choreepiscopi* [i.e. literally a country or suffragan bishop] was so magnanimous as to make me incumbent there![215]

Even ten years later in his oration given on the occasion of Basil's death, Gregory spoke of this appointment with resentment: he felt forced to accept, and he deplored his treatment by the more dominant, and he thought insensitive, Basil:

> Greatly as I admire his whole conduct, to an extent indeed beyond the powers of expression, of this single particular I find it impossible to approve, for I will acknowledge my feelings in regard to it, though these are, from other sources not unknown to most of you [the mourners at Basil's funeral!]. I mean the change and faithlessness of his treatment of myself, *a cause of pain which even time has not obliterated*. For this is the source of all the inconsistency and tangle of my life; it has robbed me of the practise, or least a reputation for philosophy.[216]

Indeed, it was this appointment that made him vulnerable to holding dioceses in plurality or moving to another without Council approval, so breaking a canon of Nicaea, which condemned those who transferred diocese without express permission, or held them in plurality. So when he was appointed Bishop of Constantinople by the new Emperor Theodosius—after the death of the pro-Arian Emperor Valens during the defeat of the Roman army at Adrianople by the Goths—others, opposed to him on theological grounds or out of prejudice, objected to his appointment to Constantinople because he was already a bishop.

Nevertheless, during this period (362–372, after his appointment to Sasima) Gregory would have interspersed his pastoral duties "with intermittent ascetical withdrawal which he claimed to have chosen as his life's direction".[217] He developed as a preacher and wrote his influential

On the Loving the Poor, and his reputation as a theologian grew, but he was still prone to periods of reclusiveness, even flight. One such period of withdrawal occurred after the death of his father in 374. He left Nazianzus where he still resided (barely ever visiting Sasima) and withdrew to a women's monastic community in Seleukia (modern Silifke) where he stayed for four years. It is probable that whilst here he had more contact with the church at Antioch, supporting Bishop Meletius, whose views on the Trinity placed him between the *Homoousian* party led by Paulinus and the *Homoean* party led by such as Demophilus of Constantinople. In addition, Gregory may well have had contact with Apollinarius of Laodicea whose Christology compromised the humanity of Christ by saying—in extreme reaction to neo-Arianism—that Christ's human mind was replaced by the *logos* of God.

It is probable that while he was in this community that Gregory began to formulate a more fully Trinitarian and Christological theology which was to prove so timely; namely that the three persons of the Trinity were consubstantial and that Jesus, though personally Son of God and of the same substance as the Father and Spirit, was complete in every aspect of his assumed humanity, "for what has not been assumed", he famously coined, "has not been healed".[218] It was while here at Seleukia that he wrote to the presbyter Cledonius back in Nazianzus with theological advice and ammunition to prevent the appointment of an Apollinarian bishop in succession to his father who typically denied the full humanity of Christ:

> For we do not part the human being from the Godhead; no, we affirm and teach one and the same God and Son, at first not man but alone and pre-eternal, unmixed with body and all that belongs to the body, but finally human being too, assumed for salvation, the same passible in flesh, impassable in Godhead, bounded in body, boundless in Spirit, earthly and heavenly, visible and known spiritually, finite and infinite: so that by the same, whole man and God, the whole human being fallen under sin might be fashioned anew.[219]

Here we have a flavour of Gregory's writing: orthodox, elegant, terse, harmonious, and exhibiting a kind of theological parallelism (e.g. *the whole man and God* fashioning anew the *whole human*). But soon this period of retreat and sojourn away from the minor conflicts of Nazianzus was broken by events elsewhere which would catapult Gregory into the fulcrum of events of the Church in the East and indeed the apex of his career.

Following the accession of Theodosius after the death of Valens at Adrianople, Gregory—this rather prickly, touchy, and vain man who "like a hothouse flower, was brilliant and blooming in warm admiration and a modicum of protective privacy but who withered under the cold blasts of stress"[220]—was called by the Church and Emperor to Constantinople. Gregory was to show both his strengths and weaknesses during this short, turbulent, and influential time (379–381), as Bishop of Constantinople

Like his predecessor Constantine, Theodosius wanted to bring peace and a settlement to the Church, and also like many of his predecessors, including Valens, he was pragmatic in looking for a result. The policy of Valens was to support a broadly *Homoian* position, "but not at any great cost to his civil administration".[221] The *Homoiousian* party, after a council at Lampascus, looked west, sending a delegation to the Western Emperor Valentinian (364–375) and making peace with Pope Liberius. The more neo-Arian party of the Anomeans, of which Eunomius was the leader, was broadly opposed by Valens. But after Valens' death the Spanish general Theodosius assumed power with the express mandate of repelling the Goths who had been victorious at Adrianople, and he also set about the settlement required in the Church with a general's élan, but with only limited patience, for the theological nuances for which the different parties stood.

In February 380, after spending some time being briefed about the complexities of Greek Christianity (he being from the West), Theodosius issued an edict "which indelicately defined orthodoxy as 'the form of religion handed down by the apostle Peter to the Romans and now followed by bishop Damasus [of Rome] and Peter of Alexandria (Athanasius's successor, who had died in 373).'"[222]

A few months later, on 24 November 380, Theodosius took possession of Constantinople and deposed the Arian Bishop Demophilus. By then Gregory had become the leading Nicene bishop in the region having already taught (mostly his Theological Orations) in Constantinople as a kind of chaplain to the Nicene community assembled at the chapel called Anastasia in the autumn of 379.[223] It was not, therefore, surprising that a Council sitting in Antioch and then transferred to Constantinople invited Gregory of Nazianzus to take up the vacant see after the sudden death of their presiding bishop, Meletius.

Gregory had come originally to Constantinoole from his convent-retreat in Seleukia, maybe via Nazianzus and his out of the way bishopric of Sasima, which he so despised, to the capital of the Eastern Empire. But being Gregory, his time in Constantinople was to be both the pinnacle of his career—as theologian and teacher—but also his final humiliation and his last ecclesiastical appointment. His stay included a strange controversy with an impostor from Alexandria, Maximus, who sought to oust him as bishop, which precipitated a further flight and a brief and messy time as the Bishop of Constantinople, a moving farewell address, and the greater part of his Orations which, in their eloquence and luminosity, described the doctrines of the Trinity, and others, for all time. It was a time of greatness and deep disappointment. Two years after his arrival, Gregory would be back in his family estate near Nazianzus writing his *Sua vita* and his poems, and polishing his Orations for posterity.

Constantinople was a city which had been recently saved from attack by the exotic-sounding mixture of "the Arab archers of Queen Mavia and by the city's impressive walls",[224] and was relieved to be back in the possession of the Emperor. It was also a city in almost permanent theological ferment. Famously, Gregory of Nyssa, also present for the Council of Constantinople summoned by the Emperor, wrote: "If you ask anyone for change, he will discuss with you whether the Son is begotten or unbegotten. If you ask about the quality of bread, you will receive the answer that 'the Father is greater, the Son is less'. If you suggest that you require a bath, you will be told that 'There was nothing before the Son was created'".[225] Relieved by Theodosius' forces, but simmering with theological speculation, subject like so many ancient cities to the vagaries of the mob, rife with rumour about factions in the Church but now hosting a Council which had moved from Antioch, Constantinople sought to put down a benchmark of orthodoxy. Constantinople received 150 bishops for a Council to settle matters finally, with Gregory only briefly presiding.

Gregory's time in Constantinople, brief though it was, was tumultuous both for him and the Church. Broadly speaking it can be divided into two main phases. The first period, which lasted a little over a year, was before he became bishop. He was originally summoned to lead the Nicene cause in Constantinople by Theodosia, the wife of a prominent senator named Ablabius. He did not arrive until after the death of Basil so as not to seem to jeopardise Basil's leadership in the province or the Eastern Empire. When he came, he preached in a hall in Theodosia's large house which Gregory called Anastasia.[226] Here some of his most famous theological orations were first given.[227] But Gregory's presence was opposed by bands of anti-Nicene monks who broke into the Anastasia and pelted the community with stones![228]

The second phase of Gregory's stay followed his virtual forced appointment as Bishop of Constantinople on 24 November 380 by Theodosius who installed him with an armed guard escort after the banishment of the previous bishop, Demophilus. The populace had real sympathy for Demophilus but now, together with many of his anti-Nicene clergy, he was sent into exile. Gregory vividly records the occasion and atmosphere in the Church of The Holy Apostles where he was all but installed then and there as bishop (his appointment had to be ratified by the Council but probably never was formally):

> Armed forces, drawn up in various aisles, invested the church. An agitated mob confronted them, like the sand of the sea, or snow, or storm tossed waves. The mood veered between hostility and entreaty; hostility towards me but entreaty where the civil power was concerned. Every place was crowded the streets the arenas, the piazzas. Men and women, children and old folk, craned down from second and third stories, Struggles, groans, tears and grumblings gave the impression of a town being sacked by force. And the noble leader was myself, sickly and decrepit, the breath scarcely left in my carcass, marching between general and army, my eyes raised to heaven. Hope sustained me as we wound our way, until finally stood in the church, I know not how.[229]

Around the same time, Gregory took over as the presiding bishop of the Council of Constantinople in succession to Bishop Miletus who had died. He had been the previous president of the Council, which had first been assembled at Antioch but which was now gathered by imperial edict at Constantinople. Gregory found the task extremely difficult, complaining that:

> The leaders and teachers of the people, donors of the Spirit, whose doctrine of salvation is poured forth from high thrones, who constantly with booming voices preach peace to everyone publicly in churches, raged bitterly against one another. And as they clamoured, gathered support, accused and were accused, jumped from their seats beside themselves, appropriated to their side anyone they could get to follow in a furious struggle for power and control (I have no words to stigmatize their goings-on), they burst the whole universe apart![230]

What made matters even worse, especially for the solitude-loving, conflict-shy Gregory, was the strange episode of the attempted appointment of a rival bishop, Maximus in a kind of ecclesiastical *putsch* by the Egyptians whom Gregory had earlier befriended, trusted, and admitted to his own intimate circle of close friends.

Maximus, a would-be philosopher of uncertain background, was put forward by the Egyptian church of Alexandria as the rightful Bishop of Constantinople, in part because Gregory had transferred from his diocese of Sasima to Constantinople without proper council permission, so contravening the fifteenth canon of Nicaea, but more because they wanted one of their own in this influential see. A delegation from Bishop Peter of Alexandria, with the support of the Pope, took part in a night-time, hastily convened consecration of Maximus while Gregory was ill nearby. This was only disturbed and prevented in its final minutes.

Understandably Gregory, who had given Maximus his confidence, time, and trust, felt deeply betrayed. As so often with Gregory in the face of this bitter conflict, he fled Constantinople only to return later, to try and explain why he had in his Oration 26, and sometime later having lost the support of the Emperor and not being able to lead the Council, he gave his farewell address to the Council in July 381. But his Farewell Oration to the Council was a moving one. In it he recounted that, whilst walking along the shores of the Black Sea, God showed him through a storm how:

> Some of the waves began to swell far out at sea and, after gradually reaching a crest, rippled to the shore and died, while others crashed over the nearby rocks and were sent flying backwards and dissipated in foam and mist. The rocks remained unshaken and unmoved just as if nothing disturbed them except the waves clashing against them ... Clearly, there was something of significance and value for me here.[231]

Those with a philosophic way of life, he said, would be like the rock which stood its ground whiles waves crashed around. Still, forced to resign, he left for Nazianzus and his family home nearby where he would spend the rest of his life.

Gregory's theological legacy consisted of the Forty-five Orations, some of which came from this period in Constantinople, together with his letters and poems, and the long autobiographical poem on his life. The Orations which carry most of his theological thought were the so called *Five Theological Orations*,[232] which were most probably given during his time in the private chapel of Anastasia before his appointment as bishop. In the later period when presiding at the Council of Constantinople as bishop he wrote his Orations on the Holy Lights for Epiphany 381, his Oration on Baptism on the feast of the Epiphany itself, and his earlier Oration on the Theophany or birthday of Christ.[233] All of which are moving addresses about the nativity and the significance of Baptism on the eve and feast day of Epiphany of 381.

Likewise, before his retirement to Nazianzus, he gave a moving farewell to the Council itself, to the city of Constantinople, and to his time at Anastasia.[234] "For nothing is so magnificent in God's sight as pure doctrine, and a soul perfect in all the dogmas of the truth", he said at his Farewell, and went on to define the essence of what he taught, "now the name of that which has no beginning is the Father, and of the Beginning the Son, and of that which is the beginning, the Holy Ghost, and the three have one Nature-God".[235] His doctrine was orthodox Nicene teaching; his style was full of classical and literary flourish, his expression often memorable and full of parallelism and paradox as with his famous description of the Son in Oration 29:

> As man he [Jesus] was baptised, but he absolved sins as God; he needed no purifying rites himself—his purpose was to hallow water. As man he was put to the test, but as God he came through victorious, yet bids us be of good cheer, because he has conquered the world. He hungered, yet he fed thousands. He is indeed "living heavenly bread". He thirsted—yet he exclaimed: "Whosoever thirsts, let him come to me and drink". Indeed he promised that believers would become fountains. He was tired—yet he is the rest of the weary and burdened. He was overcome by heavy sleep—yet he goes lightly over the sea, rebukes the winds, and relieves the drowning Peter. He pays tax—yet he uses a fish to do it; indeed he is Emperor over those who demand the tax. He is called a "Samaritan demonically possessed"—but he rescues the man who came down from Jerusalem and fell among thieves. Yes, he is recognised by demons, drives out demons, drowns deep a legion of spirits, and sees the prince of demons falling like lightening. He is stoned yet not hit; he prays, yet he hears prayer. He weeps, yet he puts an end to weeping. He asks where Lazarus is laid—he was man; yet he raises Lazarus—he was God. He is sold, and cheap was the price—thirty pieces of silver; yet he buys back the world at mighty cost of his own blood. A sheep, he is led to the slaughter—yet he shepherds Israel and now the whole world as well. A lamb he is dumb—yet he is the Word, proclaimed by "the voice crying in the wilderness". He is weakened, wounded—yet he curses every disease and every weakness. He is brought up to the tree and nailed to it—yet by the tree of life he restores us. Yes, he saves even a thief crucified with him; he wraps all the visible world in darkness. He is given vinegar to drink, gall to eat—and who is he? Why one who turned water into wine, who took away the taste of bitterness, who is all sweetness and desire. He surrenders his life, yet he has power to take it again. Yes, the veil is rent, for things of heaven are being revealed, rocks split, and dead men

have an earlier awakening. He dies, but he vivifies and by death destroys death. He is buried, yet he rises again. He goes down to Hades, yet he leads souls up, ascends to heaven, and will come to judge quick and dead.[236]

Vain, difficult, and touchy Gregory may have been at times, but his teaching at its best was engaging, passionate, full of God's presence; an oratory of high elegance, memorable and inspiring. There was about him a sense of God's presence which irradiated his communication. Ullman wrote:

> To have been in Anastasia with the friends and family of Ablabius or in the church of the Holy Apostles on the vigil of Holy Lights in 381 would have been to have been at an occasion which must have surely inspired. His tenure in office was brief, his was no ministry like Basil in the less grand city of Caesarea or Ambrose in Milan, the virtual capital of the Western Empire, nor like Athanasius in Alexandria but briefly, like one of the candles in the church of the Holy Apostles, he shone brightly but flickered simultaneously.

The Council of Constantinople, with its fissiparous bishops, still produced a Creed which was both similar and different to the Nicene Creed on which it built. The Creed itself was lost, until it re-emerged at Chalcedon in 450.[237] It did not include the phrase "from the *ousia* of the Father" in describing the Son's relationship with the Father which had been present at Nicaea. On the other hand it did speak of the Son being consubstantial with the Father, and although it speaks of the Spirit being "worshipped and glorified together with the Father and the Son," it was shy of saying that the Spirit was of the same substance as the Father and the Son. Nevertheless, the Creed was a clear break with both the *Anomean* party and the *Homoian* group—even if there were still traces of accord with the *Homoiousians*. This may have been due to Gregory's opposition to any seeming compromise in the use of the language of substance which may then have back fired somewhat; as well as being due to his backing of the wrong successor to Meletius as Bishop of Antioch in the long-running bishop squabble.

Gregory was replaced by Nectarius as Bishop of Constantinople; an un-baptised civil official who would, it was presumed, be more compliant to the youthful Emperor, still only thirty-three years old. He was to remain bishop for twenty years until the succession of Chysostom. Gregory found giving up the position of bishop difficult, still signing himself Bishop of Constantinople long after his withdrawal. Despite the general victory over Arianism it did not mean that vestiges, indeed strongholds, of Arianism did not continue in places, albeit patchily and sporadically, for years to come—as can be seen from churches in Ravenna with Arian mosaics depicting Christ as more human than divine, or the missionary movement amongst the Germanic tribes which was largely Arian.

Nevertheless the Church, orthodox and catholic, had settled its definition of the Trinity around the slogan of "one substance and three hypostases". This became something of a catch phrase which pithily described the benchmark of Nicene and now the Council of Constantinople's orthodoxy. The Cappadocians were content with it and, to a large measure, responsible for its development. The hall marks of this new orthodoxy, sometimes called pro-Nicene, are: a clear distinction between the substance and persons of the Trinity, so that whatever is said of the godhead as a whole may equally be said of each separate person; a clear expression of the generation of the Son "within the unitary and incomprehensible divine being"; and thirdly a clear expression that each person of the Trinity work inseparably.[238]

Academics since the nineteenth century have sought to label the development of Nicene theology as pro-Nicene or neo-Nicene, and theologians like Harnack sought to show the Cappadocians, and especially Basil, as rowing back from the full *homoousios* theology to a more *homoiousios* shade of Nicene theology.[239] The truth is that all theology of the Trinity was developing, as Basil himself was, in the light of different theological challenges from different schools or various theological trajectories whether in Alexandria, Antioch, Rome, or Constantinople during this period. The overwhelming need at Nicaea of showing that Father and Son are one in substance was added to by a further need to show both the unity of the one Godhead but also the distinctiveness and separateness of each person of the Godhead within the unity.

This developmental process was present in Basil who, at first, was a little uneasy in committing to *homoosious*[240] and toyed with *homoiousios* for a while (partly in reaction to Marcellus who stressed God as a single entity or monad with no recognition of his three-ness), but, in refuting Eunomius, Basil was content to return to *homoousios* as were the two Gregorys. For this process to be complete or satisfactory, not only was it necessary to demonstrate the divine substance of the Son and an understanding of his generation commensurate with that, but also a deeper understanding was needed of the Spirit and his "spiration" within the Trinty as well as his separate role within the Godhead, the world, and human hearts. To understand teaching about the Spirit, and the Cappadocian understanding of his role and work, their pneumatology must be turned to in order to complete the picture of the Cappadocian contribution to orthodoxy.

CHAPTER 5

The Cappadocians and the Spirit

Following the initial focus at Nicaea on the divinity of the Son and his consubstantial existence with the Father, the debate shifted to a more full-blown discussion of the Trinity in which each person shared the same substance but were distinct *hypostases*. This was at the heart of the struggle for orthodoxy over the sixty years from the Council of Nicaea to the Council of Constantinople in 381. This teaching about the nature of the Trinity was expressed in the West (although coming from North Africa) by Tertullian who provided the beginnings of a Latin vocabulary to speak about the Trinity (e.g. *substantia* for *ousia* and *persona* for *prsopon* or *hypostasis*).[241] Later Origen would also describe the Trinity in terms of three distinct *hypostases*, including the pre-existent *logos* and the distinct being of the Spirit who was himself a separate *hypostasis*.[242] But the beginning of a thorough-going treatment of the divinity of the Holy Spirit started again with Athanasius. Indeed just as Athanasius defended the full divinity of the Son, so too he also now defended the full divinity of Spirit.

At the start of his third exile Athanasius fled to the desert following the invasion of his church in Alexandria by the Imperial troops seeking his arrest. Athanasius slipped away on 6 February 356 from the church of Theonas, headed for the Egyptian desert, and remained in exile for six years. Emperor Constantius looked for a compromise settlement in May 359 around Basil of Ancyra's designation that Father and Son being "like in every way", but in view of the growing neo-Arianism under Aetius and Eunomius this proved wholly inadequate. Constantius was strongly opposed to Athanasius, of whom he wrote that he "was a man who had come from the lowest pits", who won over the simple people by deceit and demagoguery, and who deserved to be killed "ten times over".[243] So Constantius replaced Athanasius as Bishop of Alexandria with George of Cappadocia who, supported by the local military commander or *dux* in Alexandria, Sebastianus, violently persecuted the followers of Athanasius; thus, sowing seeds of George's own eventual execution by a vengeful Egyptian mob in 361.

Athanasius' exile in the Egyptian desert as a guest of the monks was especially fruitful in terms of his writing. He wrote his *Defence before Constantius*, his *Defence of his Flight*, and *The History of the Arians* as well his response to the Councils of Ariminum and Seleukia and his *Life of Anthony*. He also wrote his work on the Holy Spirit in form of his *Letters to Serapion* (357–359).

A group of Christians had risen up in Egypt who acknowledged the divinity of the Son but considered the Holy Spirit to be a creature. They were called by Athanasius the Tropici ("the Metaphoricals") because of the way in which they spiritualised their interpretation of scripture.[244] These letters about the Spirit were written by Athanasius to his friend, bishop Serapion of Thmuis, who had supported Athanasius a few years earlier in 353 by travelling to Milan to plead Athanasius' cause.[245] The Tropici maintained that the Spirit was unlike the Father (*anomios*) in the same way that Eunomius maintained that the Son was unlike the Father. Athanasius' response was in the form of a long letter, followed by two shorter ones to Serapion. The first half of the long letter (1–14) deals with scriptural texts used by those who deny the divinity of the Spirit. His conclusion was that the word 'spirit' in scripture with the definite article referred to the Holy Spirit but without it the term signified the human spirit. The second half of the letter (15–33) refutes the Tropici's suggestion that if the Spirit is not a creature, he must be "a brother" or "a son" of the Son himself:[246]

> It is only in the Godhead that the Father is properly (*kyrios*) Father, and the Son always Son. Just as the Father could never be the Son, so also the Son could never be Father. And just as the Father will never cease to be uniquely Father, so also the Son will never cease to be uniquely Son. So it is madness to speak, and even to

think, in any way of a brother of the Son, and to name the Father a grandfather. Neither is the Spirit called Son in scriptures, so as to be considered as a brother, nor is it called a son of the Son, lest the Father be conceived as a grandfather. But the Son is said to be Son of the Father, and the Spirit of the Son is said to be Spirit of the Father. Thus, there is one Godhead of the Holy Trinity, unto which there is also one faith.[247]

Athanasius refutes the suggestion that in some way the Trinity was like a human family with relationships that reflect a human hierarchy (i.e. father, son, grandfather, or brother) by appealing to the apophatic tradition that God is unlike human-kind. "God is not like a human being (Numbers 23:19), nor does he have a partitive nature".[248] He went on to show that the Spirit who is at work both in creation and redemption is identified in scripture with both Father and Son, and is illustrated as such in the dramatic symbolism of Baptism.[249]

Athanasius goes further. He describes Son and Spirit as being of the same *ousia* as the Father. "For just as the Son, who is in the Father and in whom the Father is (cf. John 14:10), is not a creature but belongs (*idios*) to the being (*ousia*) of the Father (and indeed you also claim to say this), so also the Spirit, who is in the Son and in whom the Son is, cannot legitimately be ranked among creatures separated from the Word, so as to render the Trinity incomplete."[250] He goes on to argue that, since we are sharers in the divine nature through the Spirit as Christians, "one would have to be crazy to say that the Spirit is of a created nature and not of the nature of God".[251]

Again Athanasius continues to write that, since the Spirit inspires the word of the Lord in the mouths of his servants and prophets, then "the Spirit indeed is inseparable from the Word",[252] and, furthermore, since it is the Spirit that imparts gifts to his body then "that which the Spirit imparts to each is provided from the Father through the Son. Everything that belongs to the Father belongs to the Son (John 16:15, 17:10); thus, what is given by the Spirit is in us, the Word who gives the Spirit is also in us, and the Father is in the Word."[253] In a real sense, to have one is to have all, and no distinction can be made between the substance or presence which each share or in which we participate, so to have a gift of the Spirit is to have a gift from the Father and the Son too. Athanasius argues for the inseparable action of the Trinity whilst maintaining their individuated existence but sharing the same substance.

So, while "residing in the desert,"[254] Athanasius affirmed that "the divine scriptures thus unanimously demonstrate that the Holy Spirit is not a creature but belongs to (*idion*) the Word and to the divinity of the Father", that the Spirit is the one in "whom the Word divinizes the things that have come into being" and "accordingly belongs (*idion*) to the one God and is of the same being *homoousion*.[255] Athanasius more or less concludes then that "the divine Scriptures unanimously demonstrate that the Holy Spirit is not a creature but belongs to (*idion*) the Word and to the divinity of the Father".[256]

What Athanasius had initiated in a letter to his friend Serapion from the Egyptian desert in his third exile before returning to Alexandria (ironically through the permission of an apostate and pagan Emperor, Julian, who rescinded the sentences of exile imposed by his predecessor Constantius), Basil would continue nearly twenty years later. Basil would also write in defence of the divinity of the Spirit, setting himself against any idea that the Spirit was a creature. He was drawn into this firstly because of another conflict with a group similar to the Tropici called the "Spirit-fighters", but also because of differences of doctrine about the Spirit with his old friend and mentor Eustathius and two other Church leaders, Apollinarius and Marcellus of Ancyra. This would involve him in painful controversy, especially with Eustathius, where personal relationships became subservient to the necessity of upholding the truth, in this case in relation to the Spirit. All of them doubted the divinity of the Spirit. What Athanasius had so clearly stated needed now to be reformulated in the light of these further threats to the divinity of the Spirit and the unity of the Trinity.

Basil and the Holy Spirit

The contours of the debate about the Holy Spirit for Basil involved a number of Church leaders, some of whom he personally knew. When they jettisoned or failed to embrace orthodoxy, Basil therefore considered them to have betrayed him personally. In several of these debates about the individuated divinity of the Son and the Spirit the search for orthodoxy is tainted by a sense of personal dismay and betrayal, no more so than in his relationship with his old travelling friend and fellow ascetic from his formative years, Eustathius of Sebaste. Perhaps it is an overstatement to say, as Philip Rousseau does about Basil, that "Bonds between people were put now at the service of bonds between churches. The shift was not accompanied, however, by happiness or success: the pursuit of so *heartless a policy* coincided with a sense of failure and personal inadequacy".[257] Perhaps it is nearer to the mark to suggest that now he was an influential Church leader, he no longer could afford to sacrifice clarity for friendship nor orthodoxy for yesteryear affection. This was part of the pain of being a leader, part of the care of all the churches, and in going down this path happiness could not be goal, as the Apostle Paul found to his cost with both the Galatians and Corinthians.

The difficulty was that, with some Church leaders, their very closeness to the Nicene settlement made them seem orthodox at first and so influenced others—especially at a distance, as in the West—when in fact their defence of the likeness of Father and Son simply led to a subordination of the identity of the Son and the Spirit to the Father. Amongst this group were Marcellus and Apollinarius, Eustathius and the Macedonians or Spirit-fighters. These are the relationships which in turn provide the contours in which theological debate took place and out of which Basil's own formulation of the status and function of the Spirit arose in his long letter to his sympathetic friend, and virtual pupil, the Bishop of Iconium, Amphilochius.

Marcellus (d. 374) and Apollinarius were two of a kind: both ardent in their support of the Nicene settlement but in such a way that stressed the unity of the Godhead in its consubstantiality at the expense of the individuated divinity of each member. Marcellus was Bishop of Ancyra but was deposed for his opposition to Arius (336), although briefly re-instated (337–339). He taught that, in the unity of the Godhead, the Son and the Spirit only emerged as independent entities for the purposes of creation and redemption. Although influential, especially in the West, he was never personally involved with Basil directly.

Apollinarius (310–c.390) was just such a person who at first sight seemed more orthodox than the orthodox. A vigorous advocate of the orthodoxy against the Arians, he was a close friend of Athanasius and became Bishop of Laodicea, but in his defence of the divinity of Christ he overstepped the mark being later condemned by synods at Alexandria 362, Rome beginning in 374, and by the Synod of Constantinople in 380. His error was to insist that in his incarnation Christ had no human spirit, it being replaced by the divine logos. Thus although Christ possessed perfect Godhead he lacked complete manhood. His Christological theories in a way anticipated, but in a different form, the controversies of a few years later between Cyril and Nestorius about how the twin natures of Christ co-existed. In addition, he did not teach the full individuated divinity of the Spirit.

There appears to have been a theological triangulation between Eustathius, Apollinarius, and Basil which seems to suggest that Basil was shabbily dealt with by his mentor, and now senior bishop, Eustathius of Seabaste. For a time Basil had been on reasonable terms with Apollinarius until his incipient Sabellianism became more pronounced. (Sabellius is a little-known cleric described by Basil in letter 207 as a Libyan who taught a Modalist view of the Trinity in early third-century Rome; i.e. he taught that the Trinity existed in temporary successive roles of the same being).

Basil initially saw Apollinarius' defence of Nicaea as attractive, although he was cautious of espousing *homoousios*, wary as he was of the more extreme position of Marcellus and being drawn to the moderate anti-Arian position. With the arrival of Aetius and Eunomius, he moved back to a more strongly *homoousios* line in concert with Gregory of Nyssa and Gregory of Nazianzus. For a time he corresponded with and became close to Apollinarius, until Apollinarius' position was unmasked. In his letter to The Westerners (no. 263) Basil complained that "his (Apollonarius') theological writings, which were constructed, not out of Scriptural proofs, but out of human arguments, but there are also his writings about the resurrection, composed in the manner of myths . . . where he tells us to return again to the worship which is according to the law, and again to be circumcised, and to observe the Sabbath . . . and in general to become Jews instead of Christians".[258]

He went on to say that Apollinarius followed Marcellus whose doctrine "contains the destruction of all our hope, neither confessing the Son in His proper person, but as having been sent forth and as having again returned to Him from who He went forth, nor admitting the Paraclete his own person".[259] In other words, Apollinarius' scheme, as in Marcellus' scheme, did not teach the individuated divinity of the Son and Spirit. Despite this letter, which is dated around 376, and is part of a submission for a delegation from the West to take evidence about the orthodoxy of those troubling the Church in the East, quite clearly Basil has broken with Apollinarius and indeed Eusthathius whom he also roundly condemns in it as "having obtained a bishopric" (on the basis of a false deposition of orthodoxy) then "immediately to have written an anathema of consubstantiation at their Synod convened at Ancyra" in 352.[260] But now Eustathius further muddied the waters: he not only encouraged others to speak against Basil but also fabricated letters to Apollinarius which smeared Basil by insinuating a close relationship existed between Basil and Apollinarius, now branded a heretic.

Basil's relationship with Eustathius was perhaps the most painful and difficult. In 358 he had toured monastic communities in the company of Eustathius in Egypt, Syria, Palestine, and Mesoptomia in what was the springtime of the monastic movement in the near East. Eustathius was an acknowledged ascetic whom Basil took fully into his confidence, introducing him to his family at Annisa and spending days in heart to heart conversation with him.[261] For a long time Basil was unwilling to credit his unorthodoxy and Eustathius' commitment to Arianism, being taken in by his guise as an ascetic, but eventually there was nothing to do but publicly break with Eustathius.

Basil's disappointment in Eustathius, which later turned to a sense of betrayal, revolved around Eustathius' understanding of the Trinity and in particular his understanding of the Holy Spirit.[262] As so often with relationships, the outcome turned not so much on a single event but a maelstrom of circumstances that eventually developed a narrow crack into a gaping fissure. There was some suspicion amongst other local leaders about Eustathius and his orthodoxy, especially by Meletius—the exiled bishop of Antioch whom Basil supported—and Theodotus of Nicopolis and, by his association with Eustathius, Basil himself. This was made more complicated by false accusations laid against Basil by two priests sent by Eustathius to Caesarea called (confusingly) Basil and Sophronius who it seems misrepresented Basil to Eustathius possibly on some aspect of asceticism.[263]

Basil wrote to Eustathius that he feared that "whatever accusation these persons may bring against us, let them be examined by you with all your acumen as to this—first, whether they have brought a formal complaint against us, secondly, whether they now attack us and finally, whether they have made their grievance against us entirely clear".[264] But at the same time Eustathius was asked by these aforementioned leaders, and joined now by Armenian Church leaders as well, for a statement of Eustathius' faith which would re-assure them of his orthodoxy in relation to the Trinity and the Holy Spirit. Basil duly met with Eustathius and got him to sign an orthodox creed or statement of faith in 373 which is recorded in Basil's letter no. 125.[265]

Although Eustathius signed the Creed, his riposte soon afterwards was to accuse Basil of Apollinarianism and forge letters about Basil's closeness to this now condemned Sabellian heretic. Correspondence at the end of Basil's collected letters (nos. 361-364) are notoriously controversial, appearing to set out a congruence of views between Basil and Apollinarius and ascribing views about the Trinity which seem unlikely for Basil to have held,[266] when, by the time of writing this after his work against Eunomius, Basil was clearly in favour again of the term *homoousios*. Although Rousseau is confident that this was a genuine correspondence with Apollinarius,[267] the style seems different; the terminology inconsistent with Basil's later Trinitarian position and, with the record of a previous forgery by Eustathius, it is quite plausible that these four letters were more of the same seeking to discredit Basil. At any rate the relationship between Basil and Eustathius had broken down, and following what Basil calls three years of silence,[268] he wrote of his break with Eustathius.

Written in 375, shortly after his writing *On the Holy Spirit*, it is particularly personal and self-revelatory, full of admiration for the ascetic life, grateful for family example—especially Macrina his grandmother—but clear that he has been the victim of slander by the publication of a letter by Eustathius he supposedly wrote to Aplollinarius in some way sharing his Sabellian views. Whatever were the exact personal contributory causes to the breakdown of their relationship, it floundered also on theological grounds. Eustathius had become the leader of the Macedonians, those who were called the Spirit-fighters (the *Pneumatomachi*) following a former Bishop of Constantinople in *c*.340, Macedonius. It was to clarify his orthodoxy about the status of the Holy Spirit that Basil embarked on his work *On the Holy Spirit*, written as a letter to his friend and Gregory of Nazianzus' relative, Amphilochius, the Bishop of Iconium (present day Konya). It was one of the longest works in Patristic writings on the Holy Spirit.

Written only a few years before his death, partly in response to questions posed by Amphilochius, *On the Holy Spirit* is undoubtedly a statement of belief in the divinity of the Spirit by Basil. It is written at a time when Basil was more confident in what he wanted to say about the Trinity and the Holy Spirit but, nonetheless, it is cautious in its approach. This caution was motivated by the theological strategy of trying to unify the more moderate factions within the Church against the Arians. It is written as a riposte both to the errors of the Macedonians or Spirit-Fighters as well as the error of Eustathius of Sebaste in likewise denying the divinity of the Spirit. It must also have been generated by the emotional controversy which accompanied Basil's break with Eustathius who, it seems, had become the leader of the anti-Spirit faction that existed amongst the later Arians in Asia Minor. These tempestuous relationships, with their accusation and counter-accusations, their call for an assertion of orthodoxy, their promulgation of creeds, and then their reneging of them at leisure, created the theological furnace or kiln in which doctrine was both fired and formed, fashioned and glazed.

The text of *On the Holy Spirit* contains both positive scriptural teaching and refutations of Basil's opponents "who refuse to rank the Spirit with the Father and the Son, those who deny the Spirit's roles in Baptism, those who number the Holy Spirit under the Father and the Son and subordinate him, and those who give the Spirit a middle position between God and Creatures".[269] Many of the earlier chapters are taken up with a refutation of the misinterpretation of prepositions about the Father and the Son, as well as the Spirit. Basil attacks both "the hair-splitting reasoning of these men concerning syllables and words"[270] and their logic chopping analysis of grammar which loses the purpose of a statement in the disquisition of its grammar. So Aetius, commenting on 1 Corinthians 8:6—"There is one God and Father, from whom all things, and one Lord Jesus Christ, through whom all are all things"—maintains that "from whom" denotes a difference of nature in the Father (from whom) to Son (through whom) or the Spirit (in whom) so that they cannot be of equal status. To build a Trinitarian theology on prepositions alone, which anyhow denote function and not status, is to confuse a difference of role with an inferiority of substance. The first eight, admittedly short, chapters are about this kind of refutation.

From these early chapters, Basil begins to build a scriptural picture of the Spirit, surveying his titles from scripture. Having recalled the Spirit's names as the Spirit of God, the Spirit of truth who comes from the Father (John 15:26), the Spirit of righteousness (Psalm 50:12), and the directing Spirit (Psalm 50:14), he writes:

> Therefore, whoever hears "spirit" cannot impress on his mind a circumscribed nature, or one subject to changes and alterations, or one at all similar to creation. Rather, he must advance to the highest heights in his thoughts and conceive of a necessary, intellectual substance that is infinite in power, unlimited in greatness, immeasurably by time or ages, and generous with goods that it has. Everything that needs holiness turns to him. All that live virtuously desire him, as they are watered by his inspiration and assisted toward their proper and natural end. He perfects others, but he himself lacks nothing. He lives, but not because he has been restored to life; rather, he is the source of life. He does not grow in strength gradually, but is complete all at once. He is established in himself and present everywhere, He is the source of all holiness, an intellectual light for every rational power's discovery of truth, supplying clarity, so to say through himself. He is inaccessible in nature, but approachable in goodness. He fills all things with power, but only those who are worthy participate in him. He is not participated in all at once but shares his energy "in proportion to faith" (Romans 12:6). He

is simple in substance, but manifold in powers. He is present as a whole to each and wholly present everywhere. He is portioned out impassibly and participated in as a whole. He is like a sunbeam whose grace is present to the one who enjoys him as if he were present to such a one alone, and still he illuminates land and sea and is mixed with the air. Just so, indeed, the Spirit is present to each one who is fit to receive him, as if he were present to him alone, and still he sends out grace that is complete and sufficient for all. The things that participate in him enjoy him to the extent that their nature allows, not to the extent that his power allows.

In this section Basil comes to a final crescendo on the work of the Spirit writing, "Just so are the Spirit-bearing souls that are illuminated by the Holy Spirit: they are themselves made spiritual, and they send forth grace to others. Thence comes foreknowledge of the future, understanding of mysteries, apprehension of secrets, distribution of graces, heavenly citizenship, the chorus with angels, unending joy, remaining in God, kinship with God, and the highest object of desire, becoming God".[271]

It is in protection of this high teaching about the Spirit that Basil advances a defence against those who contradict him. Basil maintains that "the Holy Spirit is indivisible and inseparable from the Father and the Son".[272] All three were at work together in creation. They are what Basil calls "the commanding Lord, the Word, and the confirming Spirit".[273] It is the Spirit who helps the accommodation of the Word to his people whether in the Old Testament "as in the Law, the types, the Prophets, the brave deeds in wars, the signs worked through the just or in the incarnation and ministry of the Word himself through the anointing of him by the Spirit".[274] The Spirit helped Jesus in the hour of temptation: "The Spirit was inseparably present to him when he worked miracles."[275] The Spirit founded and then equipped the Church with the fivefold ministry—"This very order has been ordained according to the distribution of the gifts of the Spirit".[276] Basil concludes "so we did not shrink from the cloud of enemies; rather we have placed our hope in the help of the Spirit and fearlessly proclaimed the truth".[277]

Basil's *On the Holy Spirit* was original but cautious. His was a clear admonition of those who made the Spirit either creature or subordinate to the Father, but his writing was careful in the use of language, especially language which might enflame or make an alliance of the centre ground against the extremes of either Arianism or Sabellianism harder. Just as in *Contra Eunomium*, Basil scarcely used the word *hypostases* of the three persons of the Trinity, except when explaining that the Seraphim in Isaiah 6:3 who "expressed the holiness of God according to nature (*phusis*)" and were "contemplated in three hypostases",[278] so in *On the Holy Spirit* Basil studiously avoided *homoousios* language, much to the chagrin of Gregory of Nazianzus, presumably to encourage more wide ranging support. Basil was careful not to use terms which could fracture possible unity whether in *Contra Eunomium* or in *On the Holy Spirit*: his strategy appears to have been to a build a coalition of support for orthodoxy against extremes whether proceeding from Arianisn or Sabellianism.

For Basil, as for Athanasius before him, "the most important pressure was to find a place for the Spirit in the Trinity as distinct from and not simply as another Son".[279] Difficulties had to be overcome, such as the way to describe the procession of the Spirit with no equivalent scriptural description as "begotten" (John 1:1ff) to use of the Spirit's procession or generation as it was of the Son. Although the description of the procession of the Spirit is not advanced very far at this time, there is no question of trouble brewing over the later question of *filioque*. "For the most part the problem is negotiated by attention to the traditional functions of the Spirit in the economy of salvation and by working with the dependence of Spirit on Son articulated there. The culmination of this strategy is found in Basil and Gregory of Nyssa where the order of the Spirit is preserved insofar as the Spirit is third in the order of every divine action, completing and bringing to fruition what the Father accomplishes through the Son".[280]

What Basil and Athanasius stress is the inseparability of the Father, Son, and Spirit in their action; so that what each does the other does, and, in regard, therefore, to sanctification, the Father acts fully through the Son and the Spirit. Understanding the Spirit's work comes from humble contemplation of the word and peering into its spiritual meaning. In this way the veil is taken away and the eye passes from merely understanding the letter to being in touch with the Spirit. This, Basil argues, is Paul's meaning in 2 Corinthians 3:17–18. "He who strips off the letter in his reading of the Law turns to the Lord—the Lord here is called the Spirit—and becomes similar to Moses whose face was glorified by God's epiphany".[281] The Spirit enlightens the humble and enquiring soul and mind.

Gregory of Nazianzus on the Spirit

If Basil blazed a trail in upholding the divinity of the Spirit with his *On the Holy Spirit*, albeit in moderate terms, both Gregorys were less circumspect. Of the two, Gregory of Nyssa wrote more extensively on the Spirit than Basil's erstwhile friend and university companion, but Gregory of Nazianzus did devote one of his Theological Orations to the Spirit, and this work is our main reference point for his understanding the Spirit's being and activity. Preached originally in the Chapel of Anastasia in Constantinople *c*.379 to a pro-Nicene congregation, it was probably further polished by Gregory in retirement after his departure from Constantinople in the sad circumstances of the withdrawal of support of the Emperor Theodosius and his consequent loss of the see. But Gregory, for all his sensitivities to conflict and opposition, had "a deep sense of the presence of God, a wonderful grasp of the essentials and ... great persuasive power,"[282] earning him the title in the Orthodox Church as Gregory the Theologian. Whether Gregory knew of Basil's earlier work on the Spirit we cannot be sure, but since it was written in the first instance to Gregory's relative through his wife, Amphilochius, Bishop of Iconium, it is fairly safe to assume that Gregory knew of it. By the time Gregory came to preach his *Fifth Oration on the Spirit*, Basil had been dead for at least a year.

It is a rather disappointing volume in terms of helping to understand Gregory's perception of the Spirit's work, but then so much at this time was mainly concerned with sketching out the essentials of the Trinity rather than explaining the function of each member. Its main concern was to defend the divinity of the Spirit and so deals with the all too familiar question of the Spirit's origin in the Godhead, his unity with the Father and Son, and some of the false teachings that existed about him. But that it is there amongst these five foundational Orations about the Trinity is essential.

Being the last of what are commonly called "The Five Theological Orations" on God and Christ, it must be contextualised. In his mind, Gregory is moving on from a defence of the divinity of the Son and his consubstantial nature with the Father to a similar defence of the Spirit against either the Sabellians, who see the Spirit only as a mode of God's being—rather than a distinct person or hypostasis—or as a subordinate part of the Godhead because the Spirit, like the Son, was generated by the Father. At the outset, Gregory moves from a confident defence of true orthodox doctrine of the Son which "has passed through the midst of its adversaries unscathed by their stones"[283] to answer this rhetorical question, "But what do you say", they ask, "about the Holy Spirit? Where did you get this strange, unscriptural "God" you are bringing in?" Straightway Gregory argues that what is said about one member of the Godhead should be said about all:

> "For our part we have such confidence in the Godhead of the Spirit, that, rash though some may find it, we shall begin our theological exposition by applying identical expression to the Three". So, "He was the true light that enlightens every man coming onto the world"—yes, the Father. "He was the true light that enlightens every man coming into the world"—yes, the Son. "He was the true light that enlightens every man coming into the world"—yes, the Comforter. These are three subjects and three verbs—he was, he was and he was. But a single reality was.[284]

Perhaps this was a classic insight into Gregory's methodology. It was scriptural but the interpretation was guided by the premise that what might be said of one member of the Trinity—and here John is speaking clearly about the Incarnate Word (John 1:4)—should be said about all. In the fevered theological climate in which he operated, to have interpreted this verse as applying uniquely to the Son may have risked the unity of the Godhead.

Turning to the origin of the Spirit and whether he was ingenerate or generate, one of the vexed questions endlessly debated in this period,

Gregory is equally clear: "If there was a 'when' when the Son did not exist, there was a 'when' when the Holy Spirit did not exist. If one existed from the beginning, so did all three. If you cast one down, I make bold to tell you not to exalt the other two. What use is incomplete deity?"[285] He goes on to say that the consequences of the Spirit not existing from the beginning meant that he too is a creature and says "If he did not exist from the beginning, he has the same rank as I have (i.e. a creature), though with a slight priority—we are both separated from God by time. If he has the same rank as I have, how can he make me God, how can he link me with deity".[286] (This final thought "how can he make me God" is in fact strongly present in the Fathers, e.g. Irenaeus, "He became as we are so that we might become as he is"; this thought is also strongly present in Athanasius.)

Gregory then shows the fallacies of those who do not hold to the godhead of each member of the Trinity. Some, he says, delineate the Trinity as follows: they say "one is infinite in substance and power; one is infinite in power but not substance, and one infinite on both counts. These people copy, if in a slightly different form, those whose names 'Creator', 'Co-worker' and 'Minister', alleging that the rank inherent in the names coincides with the quality of realities."

The next question that Gregory turns to is: "The Holy Spirit must either be ingenerate of begotten. If he is ingenerate, there are two un-originate beings. If he is begotten, we again have alternatives: either begotten from the Father or from the Son. If from the Father there will be two sons who are brothers".[287] Gregory uses irony, invective, and sarcasm for those with such arguments: "Make them (Son and Spirit) twins if you like, or one older than the other, since you have a penchant for corporeal ideas. If he is begotten from the Son, our God apparently has a grandson, and what could be odder than that?"[288] Gregory then explains the argument for the procession of the Spirit, later to be such a stumbling block between the Western and Eastern Church but now not an issue. The teaching of the procession of the Spirit is neither ingeneracy nor generacy but a midpoint between the two, based on our Lord's teaching.[289] Again Gregory neatly, typically, and succinctly encapsulates it in almost epigrammatic form: "In so far as he proceeds from the Father, he is no creature; in as much as he is not begotten, he is no Son; and to the extent that procession is the mean between ingeneracy and generacy, he is God. As to what 'proceeding' actually means, it is God's secret and "what competence have we here?". If we do not understand what is under our feet (i.e. how many grains of sand there are), Gregory argues, what hope have we of understanding the procession of the Spirit? Once again the apophatic theology, or the un-knowability of God, prevents us from ever describing fully the mystery of his existence.

Whereas Basil was shy in describing the Holy Spirit as of the same substance as the Father and Son, maybe for reasons of seeing to draw those cautious of that term into a single party, Gregory had no such hesitation or shyness. So, in section 10 of Oration 5, he writes: "What, then? Is the Spirit God? Certainly. Is he consubstantial? Yes, if he is God".[290] And having roundly stated this, Gregory goes on to use some analogies to demonstrate that is possible to share the same *substance* whilst being individual persons. Just as in the human family, we share the same substance yet we are different individuals or personalities, so Adam's family share the same substance but are different personalities.[291] This is a well-used analogy, which Basil also deploys in defence of the consubstantial nature of the Father and the Son. Because they are of the same substance they are not three Gods, "though they are three objects of belief, they derive from the single whole and have reference to it. They do not have degrees of being of being God or degrees of priority over against one another . . . To express it succinctly, the Godhead exists undivided in beings divided. It is as if there were a single intermingling of light, which existed in three mutually connected Suns".[292] Other analogies such as a single Greek word which has several meanings like a "crab, a pair of tongs or the sign of the zodiac, Cancer, are used. Or again a single word can variously mean a dog, a dog-fish, or the dog-star in the sky".[293] Analogies like these often make the sublime trite though illustrating a common principle of diversity existing in unity.

Finally, Gregory issues a whole cascade of scriptures to demonstrate both the divinity and activity of the Spirit. Introducing this Gregory tersely says, "But now you shall have a swarm of proof-texts, from which the Godhead of the Holy Spirit can be proved thoroughly scriptural at least to those not utterly dense or utterly alien to the Spirit . . . I shudder to think of the wealth of titles, the mass of the names, outraged by resistance to the Spirit. He is called 'The Spirit of God, Spirit of Christ, Mind of Christ, Spirit of the Lord, and Lord absolutely . . .'".[294] He concludes "to the best of my powers I will persuade all men to worship Father, Son, and Holy Spirit as the single Godhead and power, because to him belong all glory, honour, and might for ever and ever. Amen."[295] So concluded Gregory's Oration in the Anastasia Chapel in 379 or early 380; no doubt it was further polished in his rural retreat following his removal from the see of Constantinople. But just a few years later his namesake, Gregory of Nyssa, released his own contribution to the debate about the Spirit.

Gregory of Nyssa on the Holy Spirit

Gregory of Nyssa's contribution to the debate over the divinity of the Spirit and the Spirit's full inclusion in the Godhead was not as extensive as Basil's but was more polemical. While Basil wrote on the occasion of his break with Eustathius and Gregory of Nazianzus wrote just prior to the Council of Constantinople, Gregory of Nyssa—it is generally thought—wrote his defence of the Holy Spirit or *Against the Followers of Macedonius* after the defining definitions of orthodoxy of the Council of Constantinople.[296] Gregory of Nyssa was writing, therefore, after the doctrine of the Trinity had been more firmly established, and not in the more febrile atmosphere of the debates with the Sabellian Apollinarius or in the context of the breakdown of longstanding and complex friendship with Eustathius, as was the case with Basil.

Gregory of Nyssa, in writing his treatise or defence of the Spirit, had in mind the earlier heresy attributed to Macedonius, the Bishop of Constantinople, who, it appears, did not grant full divinity to the Spirit. "It is not entirely clear how his name came to be connected with a movement that sprang to prominence so much later. The main contention, which Gregory is concerned to rebut, was that the Holy Spirit occupied a mediant position between creature and creator".[297] So Nyssa wrote, "We confess that the Holy Spirit is of the same rank as the Father and the Son, so that there is no difference between them in anything, to be thought or named, that devotion can ascribe to a Divine nature . . . He has in all else an exact identity with them".[298] Based purely on the scriptures,[299] Gregory rests his case for the Divinity of the Spirit. He argues that, just because the Spirit is delivered third of all to the disciples, it is quite erroneous to think he is less.[300] The Spirit was not separate from Father and Son in creation or redemption: "We are not to think of the Father as ever parted from the Son, nor to look for the Son as separate from the Spirit . . . If these persons then are inseparable from each other, how great is the folly of these men who undertake to sunder this indivisibility by certain distinctions of time, and so far to divide the Inseparable . . ." So Nyssa magisterially concludes this point about the Spirit's activity in creation as follows: "For neither did the Universal God make the Universe 'through the Son' as needing any help, nor does the Only-begotten God work all things 'by the Holy Spirit', as having a power that comes short of His design; but the fountain of power is the Father, and the power of the Father is the Son, and the spirit of that power is the Holy Spirit; and creation entirely, in all its visible and spiritual extent, is the finished work of the Divine power".[301]

Just as each member of the Divine Trinity were involved in creation so likewise in redemption and sanctification. Gregory says that, in Baptism, it is not the water that gives life but "that which gives life to the baptised is the Spirit". He goes on "If, then, life comes in baptism, and baptism receives its completion in the name of the Father, Son, and Spirit, what do these men (the Spirit-fighters) mean who count this Minister (the Holy Spirit) of life as nothing ?"[302] For Gregory, the Spirit is none other the actual Kingship in the rule of the Father. For just as the oil of anointing is the symbol of kingship (the most intimate, private, and culminating action of coronation, as in the crowning of Elizabeth II) so likewise that oil of anointing in Church life is a symbol of the kingship of the God in the Spirit.[303] Gregory goes on to argue that the Spirit is the actual presence of the Kingship of God, the one who mediates it and makes that kingship real and present: "For as between the body's surface and the liquid of the oil (anointing the body) nothing intervening can be detected, either in reason or in perception, so inseparable is the union of the Spirit and the Son".[304] The inseparability of the Trinity in person and action, but the distinctiveness of their ministry appears to be profound principles of Gregory's understanding of the Trinity. The Spirit is both fully present in the divinity of the Godhead but ever-active in making known that divinity: "He ever 'searches the deep things of God', ever 'receives' from the Son, ever is being 'sent', and yet not separated, and being 'glorified' and yet he has always had glory. It is plain that, indeed, that one who gives glory to another must be found himself in possession of super-abundant glory." With such teaching and with such happy expression, Gregory exalts the ministry of the Spirit.

If by 380 much of the struggle for orthodoxy was nearly over, then what followed was more like a mopping-up operation after a long and arduous campaign with many fixed battles, many setbacks and disappointments. The success of their campaign would not have been possible without the linking of ortho-praxy to orthodoxy. Despite their many differences, squabbles, and misgivings, and despite the differing degrees of boldness with which each asserted their orthodox teaching, the three deployed wisdom not just in what they taught or defended doctrinally but in the how they lived, cared, and conducted their own spiritual journey, immersed themselves in issues of social justice and kept a wider theological perspective than the even the great issues that beset them. It was because orthodoxy was linked to ortho-praxy that the Cappadocians had such wide appeal. It is time to look more carefully at how they lived as well as what else they believed about humankind and its creation, the environment, and human destiny.

Part II: The Orthopraxy of the Cappadocians

CHAPTER 6

Being Ourselves

Although the Cappadocians' main struggle was with those who denied the orthodoxy of the Trinity, they were not blinkered or subject to a kind of single-issue tunnel vision. Undoubtedly the main theological debate of the age raged around a proper understanding of the Trinity and the full statement of the divinity of the Son as well as the Holy Spirit in the unity of the Godhead, but they came to these issues from a grounded orthopraxy which gave them balance, a connectedness with ordinary lives despite their privileged backgrounds, a spirituality, and a vision of the Church, which both sustained their lives and provided healthy sustenance for the orthodox Christian community.

In other words, they offered a discipleship which included a deep understanding of the origin, potential, and struggles of human life. They put forward a spirituality which was both demanding and appealing (if also speculative and deeply influenced by Platonic concepts in the case of Gregory of Nyssa). They demonstrated a form of Christianity which placed a high premium on community, especially the monastic setting and a resolute care of the poor. Finally, they laboured for outcomes of holiness and truth within the fragility of a Church harassed by heresy, beset by problems of existing within an Empire often hostile to its ideals, and, like all human movements, subject to the vagaries, misunderstandings, and vanities which beset all but the most saintly. The Cappadocians may have been tireless in their struggle for orthodoxy but they were not free from the pressures that came from wrestling with forces which frequently seemed, and were, well beyond their control, and with people whom seemed to, or did, betray them. At times, these pressures all but overwhelmed them.

Having looked at some of the historical and theological narrative which was the Trinitarian controversy of the middle of the fourth century, it is now time to appreciate their wider sympathies, interests, and doctrinal understanding which gave them the ballast and stability, human, spiritual, and devotional, to engage in prolonged spiritual combat over these years. To begin with, we shall look at their understanding of creation and the nature of the human condition, to look at what the Cappaodocians thought it meant to be *fully human* or to be all that God intended.

Of the three Cappadocian Fathers, the two who wrote most about these issues, and therefore whom we shall consider in this context, are Basil, and Gregory of Nyssa. From Basil's writings, we shall consider his two homilies *On the Human Condition*.[305]

Furthermore, we also shall reflect on Gregory of Nyssa's writings and begin to appreciate his Platonic dialogue, *On the Soul and Resurrection*. Together these works make a substantial contribution from the Church Fathers to the doctrine of man and of creation: our origin, role, and calling in creation together with reflections on the entry of evil into the world. They present a seriously argued world view distinct from the Greek cosmogony and based especially on the creation narratives of scripture, the resurrection, and the more general insights of biblical revelation on God's purpose for creation. It was their commitment to the authority of the scriptures that made their cosmogony so different from that of the Greeks which, in the ancient world, was the starting point for understanding both creation and humankind's role within it.

The Greeks had provided a remarkable world-view based on their philosophy and, in part, from the acute observations of their most celebrated "scientists", such as Aristarchus of Samos who maintained, some two millennia before Galileo, that the earth and the planets went around the sun.[306] If some of their observations about the sun and planets took millennia to substantiate, and even then in the teeth of opposition from the papacy, the Greek's more general cosmogony or metaphysical understanding of creation was overtaken in Christian circles by the biblical narrative of creation. Plato's cosmogony, as stated in *Timaeus*, was highly influential. Plato thought that God made the soul first and then the body, so something eternal pre-existed the material world which itself was not made *ex nihilo*, as Aristotle would later maintain: essence existed before the substance, the ideal before the material reality, or the soul before the object. For Plato, every star has a human soul, the soul is sensible, having love, fear, and anger; if the person is able to live in harmony with these competing emotions then he or she will inhabit the stars too, but failure to do so will result in more inferior creations until reason eventually overcomes and the soul is restored to its true destiny. The elements of the universe are not earth, fire, and water but geometric shapes based around two kinds of right-angled triangles (half a square and half an equilateral triangle), these triangles are the means of constructing the constituent parts of the earth and universe. If this theory of geometric formation was wrong nevertheless, the concept of matter being composed of constituent particles, and that these parts or "particles" were in fact the elements of the universe's existence was prescient. Plato's mixture of metaphysics and physics set a challenge for all future theologians and physicists to show the boundaries of each in the explanation of the universe. At the end of *Timaeus*, Plato summed it all up as follows:

> We may now say that our discourse about nature of the universe has an end. The world had received animals. Mortal and immortal, and is fulfilled with them, and had become a visible animal containing the visible—the sensible God who is the image of the intellectual, the greatest, best fairest, most perfect—the only begotten heaven.[307]

The Hexaemeron and Basil's Addresses on Human Origin

Basil's task in his *Hexaemeron*, nine lectures on the creation narrative of Genesis, was to start to draw the boundaries between the Creator and the Creation, the invisible and the visible, and between the physics employed in creation and the power and will of the one who created these laws. Basil gave an *apologia* in the *Hexaemeron* for a Judaeo-Christian doctrine of creation from the opening chapters of Genesis against the background of Greek cosmogony without any of the scientific research that has been part of the progress of humankind over the last seventeen hundred years. Nevertheless, he faced similar issues to a modern Christian theologian understanding the complexity, beauty, and dependability of laws governing matter and the universe whilst maintaining from scripture that these physical laws are God's agents of creation and providence now. At the opening of the London Paralympics, Professor Stephen Hawking re-posed the age-old questions about the origin and purpose of the universe but with scientific knowledge about the Big Bang and evolution, unknown to Basil or Gregory of Nyssa. Although the state of knowledge could not be more different between then and now, Basil was answering questions about the origin and purpose of the universe and God's troublesome creature, Man, which are as relevant now as they were then. Because the issues are similar, even if the state of knowledge is different, Basil's expositions of the opening chapters of Genesis seem in some respects remarkably modern and topical, if in other ways they seem quaint and folksy.

Basil first establishes, in his nine lectures which make up the *Hexaemeron*, the authority of the text or scripture he will be using as a foundation for his teachings about creation. So before "weighing the justice of these remarks (namely that "in the beginning God made the heaven and the earth", Genesis 1:1) and before examining all the sense contained in these few words", he says, "let us see who addresses us".[308] Moses is the one who addresses us; of whom God said, "If there be a prophet among you, I the Lord will make myself known unto him in a vision, and will speak unto him in a dream. My servant Moses is not so, who is faithful in all mine house, with him will I speak mouth to mouth, apparently and not in dark speeches" (Numbers 12:6–8). But behind Moses lies the inspiration of God himself, thus Basil concludes, "Let us listen then to these words of truth written without the help of 'the enticing words of man's wisdom' by the dictation of the Holy Spirit; words destined to produce not applause of those who hear them, but the salvation of those who are instructed."[309] In other words, this teaching is not merely for the philosophy lecture halls but rather for the catechism of the baptismal candidate.

At the outset, in these lectures Basil contrasts the competing ideas of the Greeks about the origins of the universe with the simple authority of this statement: "The philosophers of Greece", he says, "have made much ado to explain nature, and not one of their systems have remained firm and unshaken each being overturned by its successors".[310] The variability of human ideas against this simple statement about God's creative power creating all things is at the heart of Basil's argument. Not only so, but Basil also draws the conclusion in his first Homily from this text—*In the beginning God made the Heaven and the Earth*—that "that which was begun in time is condemned to come to an end in time", meaning that just as God made the beginning he too will make an end or will renew what he has made. Time was the consequence of creation and likewise time, for Basil, will presumably be merged with eternity in its ending.

But Basil gives further cause, and pause, for thought about God's creation and gives further reflection about the concept of *ex nihilo*. It is not quite as simple as saying that before creation *nothing* except God existed, for Basil says, "It appears indeed that even before this world an order of things existed of which our mind can form an idea, but of which we can say nothing, because it is too lofty a subject for men who are but beginners and are still babes in knowledge".[311] He goes on to explain that a world existed which was invisible and equally created by God which existed in parallel to this one. Thus Paul says that "by him were all things made that are in heaven, and that are in earth, visible and invisible whether they be thrones or dominions or principalities or powers or virtues or hosts of angels or the dignities of archangels".[312] Clearly, for Basil, a parallel, invisible order existed beyond our comprehension but on which the created visible order or universe was contingent. Hence he says "the birth of the world was preceded by a condition of things suitable for the exercise of supernatural powers, outstripping the limits of time, eternal and infinite".[313] "To this world at last it was necessary to add a new world (our world), both a school and training place where the souls of men should be taught and a home for beings destined to be born and to die".[314] Basil gives us the idea that this world is contingent on a parallel spiritual world where the hierarchy of heaven exists. This world uniquely and significantly is a vale of soul-making, especially after the Fall, and is the place where human salvation is both provided, received, and worked out.

The next eight homilies or lectures contain both an exhortation to consider the works of creation (see Psalm 19:1–2: "The heavens declare the glory of God; the skies proclaim the work of his hands. Day after day they pour forth speech; night after night they display knowledge") and what that creation teaches us. But whenever theologians move from the "why" to the "how" of creation they often become the fall-guys of their own ignorance. This was true of Basil as of others. Despite his close observation of nature and his knowledge of geography and contemporary science, his scientific outlook was obviously primitive compared with a modern's. For instance, he refers to the leader of a hive of bees as a king bee[315] or, on a few occasions, refers to the North Sea around Britain as a "being very shallow and, lying exposed to violence of the winds, has few beaches and shelters".[316] Basil had obviously heard rumours of the gales that blow around Britain and in the Bay of Biscay![317]

However, when it came to encouragement to observe and consider creation, Basil was vivid and engaging in his rhetoric, and often very eloquent and moving in his desire for his listeners to learn from it. At the beginning of the *Fourth Homily* he compares the enthusiasm of the pagan for the magic arts and chariot racing with the comparative lack of interest of the Christian in the wonder of creation:

> There are some communities that feast their eyes on the manifold spectacles of conjurors from the dim morning twilight until evening itself. Nevertheless, they never have their fill of listening to soft and dissolute melodies, which undoubtedly engender in souls great impurity. Some of those who are mad with love of horses, wrangle over their horses in their sleep, unyoking the chariots and transferring the drivers, and they do not at all leave off their daytime folly even in their dreams. And we, whom the Lord, the great Wonder-worker and Craftsman, has called together for a manifestation of His works, shall we become weary in contemplating or reluctant to hear the eloquence of the Spirit? Rather, shall we not, standing around this vast and varied workshop of the divine creation, and going back in thought, each one, to the times past, *contemplate the orderly arrangement of the whole*?[318]

His homilies not only encouraged contemplation of creation but also sought to explain how the six days of creation—before God rested—may have occurred, and, in the process of this teaching, he rebuked other theories of creation which he regarded as erroneous. In this respect, not only did he seek to show the error of Greek theories of creation emanating from Plato but he also sought to overturn other pagan or non-biblical assumption about the universe. In describing the creation of the world in his second homily, he is at pains to show that the *darkness* mentioned in the biblical account (see Genesis 1:4–5) in no way referred to the presence of evil at creation (a Manichaean view) rather than simply the absence of light. He concludes, "No one who is in the world will deny that evils exist. What, then, do we say? That evil is not a living and animated substance, but a condition of the soul which is opposed to virtue and which springs up in the slothful because of their (humanity) falling away from good."[319] Or again in teaching about the creation of the lights of heaven (Homily 6) Basil uses the opportunity to pour scorn on the astrological influence of the Zodiac on the destinies of individuals and communities. So he cogently argues "If truly the origin of our vices or virtues is not within us (but pre-determined by the zodiac) but is the unavoidable consequence of our birth (i.e. what star we are born under), the lawgivers who define what we must do and what we must avoid, are useless. In fact the wrong done is not attributable to the thief, nor to the murderer, for whom it was an impossibility to restrain his hand, even if he wished to, because of the unavoidable compulsion which urged him to the acts . . . But the great hopes of us Christians will vanish completely since neither justice will be honoured nor sin condemned because nothing is done by men through their free will".[320] But there were times when Basil's didactic aims got the better of him as when, in seeking to allay the power and allure of the sun and so prevent it being made in any way divine, he argued that the earth without light or sunshine had power to generate its own vegetation. So he said, "Let the earth bud forth by itself, needing no assistance from the outside. Since some think that the sun, drawing the productive power from the centre of the earth to the surface with its rays of heat, is the cause of the plants growing from the earth, it is the cause of the plants growing from the earth; it is for this reason that the adornment of the earth is older than the sun, that those who have misled may cease worshiping the sun as the origin of life. If they are persuaded that before the sun's generation all the earth had been adorned, they will retract their unbounded admiration for it, realizing that the sun is later than the grass and plants in generation".[321]

Perhaps the most endearing feature of Basil's lectures on creation was the spiritual and life-lessons he draws from observation of the created order, its physical bodies, animals, plants, fish, and birds. In this respect the lectures are a bit like a biblical Aesop's fable in which deductions drawn from the characteristics of the created order are used to instruct the faithful. Such examples are plentiful. So "whenever you see a grassy plant or flower, think of human nature, remembering the comparison of the wise Isaiah, that 'all flesh is as grass, and all the glory of man as the flower of the grass'".[322] For the short span of life and the briefly-enduring pleasure and joy of human happiness have found a most apt comparison in the words of the prophet. Today he is vigorous in body, grown fleshly from delicacies, with a flowerlike complexion, in the prime of life, fresh and eager, and irresistible in attack; tomorrow that same one is piteous or wasted with age, or weakened by disease".[323] Or again he sees passion in reproduction in the plant world as illustrative too of human behaviour in marriage; "They (gardeners) divide even the palms into males and females. And at times too, one may see the so-called female among them letting down its branches, as if with passionate desire, and longing for the embrace of the male, at which caretakers of the plants then throw the branches a certain kind of seeds of the males called *pesnes*. Then as if it is consciously perceptive of fruition, it again raises its branches erect and restores the foliage of the plant to its proper".[324] Basil leaves us with the sense that is as if the whole of creation is impregnated with the desire to multiply, and this is the divine mandate.

Finally, in talking about fish and those that live in the sea Basil draws more analogies with human life:

> Since you have already perceived much wickedness and plotting in weak animals, I want you to avoid imitating the evildoers. The crab longs for the flesh of the oyster; but, because of the shell of the oyster, it is a prey hard for him to conquer. Nature had fastened the tender flesh in an unbroken enclosure. Therefore, the oyster is called "sherd-hide". Since the two enveloping shells, fitted exactly to each other, enclose the oyster, the claws of the

crab are necessarily of no avail. What does he do then? When he sees it pleasantly warming itself in spots sheltered from the wind and opening its valves to the rays of the sun, then stealthily inserting a small pebble, he prevents it from closing and is found to gain through inventiveness what he fell short by strength. This is the wickedness of the creatures endowed with neither reason nor voice. Now I want you although emulating the crab's acquisitiveness and their inventiveness, to abstain from injury to your neighbours. He who approaches his brother with deceit, who adds to the troubles of his neighbours, and who delights in others misfortunes, is like a crab. Avoid the imitation of those who by their conduct convict themselves. Be satisfied with your possessions. Poverty with an honest sufficiency is preferred by the wise to all pleasure.[325]

Likewise Basil warns of the behaviour of the octopus, which:

Assumes on every occasion the colour of the rock to which it fastens itself. As a result, many of the fish swimming unwarily fall upon the octopus as upon a rock, I suppose, and become an easy prey for the cunning fellow. Such in character are those men who always fawn upon the ruling powers and adapt themselves to the needs of every occasion, not continuing always in the same principles, but easily changing into different persons who honour self-control with the chaste, but incontinence with incontinent, and alter their opinions to please everyone . . . Such characters the Lord calls ravenous wolves which show themselves in sheep's clothing.[326]

These are just some of the many lessons drawn by Basil from the characteristics of created forms.

Nor was Basil, like many preachers, above teasing his audience a little about the length of his addresses. He says, "to detain you longer is to withdraw you a longer time from evils".[327] In other words, the longer he spoke the less time they had for "the gaming tables" or other sinful pastimes.[328] So Basil says, "let us avail ourselves of a bodily fast", and, "since you have frequently served the flesh for pleasure, today persevere in the service of the soul".[329] Or again he teases his listeners by saying that his teaching will drive them to righteous sleep: "While partaking of your food, may you discuss at table the stories which my words reviewed for you early in the morning and throughout the evening; and falling asleep while engaged in thoughts of these things, may you enjoy the pleasure of the day, even while sleeping, so that it may be possible for you to say, 'I sleep and my heart watcheth' since it has meditated night and day on the law of the Lord, to whom be glory and power for ever. Amen."

Basil's *Hexaemeron* was to be popular long into the middle ages until the scientific revolution of the seventeenth century and the onset of Newtonian physics, when a new understanding of the opening chapters of Genesis emerged to be further changed by the onset of Darwinianism and then, more recently, quantum physics. But his *Hexaemeron* would be incomplete without the final two addresses, which may have been given at quite a different time, on "The Origin of Humanity".

The Cappadocians, and especially Basil and Gregory of Nyssa, realised the significance of the moment when God paused before the creation of humankind. Gregory fully understood the gravity of it and spoke of the drama of that moment when a divine consultation in the Trinity took place before the pinnacle of God's creation was given the central and sovereign role in it.[330] The significance of the saying "let us make man" in the midst of the Trinitarian controversies of the fourth century was not lost on either. "Basil explains that this (act of human creation) supports the Nicene faith by identifying the Son and the Spirit as co-creators with the Father. Moreover, in his understanding it strongly affirms the dignity of humankind, disclosing it as a masterpiece of divine craftsmanship ... Yet perhaps this point has a further implication as well. If our creation according to the divine image emerged from the shared deliberation and activity of the divine persons then our core human identity is rooted in the mutual relationship, love, communion that constitutes the life of the Trinity itself?"[331] Gregory of Nyssa makes the additional point that, unless the persons of the Trinity were one themselves, they would not have a single image to confer on humanity but several: the Godhead's unity results in a single image being given to humankind.[332] Indeed, as Basil remarks, the fact that it says "Let us make" rather than "and they made" means "that you would not receive an occasion for polytheism. For if the person (the Godhead) is introduced as multiplicity, people would have become heedless in heaping up for themselves a great crowd of gods. Yet it says, 'Let us make', that you may recognise Father, Son, and Holy Spirit".[333]

Having reflected on the pause of the Godhead before creating humankind, Basil considers how that divine image is manifested in his creation and the calling that they are given. Firstly, he contemplates the greatness of God and the image, therefore, in which we are created. "Do not imagine a shape in regard to him. Do not diminish the great one in a Jewish way . . . He is incomprehensible in greatness . . . Nothing is with God as it is with us".[334] Basil then gives three ways in which the image of God is present in us. First it is set within our post-Fall corruptible nature; the unchanging is set within the changing. But the image is most akin to reason which exists within the whole body but is distinct from it. "But in what is the ruling principle? In the superiority of reason".[335] Therefore there is a dual reality to human life: "the body is an instrument of the human being, an instrument of the soul, and the human being is principally the soul itself".[336] And reason is what gives superiority or God's image to the human soul.

Secondly, humans were given innate sovereignty or the right to rule. "Why whenever the dolphin observes that a human is nearby, although the dolphin is the most royal of aquatic beasts, it stands in awe."[337] Basil gives innumerable examples from animal, bird, and sea life of the way this rule is exercised through intelligence, ingenuity, and cunning.

Thirdly, the image of God is restored, burnished, and enhanced by growth in Christ in the Spirit. Basil notes that God honoured humans by enabling them to become fashioners of the divine likeness within themselves. Of the Spirit's work in humans Basil says elsewhere, "Spirit-bearing souls illumined by the Spirit themselves become spiritual and send forth grace to others. From this comes foreknowledge of future events, understanding of mysteries, comprehension of hidden things, distribution of gifts heavenly citizenship, dancing with angels, joy without end, abiding in God, likeness to God, and the summit of desires, becoming god".[338] The Word too will help this image-making in humans: "When I wish to make you like God, (why) do you flee the word which divinizes you, stopping your ears, that you may not hear saving words?"[339]

In the second of his addresses on the origin of humankind, Basil concentrates on the second creation narrative of Genesis 2. For Basil, the simple distinction between the two narratives was that in Genesis Moses records what God did, whereas Genesis 2 shows how he did it. It focuses on the creation of humans from the dust of the earth and the breath of God, the breath of life.[340] "Above light, above heaven, above luminaries, above all things is the creation of the human being, for the lord himself took it". Our body is quite worthy to be entirely moulded by his own hands; He did not command an angel. The earth did not automatically cast us forth as it did the cicadas. He did not tell the ministering angelic powers to make this or that. But by his own hands, as an artist he took earth. When you focus on what is taken, what is human being? When you understand the One doing the moulding, the human is great indeed; he is nothing because of the material but great through the honour".[341] The dust of our humanity, Basil says, speaks of humility, and so, in our view of the powerful, prestigious, or proud (dressed in the purple you, might say): "when you see these (proud) rulers, preceded by a herald with an uplifted voice, when you see them terrorising one and torturing another, confiscating one's property and delivering that one to death, do not fear what you see, do not be dismayed by these who command that these things happen, do not let your imagination astound you. Take to heart that God molded the human being, dust from the earth.[342] Humans are of the dust or earth, but made upright so as to look to heaven, with eyes defended by eyebrows and eye-lashes to enable direct gaze at heaven."[343]

Humans were called to growth: growth of the body and growth of the soul—"growth into God".[344] The process whereby this growth occurs is stretching out to what lies ahead. It includes "growth in visions, acquisition in piety, extending toward the better, *as we ever reach toward truly existing things.*"[345] Basil says to fill the earth has a spiritual meaning: "Let the hand be filled with good works. Let the eye be filled with good works. May the feet stand ready to visit the sick, journeying to fitting things. Let every usage to our limbs be filled with actions according to the commandments. This is 'to fill the earth'".[346] But their goal is rest or glory and they should remember that on the seventh day God rested and this is a picture of heaven where "there will be no more works of this world in that day, no more marriages, no more business dealings, no more agriculture . . . the desires of youth have been stilled, there is no proposal of marriage; no more desire for procreation; regarding gold, no concern".[347]

Gregory of Nyssa

Gregory's two main works dealing with the doctrine of man, *On the Soul and Resurrection* and *On the Making of Man*, appear to be written shortly after Basil's death in 380 and probably before the Council of Constantinople. Gregory had suffered the loss of his older brother, for whom he mourns, and his writing *On the Making of Man* may be an intentional completion of Basil's work *Hexaemeron*, whilst his work *On the Soul and Resurrection* may have been occasioned by his brother's death and is set in a Platonic dialogue with his gravely ill and dying, but ever clear-minded sister, Macrina.

In *The Making of Man* Gregory is explains the creation, role, metaphysical anthropology, physical life, and destiny of humankind. It explores what it is to be made in God's image, the royal gift of governing creation granted to man, the unique feature of the mind and reason which distinguishes him from the animal world, the meaning of the soul and its relationship with passions and the promise of resurrection. It is a wide ranging, at times highly speculative, sometimes extremely medical (when dealing with human physiology), philosophical and spiritual work.

Gregory is prepared to speculate about the existence of man before the Fall, and in doing so goes beyond the descriptions of man's origin in Genesis, or least makes inferences from the consequences of their fall about life in Paradise. Thus, when man was first made in the image of God, it excluded the concept of sex; humans would increase like angels. So "before sin" entered the world "there is no account of birth, or of travail, or of the desire that tends to procreation, but when they were banished from Paradise after their sin, and the woman was condemned by the sentence of travail, Adam thus entered with his consort upon the intercourse of married life, and then took place the beginning of procreation".[348] In this post-Fall state, the fear of death provoked procreation "for the fear of death impelled their nature to provide succession".[349] Following the Fall we are "evidently frail, short-lived, amoral if not actually perverse, and sexually differentiated into male and female".[350] We are driven by passions most notably "our inclination to material things" and now have "a liability of passion",[351] whereas God is sexless, almighty, eternal, wise, and good: the fount of all goodness.

The distinguishing feature of Gregory's understanding of our being made in the image of God is our freedom. He argues "thus there is in us the principle of all excellence, all virtue and wisdom, and every higher thing that we conceive: but *pre-eminent among all is* the fact that we are free from all necessity, and not in bondage to any natural power, but have decision in our power as we please; for virtue is a voluntary thing, subject to dominion".[352] This freedom was abused at the Fall bringing about the tarnishing of the Image of God in us and our distancing from the Archetype who is the fount of all good.[353]

Man is distinguished from the animals by being upright so as to look to the heavens and despite his evident weakness—"destitute of natural weapons"[354] says Gregory—he is invested with reason which pervades and distinguishes his life, and is equipped by means of sensory perception. But this reason and its use resembles the archetype in whose image we are made by being beyond understanding. The following is an apt description of Gregory's reasoning, showing it as both the motive force of our being as well as the incomprehensibility of what exactly it is. He asks the question "What then is, in its own nature, this mind that distributes itself into faculties of sensation, and duly receives, by means of each, the knowledge of things?" His answer is that we cannot fully describe this faculty of mind in the same way that we cannot describe the one in whose image we have been given it. "For if, while the archetype (God himself) transcends comprehension (the aphophatic idea), the nature of the image were comprehended, the contrary character of the attributes we behold in them would prove the defect of the image; but since the nature of our mind, which is the likeness of the Creator, evades our knowledge, it has an accurate resemblance to the superior nature, figuring by its unknowable-ness the incomprehensible Nature."[355]

Gregory makes freedom (at least in his earlier writings about man) the touchstone of the image of God in man. He grants that reason, fed by sensory perception, distinguishes us from the animal world and gives humans sovereignty or "royalty" as he calls it. He makes a stab at describing the physiology of a human being with a graphic description of human organs which testify to having been present at dissections like those performed a millennium later in the presence of Leonardo da Vinci or Rembrandt.[356] But his greatest emphasis in his spiritual anthropology is kept for the soul. For him, the soul is to the body what God is to the universe, the centre of our destiny and existence. Although he writes about the relationship of soul and body and resurrection in *On the Making of Man*,[357] he reserves *his* most profound dissertation on the Soul for his dialogue with his dying sister Macrina, *On the Soul and Resurrection*.

Gregory wrote *On the Soul and Resurrection* as a Platonic dialogue with his already dying sister shortly after the death of his brother Basil on 1 January 379. This work has many parallels with Plato's *Phaedo* and his *Symposium,* also written as a dialogue with a wise woman teacher Diotima. Gregory attempts to present the doctrine of the bodily resurrection in terms of the Platonic philosophical tradition.[358] Whether Gregory succeeded is debatable; his starting point appears to be Greek philosophy, and especially Platonic and neo-Platonic ideas filtered through the influence of Origen. For the Greeks and Origen alike, the idea of a bodily resurrection was difficult: the soul was all important and the body generally thought of as a drag upon its virtue. For them to be free from the body was liberation in the progress of the soul. The whole discussion is given both poignancy and intensity by the fact that Macrina's body is visibly weakening as they speak.[359]

During the course of the dialogue, a number of issues are discussed: the origin of the soul, its inception in the body, the role of the emotions in relation to the soul, the nature of the soul after death, and the meaning of resurrection. Although taking into account scripture in different places, his methodology is to work from Greek philosophical ideas and develop them only tentatively in the light of scripture and the story of Jesus, but most Christian authors would begin from scripture and let its principles shape our understanding of the meaning of resurrection. The journey of the soul seems to be what most concerns Gregory and explaining his faith within the framework of Platonism. In the light of her weakening body, Macrina says, "the soul is an essence which has a beginning; it is a living and intellectual essence which by itself gives the organic and sensory body the power of life".[360] As is said toward the end of the dialogue "the soul and the body have one and the same beginning",[361] with the soul being like a cutting planted in the earth of the body in which it grows. There is no pre-existent substance from which the soul comes as some Platonists and Manichees believe, rather God creates soul and body as one. Thus "just as the growth of a sprouting seed proceeds gradually to its goal, in the same manner also when a human being is formed the power of the soul appears according to the measure of the body".[362] In other words, soul and body grow together, with the intellectual power or mind being in the soul and its understanding being fed by sensory-perception. Furthermore, the dialogue discusses whether they are attached to the soul and the body. Macrina comes up with the surprising conclusion that, "since clearly no such thing as desire or anger appears in the divine nature, logically one would suppose that these are not essentially united with the soul".[363] They go on to say that reason, part of the soul, is to be striped of these faculties and to exist without them, for "they are external things (desire and anger) which happen to our nature and do not belong to its essence".[364] The resulting concept of mankind is Platonic and hardly does justice to Christian views of man being an integration of mind, heart, and spirit making up the Hebrew concept of soul or living being.

    The great question that Gregory addresses, given the circumstances of the dialogue, is what happens to soul and body at death? Macrina or the Teacher replies to this question by saying that the soul passes from the visible (clothed with a body) to the invisible,[365] just as some of the earth passes into shade or darkness when not facing the sun, so the soul is invisible after death. But Gregory goes further; resurrection for him is essentially restoration of the body to its pre-Fall state. "I think that the Apostolic word agrees with our idea of the resurrection and shows what our definition means when it says that the resurrection is nothing other than restoration of our nature to its original state".[366] The soul dissolves from the body in the same way that mixed colours on a palate separate to their original form or clay used in pottery returns to its original condition.[367] He goes on to say about this restoration which is resurrection that, "If the Power which governs the universe should send to the dissolved elements the signal for coming together, then by one power of the soul the diverse elements will be drawn together. In the concurrence of its own elements the rope of our body will be braided by the soul".[368] He rules out any concept of re-incarnation of the soul in other humans or animal forms—that remains quite outside his doctrine of resurrection.

What will be lost in this new existence is that "garment of skin" which we had to wear as humans, or fallen humans (Gregory believing that such things did not exist in Paradise). So he says, with seeming relief, "we throw off every part of our irrational skin (when I hear skins I interpret it as the form of irrational nature which we have put on from association with passion) along with the removal of the garment. These are things which we have received from the irrational skin: sexual intercourse, conception, childbearing, dirt, lactation, nourishment, evacuation, gradual growth to maturity, the prime of life, old age, disease, death".

Furthermore, Gregory says that this process of disassembly of soul and body at death, and re-assembly of soul and new body in resurrection involves a process of purging or purgatory. He compares the soul at death as being like dragged from an earthquake with mess and bruises inflicted on it which must be cleansed, or like a muddy rope being dragged through a narrow hole which sloughs off the extraneous mud in the process, or like a goldsmith refining gold. This is all like the cleansing of the soul after death. The more mud, the deeper buried in the debris of an earthquake, the more painful the purging of the soul. Judgement is not primarily about the punishment of sinners but the separation of good from evil.[369] "Evil must be altogether removed in every way from being, and, as we have said before, that which does not really exist must cease to exist, since, for Gregory, evil "does not exist by its nature outside of free choice, when all choice is in God, evil will suffer a complete annihilation because no receptacle remains for it".[370] In these ways Resurrection, in terms of the restoration of the original, will result, but it was essentially a Platonic view woven onto a curtailed Christian vision that Gregory ended up with. Resurrection for the Apostle Paul was more than restoring the original; it was a brand new world order.

This chapter is not about orthopraxy, right conduct; it has been about the Cappadocian's understanding of creation and especially the creation and destiny of humankind which is the preliminary understanding and groundwork for their orthopraxy. However, only a proper understanding of creation and the destiny of man can be the starting point for the Cappadocian's work and teaching about the spiritual journey, the care of the poor and each other in community, and their vision for the Church in their society.

CHAPTER 7

Social Justice and the Monastic Life

Unlike his younger brother, Gregory, who was able to pursue the life and teachings of a mystic quietly, especially during his years of exile from the Diocese of Nyssa (374–378), Basil had no such freedom, nor the same inclination. It was true that, having returned from Athens, Basil started a life of contemplation, the philosophic life, at Annisa, but separate from his sister Macrina's family monastic establishment. He was not to be there for very long. A combination of events including his own innate desire to lead the Church in the defence of orthodoxy, and his natural ability to administer and organise the Church in its mission, meant that when the call to priesthood came from Eusebius of Caesarea, Basil responded.

After six years of retreat at Annisa he accepted the responsibility of ordination as a presbyter and began his ministry in Caesarea in 365. He was to remain in office in Caesarea—apart from a brief spell away near the beginning because of a conflict with Eusebius—as either a priest or bishop for the remainder of his life. During this time he remained at the eye of the storm: in the defence of Nicene orthodoxy and, with his strong inclination to what we would call today social justice, in the provision of care in a systematic way for the sick, hungry, or starving in the city.

Basil is still remembered by the local Islamic population. His Feast Day is celebrated in the town and he is remembered in particular for his care of the poor. To the local population, this sphere of his ministry is cherished, and this is not surprising given the strategic way in which he sought to care for the poorest in his city. He left a lasting impression of care for the disadvantaged that spans almost two millennia. This care was combined with an ascetic life; he remained a monk-bishop throughout his ministry from consecration onwards. But, for Basil, a monastic life, given his call to urban ministry, could not be an isolated retreat leading to a mystical and personal encounter with God described in the terms used by his younger brother from either the Song of Songs or the Life of Moses. In first a priestly and then an episcopal office in an important town, Basil saw his vocation as both defending orthodoxy and serving the poorest in his parish and then his diocese. He did the latter by seeking to shame or teach the wealthier citizens to distribute help to the poor through powerful homilies, and also by setting up a systematic method of support called the *Basileiados* which had strong ascetic overtones. It was a powerful combination of teaching and practical action. His ascetical teaching as well as Gregory of Nazianzus' oration on Basil[371] provide more than a glimpse of Basil's charitable work.

Basil's Homilies on Social Justice

In 365 Basil was ordained to the priesthood in Caesarea; a few years later in 369, and before he became a bishop, Caesarea was struck by a devastating famine. The famine in Cappadocia provoked passionate preaching by Basil on the need for a just response from the better off in society. Without being able to precisely date these homilies on social justice there can be little doubt that they were precipitated by the scenes of starvation following the failure of the harvests. These Homilies were titled as follows: *To the Rich, I will tear down my barns, In time of Famine and drought,* and *Against those who lend at Interest.*

The famine deeply affected Basil himself and he had first-hand experience of its devastation. He described vividly the effects of famine in his homily *In Time of famine and drought*. He writes, "I saw the fields and wept bitterly for their unfruitfulness; I poured out my lament, since the rain does not pour down upon us. Some of the seeds dried up without germinating, buried by the plough beneath clumps of dried earth. The rest, after just beginning to take root and sprout, were withered by the hot wind in a manner pitiful to see. Thus someone might now aptly invert the words of the Gospel and say, "the labourers are many, but the harvest is scant".[372] He goes on to describe the devastation of famine in order to move his hearers towards generosity:

> The disease of those who after starving, namely hunger, is a terrible form of suffering. Hunger is the most severe of human maladies, the very worst kind of death. The other hazards to human life do not involve extended torment: whether in case of death by the sword, which brings about a swift end, or roaring flames, which swiftly extinguish life . . . But starvation prolongs pain and draws out the agony . . . The body becomes dehydrated, its temperature drops, its bulk dwindles, its strength wastes away . . . The voice becomes weak and feeble. The eyes become diseased and are rendered useless, sunken in their sockets like fruits that shrivel up in their skins. The belly is empty, shrunken to nothing possessing no girth nor the natural tone of the bowels, so that the bones of the spine are visible from the front".[373]

In response to such suffering, what does Basil call for? Like most in his generation, Basil saw natural disasters as a consequence of sin just as he saw the destruction of Jerusalem as a punishment for the Jews rejection of Jesus (however poor a response Basil's biographer Rousseau sees this teaching on disaster, it was commonplace then).[374] Basil therefore writes, "Let us now examine our lives, both individually and corporately; let us regard the drought as a guide leading us to remembrance of our sins . . . Let us truly account this catastrophe as having occurred primarily because of our own sins . . . or as a test of soul."[375] As he succinctly puts it "this is why the fields are arid: because love has dried up".[376] In response to the calamity, not only does Basil call for repentance and asks for intercession but he bemoans the poor response: "Few there are who have gathered to pray for me, and those who have come are drowsy, yawning, peering around incessantly, counting the minutes until the cantor finishes the verses, until they are released from church and the duty of prayer as from a dungeon!"[377]

Furthermore, Basil calls for a communal sharing as in the early Church.[378] He asks for a redistribution of wealth: "re-distribute your surplus to the needy"; share bread with those who come knocking on your door and do not hoard or be self-indulgent.[379]

The famine was the trigger both for this teaching to the citizens of Caesarea about social justice, and the foundation of the *Basiliad* as a city for the poor. Other homilies, such as *To the Rich* and *I will tear down my barns*, continue the themes found in *In a time of famine and drought*. These themes were: the need to obey Jesus' teaching on simplicity; to adopt what we would now call now a sustainable lifestyle through redistribution of surplus; and the fact of our mortality and the avoidance of all self-indulgence. These themes guided Basil's teachings.

A governing principle of his teaching was the need to re-distribute surplus wealth or goods, and this point was directly and easily made from the Parable of the Rich Fool[380] who, when faced with a surplus, decided to tear down his barns and build larger ones. For Basil, this was absurd: "What could be more ridiculous than this incessant toil, labouring to build and then labouring to tear down again".[381] He goes on to say "If you want storehouses, you have them in the stomachs of the poor. Lay up for yourself treasure in heaven".[382] For Basil, the wealthy who will not share with those in need are like thieves taking from another what in the Lord's eyes is rightfully theirs. Nor will piety without generosity avail; after all, Basil says, "I know many who fast, pray, sigh and demonstrate every manner of piety, so long as it costs them nothing, yet would not part with a penny to help those in distress. Of what profit to them is the remainder of their virtue?"[383]

Basil's greatest invective was reserved for those who exploited others' poverty for financial reward, and these were those who lent at interest to the poor. Basil takes one sentence from Psalm 14 which says "They do not lend at interest" and preaches upon it. He says usury is a sin denounced often in scripture in both the Law and the prophets. "For in truth it is the height of inhumanity that those who do not have enough even for the basic necessities should be compelled to seek a loan in order to survive, while others, not being satisfied with the return of the principal, should turn the misfortune of the poor to their own advantage and reap a bountiful harvest".[384]

He cautioned those who took loans against such action. "It is better to care for your needs little by little with your own devices, than to be raised up all at once by outside means, only to be completely stripped of all you have".[385] And those who take out loans live constantly in fear: "If you knock at his door, the debtor is underneath the bed in a flash. His heart pounds if someone enters the room suddenly. If a dog barks, he breaks out in a sweat, seized with terror, and looks for some place to hide". And with slightly jaundiced words he says, "The one who caters for the desires of a woman goes to the banker!"[386] Rather, those with excess wealth should give it away: "Give away that portion of your silver that is lying idle, do not burden it with interest rates, and it shall be well with you both; you will have the certainty that money is well guarded, while the one who receives it will have the profit from its use".[387] But Basil was far from content to leave his efforts to help the poor to the effects of his preaching on issues of social justice. He went much further creating, or quite possibly extending, a community based on an ascetic or monastic way of life called the *Basiliad*, a "new" community for the care of the poor named after him.

The *Basiliad* and Monasticism in Caesarea

Monasticism had different expressions according to local climate, environment and spiritual vision. In Egypt, the monastery of Pachomius was quite simply called "the village", transporting into the desert "the all-absorbing routines of the villages of the *oikoumene*".[388]

In Syria also, the tradition of the lone ascetic or *ihidaya*, who were not unlike the *apotaktikoi* (renunciants) in Egypt, grew. They were like monks, *monachos*, and had often renounced normal life, separating from wife and family. According to Ephrem the Syrian, such people served the Church as a group of *ihidaye* in a covenant, monastery, or *qyma*. In Nisibis, bishops often exercised their pastoral ministry through the members of the *qyma*. Different models of monastic or ascetic life developed in these areas, and, within Egypt itself, varying landscapes created conditions for differing types of monasticism.

Another style of monasticism developed in Cappadocia, Pontus, and Asia Minor. Here one of the chief factors in its development was the weather. If in Athanasius's famous description of Egyptian monasticism "the desert became a city", one might well affirm that for many ascetics of Asia Minor the city became their desert. Describing early monasticism in Galatia, Cappadocia, and the neighbouring provinces, Sozomen commented that, unlike the holy men of Egypt and Syria, the monks of this region "for the most part dwelt in communities in cities and villages." He explained "the severity of the winter which is always a natural feature of that country, would probably make a hermit life impractical."[389] One of the results of this was the emergence of monastic communities in cities and particularly in Constantinople. The monastic historian Gilbert Dragon makes a "convincing case for the distinctiveness of the monastic movement in the city".[390] What was true for Eastern Capital of the Roman Empire would soon become true for Caesarea under Basil's energetic and practical episcopal leadership.

Caesarea in Cappadocia was an important and strategic town sitting as it does on the East-West and North-South trade routes connecting Iconium in the West to Melitene on the Euphrates in the East and Constantinople and Ancyra in the North with Tarsus and Antioch in the South. It was here in this populous city, famous for its commercial, artisan and, intellectual life, that Basil was to create a pattern of monasticism unique in its vision and scale in the Roman world. Although his older friend and fellow ascetic Eusthahius had formed groups of ascetics in cities in Anatolia with a view to helping the poor,[391] Basil was to surpass those communities in scale and practical governance. Basil's foundation was spurred into being by the famine of 369, but Basil, ever the practical organiser and carer of the poor, instituted in his *Basiliad* an urban monasticism devoted to the care of the poor and sick which was arguably unique in the province. It was, in many ways, the precursor of the work of the Augustinian friars who worked in the cities and towns in medieval Europe seven hundred years later and who founded in London the hospitals of St Thomas and St Bartholomew.

The *Basiliad* is praised in Gregory of Nazianzus' funeral oration. He said, "Go forth a little way from the city, and behold the new city, the storehouse of pity, the common treasury of the wealthy where disease is regarded in a religious light, and disaster is thought a blessing, and sympathy is put to the test".[392] On the edge of the city he founded this hospice, part hospital for the sick, part shelter for the poor, and part feeding station for the starving. He used the remainder of his paternal inheritance to found it, and made it the chief object of his philanthropy and care of the poor in conjunction with his teaching on the subject. "For by his word and advice he opened the stores of those who possessed them, and so according to scripture dealt food to the hungry and satisfied the poor with bread".[393] He personally washed the feet of the poor and became like a second Joseph in distributing food to the hungry.[394]

Once a bishop, Basil used his status to raise funds for the hospice, gaining grants from the Emperor Valens, and so developing it into a large complex of buildings, including his residence. At the centre of this city of care was not only the bishop in monkish attire, his simple brown tunic his only vesture, but with him a community of monks who put this vision into practice. In this community, Basil had founded a vision of ascetic monasticism with an engaged vision of social care that far out lasted his own episcopacy. It was also a community to which he gave practical operating rules in his *Great Asceticon* with its *Longer and Shorter Rules* and the earlier *Moralia*. Basil, like many of his contemporaries, was a monk-bishop who *renounced the world to lead the Church* (see Andrea Sterk's book of this title).

The Ascetic Writings

Of the three Cappadocians, Basil undoubtedly wrote most on the ascetic life, as opposed to the life of mystical prayer and study which was more the preserve of his brother, especially in the context of community. But rather than writing for a specific monastic community already in existence, Basil, both in his ascetic writings and his homilies, appears to be addressing all Christians when advocating an ascetic life and a life of virtue. He never used the word monk and his "rules" evolved over his own lifetime and beyond.[395] The monastic ideal developed variously in the Middle East, with Syria, Egypt, and later Asia Minor developing their variant ideals according to the climate, terrain, and their relationships with the wider Church.

In Asia Minor, ascetic groups sprung up in towns in association with Eustathius, with whom Basil had toured monastic communities in Egypt and elsewhere and from whom Basil broke due his later teachings on the Holy Spirit. A Council held at Gangra, variously dated either before 341 (Sozomen) or after 360 (Socrates), handed down canons designed to curb excesses in monasticism that had developed in Asia Minor and further afield.[396] Such canons were those which condemned contempt for legitimate marriage and the "concomitant exaltation of singles and virginity",[397] and women who had deserted their husbands for a monastic life, cut their hair as a sign of submission or wore male clothing.[398] It seems only a small step from the teaching of Gregory of Nyssa's treatise on *Virginity* to these excesses, in which both husband and wife deserted their spouses and children on the pretext of following the ascetic life.[399] Even Basil seemed ambivalent about the blessings, or rather the spiritual dangers, of the married state, writing as follows:

> Do not relax your efforts, therefore, you have chosen the companionship of a wife, as if you were at liberty to embrace worldliness. Indeed, you have need of greater labours and vigilance for the gaining of your salvation, inasmuch as you have elected to dwell in the midst of the toils and in the very stronghold of rebellious powers, and night and day all your senses are impelled toward the desires of the allurements of sin which are before your eyes ... How will you, stationed in the very thick of the battle, be able to win the contest against the Enemy?[400]

Nevertheless, Basil was keen to regularise the boundaries of the ascetic life and did so especially in two of his letters (nos. 22 and 173) which deal with this subject, as well as in the *Rules—Longer and Shorter*.

In the first of these letters—no. 22—Basil appears to be laying down the way in which the ascetic life should be pursued. What is especially striking about this letter is that Basil almost wholly identifies it with the life of an ordinary Christian and the characteristics of this life are entirely described from scripture. The aim seems to be simplicity of lifestyle, moderation in speech, willingness in work, and thoughtfulness about "his heavenly vocation". "The Christian", writes Basil, "should not be ostentatious in clothing or sandals, for all this is idle boasting. He should wear cheap clothes according to the need of the body. He should consume nothing beyond what is necessary or which tends to extravagance, for all this is abuse." Indeed, he should not be "deceived by the filling of his belly, for nightmares come from this."[401] If these brothers were living in a community of some sort there was no rule of life given here, more a handbook on how to relate to each other rather than one which lays down rules for community living as Benedict would do later.

His other letter (no. 173) on the ascetic lifestyle was written in 374 to a Theodora who was a canoness. Here Basil calls this life of virtue or ascetic life *the evangelical life*. Many choose it but very few manage to live it. What Basil is looking for is "constancy in self-control, assiduity in prayer, sympathy in fraternal charity, generosity toward the needy, subjection of pride, contrition of heart, soundness of faith, equability in despondency, never letting pass from our minds the remembrance of the awful tribunal, towards which we all indeed are hastening, though very few are mindful of it or solicitous about what the issue there from shall be".[402] Perhaps it is understandable that few found these responsibilities possible to fulfil. Elsewhere in some of his *Homilies,* the *Moralia,* and the *Short and Longer Rules* which form the *Asceticon,* Basil and his associates gave a thorough description of the ascetic life, lived-out in community, and surely with the brothers of the *Basiliad* in mind.

In his homily entitled *An ascetical discourse and exhortation on the renunciation of the world and spiritual perfection* there is both general and practical instruction about how to conduct the ascetic life in the context of community. Some of it sounds a little quaint to our ears, with other advice eminently sensible. So he writes: "Do not accumulate a heavy burden of sins for yourself by having too soft a bed or by the style of your garments, or shoes, or any other part of your dress; by variety of food, or a table too richly appointed for your stage of self-renunciation, by the way you stand or sit, or being too negligent or too fastidious with regard to manual labour".[403] Likewise, gluttony is to be avoided, and, when it is your turn to serve the monks, have ready "a word of exhortation and comfort for love of those whom you serve, that your ministry seasoned with salt may be acceptable".[404] Always take the more lowly seat in the refectory, do not butt in on conversations, do not be inquisitive, and, lastly, "if you are youthful in body or mind, fly from intimate association with comrades of your own age and run away from them as fire. The Enemy has, indeed, set many aflame through such means and consigned them to the eternal fire, casting them down into the loathsome pit of the five cities on the pretext of spiritual love. Even those who have come safely through every wind and tempest on the sea and are safe in port he has sent down into the deep, together with the ship and crew. At meals take a seat far away from your young brother; in lying down to rest, let not your garments be neighbour to his; rather, have an elderly brother lie between you." He goes on to say, in making conversation with a young brother, do not gaze fixedly into his face nor meet him on the pretext of private meditation on the scriptures, "but be fully convinced, by the oft-repeated experience of those who have fallen and have clearly demonstrated it to be so, that it is of itself an offensive act".[405]

The main provision for governing what we would call monastic life was the *Long Rules*, probably initiated by Basil but added to by his successors. The Rules were comprehensive in nature, governing admission to the community, its community life revolving around prayer (seven times during the day and night), labour, rules about clothes, laughter (not too much—rule 17), eating food, how to sit at table, the actions of the superior, how to handle dependent relatives (32), how to converse with consecrated women (33), treatment of those who leave the brotherhood (36), selling of produce from the farm, who should be allowed to go on journeys from the monastery (44), discipline, and the resort to medicine. Basil appears to agree with the moderate use of medicine but not if it becomes a distraction (55). These rules, together with Basil's homilies on *Envy, Anger, Humility*, and *Detachment*, formed a true *Asceticon* or library of ascetic works on the call to a life of renunciation. It is a powerful legacy on what would generally now be known as monastic life.

Gregory of Nazianzus and Gregory of Nyssa on Social Justice and Renunciation

Both Gregory of Nyssa and Gregory of Nazianzus were greatly influenced by Basil when it came to the monastic or philosophic life but neither had quite the same motivation or opportunity as Basil for putting these ideas into practice in such a communal way in the cause of service to city, although it is true that Gregory supported philanthropic work in Nazianzus generously. For Basil, his initial retreat at Annisa in Pontus had been more for his own personal progress in what was often called the pursuit of a *life of virtue*; once he became committed to Caesarea—first as presbyter and then bishop—he saw the way a brotherhood of like-minded "monks" could take forward the work of the diocese in both the care of the poor and the mission of the diocese to the city. He thus constructed or greatly extended the *Basiliad*.

Both Gregorys had experienced Basil's life of retreat and renunciation in Annisa to some degree: his brother, although belonging more to his sister Macrina's establishment nearby, must have visited Basil often, and Gregory of Nazianzus fled to Annisa after his "forced" ordination as priest by his father in 362 as well as having been there before. But the type of retreat or renunciation which they sought was significantly different to Basil's. When Gregory of Nazianzus visited Basil in his Pontus fastness, he teased him in letters written subsequent to the visit. "He writes to Basil with carefully elegant humour, designed at once to express his admiration for but his total inability to adopt such a lifestyle, but without offending his friend's sensibilities".[406] Gregory wrote:

> On my part I stand in admiration of your Pontus and its Pontic darkness; your place of abode—so worthy of an exile: the hills over your head and the desert underneath; the wild beasts that serve to test your faith; even your rathole of a house with its sonorous titles like "Place of Contemplation" and "Monastery" and "School". What impressive forests of overgrown brush you have. Your precipitous mountains encircle you not so much as a crown, more like a prison. Your air comes in rationed doses, and

the sun which you long for so much, you can peer at like someone looking up a chimney.[407]

And the food was no better, complained Gregory. "My poor teeth, slipping on your hunks of crust, and then bracing themselves, ready to pull themselves out as if they were stuck fast in sucking clay."[408]

No, Gregory "did not want his solitude peopled with eager groups of former serfs and aristocrats mingling together to plant root crops and dig wells and such like".[409] He wanted solitude; he wanted the philosophic life, retreat, and contemplation for study and writing but not in such extreme conditions and not in such a mixed social milieu. Although Basil was as well born, Gregory wanted a more refined monasticism. He wanted to be the scholar-monk at the centre of a family-run monastery in which the family provided protection and hospitality, and where there was time to pursue prayer, contemplation, scholarship, and writing without the intrusion of labour or distracting relationships. If Basil provided a unconscious model for the Augustinian order or even the Franciscans in their early days, Gregory of Nazianzus would have served as a model for the Cistercians or Dominicans. To press the analogy, Gregory of Nyssa would have been a model for the Carmelites.

Where Basil saw the monastery as the way of dealing with the poor, the diseased, and the dying, Gregory saw it as the way of furthering thought and prayer. In the future monasticism would be expressed in both strands in city, town, or deserted countryside. The *Basiliad* in Caesarea and the city monasteries in Constantinople after the fifth century were examples of communities more intent on scholarship.[410] But such an attitude in Gregory did not in any way mean the neglect or overlooking of the poor, for both in his Oration 14 *On the Poor* and in his *Will* he demonstrates his care of the destitute.

Gregory of Nazianzus

The principles that guided Gregory in his attitude to the celibate life, his renunciation of the world, his commitment to a life of solitude, scholarship, and quietness, and his philanthropy towards the poor, were not dissimilar to those of Gregory of Nyssa. They formed a kind of perfect circle for Nazianzus in which the greatest of his callings, to defend the orthodox faith expressed in the Trinity, took place. The monasticism, if it can be called that, which Gregory preferred was best expressed by the term *the philosophic life*. Nevertheless, he was prepared to use both his eloquence and commitment to the poor to raise funds for Basil's great project, the *Basiliad*. So in either 366 or 367, soon after Basil's ordination as priest and his arrival in Caesarea, Gregory went to the city to help Basil in his new work. The idea of a hospice for the sick and especially for lepers had originated with Basil's predecessor as Bishop, Eusebius, but it was taken on and extended greatly by Basil,[411] and given yet greater urgency and focus by the great famine in 368. In support of Basil's work Gregory wrote an oration called *On Love of the Poor*. As with many travelling rhetors of the time, Gregory was prepared to take this "fund raising" oration to many places in the area to secure support for Basil's hospice. It was most probably designed to catch the attention of the Imperial and governing classes in the neighbourhood and to gain their support. One such individual was Sophronios, an imperial official who held high office in Caesarea and would eventually become the Master of Offices in Constantinople in the secretariat of the Urban Prefect. Gregory offered him his *Oration on the Poor* in return for the favour of Sophronios's patronage of his adopted heir and husband of his beloved niece, Alypiana.[412]

On Love of the Poor, for Gregory, is part of the economy of salvation. It proceeds from a proper understanding of wealth, a proper understanding of the fragility of all human life, our knowledge of future judgement, and the complete dependence of the poor themselves on philanthropy. "As such it is a keynote piece of political thought, as well as a decisive theological essay in which Gregory sets out his mind on social altruism that characterises the inner spirit of the religion of Christ. It was something that he was willing to lend to Basil's particular cause of the Caseraean project, but something from the outset which he designed on a larger scale for his work as a Christian—philanthropist and Bishop-*Philoptochos* (friend of the poor)".[413]

The oration is a highly crafted, engaging and moving piece or writing: "He plays his audience like a musician".[414] He shows his audience varying groups deserving pity and compassion: widows and orphans, exiles, slaves, those burdened by greed, crime, or taxation but then he presents the worst of all groups—lepers. "There lies before our eyes a dreadful and pathetic sight, one that no one would believe who has not seen it: human beings alive yet dead, disfigured in almost every part of their bodies, barely recognizable for whom they once were or where they came from. By way of identification they keep calling out the names of their mothers and fathers, brothers, places of origin. A mother cries, 'Hapless child of a heart-broken mother!' She sobs. The disease has taken its bitter toll of us both. My poor child!"[415] And the challenge for Gregory is stark, "What shall we do? Will they [the lepers] continue to suffer in the open while we lounge within luxurious homes bedecked with stone of every description, resplendent with gold and silver and the inlay of delicate mosaic and varied fresco that charm and beguile the eyes?"[416] Gregory appeals for generosity and compassion. He shows how philanthropy more than anything else displays and restores the *eikon* of God in his followers, not only bringing mercy to others but allowing God to treat the benefactor compassionately too. Gregory refutes wicked misunderstandings about poverty: for instance, saying that poverty is part of the providence of God[417] or results from moral turpitude,[418] or providence is handicapped by limited resources.[419] Rather Gregory says we are to be good stewards of what God has given, to repay God's lavish kindness which has been poured upon us in a multitude of blessings,[420] and to share rather than hoard as God shares his blessings with all.[421]

For Gregory, only almsgiving can restore to humans that condition of freedom which was lost at the Fall, which alone sets us free from self-interest and restores the tarnished image of God. In other words, if you give to those who can give you nothing and have no claim on you except there common humanity then you become what you were first intended to be. In words that echo the whole Orthodox notion of *theosis*, Gregory says, "Come to be a god to the unfortunate by imitating God's mercy".[422]

What Gregory preached in this great Oration he was able to do both in his own life but more especially in his death and through his will. Gregory's will is one of the few that we have from antiquity. In fact his will "is the oldest extant will made under Roman Law".[423]

Signed in the presence of six Cappadocian bishops and Presbyter Cledonius—to whom Gregory had written earlier about Christology and the threat from Apollinarius—this will was witnessed on the day before the *kalends* of January (i.e. 31 December), most probably in Cappadocia but with Gregory still referring to himself as Archbishop of Constantinople, invoking a courtesy title following his resignation, which he found hard to relinquish.

The main clause of his will was to give "all his possessions to the Catholic Church which is in Nazianzus, for the service of the poor who are under the care of the aforesaid church". In this way his parents' estate was devoted to the poor. Further bequests, including his horses, were made to Gregory, a monk and deacon in his household, who became his heir but who was still instructed to pass on everything to the local church. Some household servants or slaves were freed, like Theodosius, the notary, and Eupraxius. Each was given five gold coins. His favourite niece, Alypiane, was given clothes, silks, and linens from his brother Caesarius' estate, and an especially generous legacy was given to Evagrius Ponticus, a deacon who, after prominence in the imperial court in Constantinople, gave it all up to become an influential ascetical writer and monk in the desert at Scetis in Egypt.

What Gregory taught in his lifetime he completed in his death, his celibate life meant that his family had become the church at Nazianzus and amongst them chiefly the poor. As he wrote in his Oration, *On the Love of the Poor*, "as long as you sail with the wind on your back, give a hand to the castaway. As long as you are prosperous and whole, help the one in distress".[424]

CHAPTER 8

The Ascent of the Soul

The Cappadocians were fighters for the Trinity and Nicaea, but first and foremost they were followers of the Way in a particular tradition. That tradition was articulated by the Apostle Paul in the provinces of Galatia and, possibly, Pontus, and was embodied in Christian communities in the first century AD in such places as Pisidia, Antioch, and Iconium. In living memory their faith was shaped by Gregory Thaumaturgus, the Wonder Worker, and his followers (a shrine still exists to him in the Hagia Sophia in Istanbul consisting of a stoop for holy water or oil in a pillar in that great church) who exerted a powerful influence in these Cappadocians' families.

When defending himself in a letter written in *c*.375 during his episcopate to the Neocaesareans (a town towards the Black Sea on the river Lycos—today the Kelkit river) against accusations of meeting with semi-Arians, Basil recalls his early spiritual formation as an argument for his orthodoxy.[425] Basil writes, "and what could be clearer proof of our faith than that we were brought up by our grandmother, a blessed woman who came from amongst you? I mean the illustrious Macrina, by whom we were taught the sayings of the most blessed Gregory (as any as she herself retained, preserved to her time in unbroken memory) and who moulded and formed us while still young in the doctrines of piety".[426] Only having mentioned both Macrina and Gregory does Basil then go on to speak of Athanasius' endorsement of his policy of reconciliation with former Arians in a letter in his possession from Athanasius, in which Athanasius expressly supports receiving into fellowship any who reject Arius and support Nicaea.[427] As proof of his orthodoxy to the Neocaesaraeans, Basil recalls his spiritual pedigree granted by his family connection to Gregory Thaumaturgus and the support of Athanasius. He is quite clear about the widely accepted orthodox tradition in which he stands.

The point is that Basil and his family, together with Gregory of Nazianzus and his family, stood in a tradition of faith which came to them through Gregory the Wonder Worker who himself had been taught and strongly influenced by Origen in Caesarea in Palestine from 233. But Origen's influence on the Cappadocians clearly diminished as time went on. For instance, only a little of Gregory the Wonder Worker's panegyric on Origen was included by Gregory of Nyssa in his subsequent life of Gregory Thaumaturgus. Later Basil and Gregory of Nazianzus—who together had written the *Philocalia* (an assembly of Origen's teaching) whilst on retreat by the river Iris in Pontus, hardly ever mention Origen directly in their writings.[428] Nevertheless Origen remained a strong background influence on their development.

Spiritual roots

In understanding the formation of their spirituality we must begin with their two families; in both families the female influence seems especially strong. In Basil and Gregory of Nyssa's family, the two Macrina's were central. The older Macrina (Basil's paternal grandmother), to whom Basil referred in his letter (no. 204), was the one who passed on the teachings of Gregory the Wonder Worker to the family and who seemingly set the tone of piety in his family. Gregory of Nazianzus, in his Funeral Oration for Basil, writes of Basil's parents, "The union of his parents, cemented as it was by a community of virtue, no less than by cohabitation, was notable for many reasons, especially for generosity to the poor, for hospitality, for purity of soul as the result of self-discipline, for the dedication to God a portion of their property".[429] But it is Basil's sister, Macrina, who had such a profound influence, if not so much on Basil as upon Gregory of Nyssa, the second youngest of five brothers. This was made clear by Gregory of Nyssa's *Life of Macrina*. Gregory also spoke warmly of his mother's piety and her strong influence in his family in his own funeral oration for his father.[430]

Gregory of Nyssa is under no allusion as to the importance of Macrina on their family, Basil included. In a rare and candid glimpse into family life and the different characteristics of the siblings, he writes of Basil as follows:

> When the great Basil, brother of the girl we have been speaking about, came back from the school where he had been trained for a long time in the discipline of rhetoric. Although she took him in hand he was monstrously conceited about his skill in rhetoric, contemptuous of every high reputation and exalted beyond the leading lights of the province by his self-importance, so swiftly did she win him to the ideal of philosophy that he renounced worldly appearance, showed contempt for the admiration of rhetorical ability and went over of his own accord to this active life of manual labour, preparing himself by means of complete poverty a way of life without impediment towards virtue.[431]

Whether this was overstated by Gregory of Nyssa we cannot be sure, but it catches both the strong influence of Macrina and the touch of overbearing manner of which Basil was from time to time guilty, especially with family and friends, in expecting their allegiance. This attitude was not left unchallenged by his equally determined sister! This combination of family spirituality, Basil's own experience of the monastic life whilst on an ascetic tour with Eustathius, and the fact of owning land made an experiment possible in "the philosophic life" in Cappadocia.

The Origins of the Philosophic or Ascetic Life in Cappadocia

Quite why the movement to the desert or wild places and the ascetic life began we cannot quite be sure, but it began in the mid-third century. According to Jerome (c.342–420), Paul of Thebes began the movement to live ascetically at some point in the 250s during the persecutions of Decius and Valerian.[432] The biblical examples for such a lifestyle are to be found in the flights of Elijah, the Life of John the Baptist, the Temptations of Jesus, and the life and deprivations of the Apostle Paul. Initially such a movement to the wilderness may have been to avoid persecution but it soon found more positive spiritual purpose.

Jerome writes simply that "a certain Paul of Thebes was the originator of the practice . . . of the solitary life".[433] Soon this *askesis*, or "training" as it means, was taken up across the Eastern Mediterranean. It involved the sacrifice of money, sex, and comfort. Later this would be crystallised in monasticism in the vows of poverty, chastity, and obedience and, in the West, enshrined in Benedict's rule, amongst others. An ascetic's life revolved around the search for God in isolated, deserted places where a concentration on prayer, contemplation, and scripture could take place as well as being a pointer to the wider Christian community and secular world of the perfection humanity might obtain in such a discipline.

Asceticism in various forms developed over the early parts of the fourth century. In Egypt Anthony was made famous by Athanasius who spent his Third Exile (356–362) amongst the monks of the desert, including Anthony himself. He wrote Anthony's biography and encouraged others to similar forms of asceticism. Anthony retreated further and further into the desert "until he retreated to inaccessible tombs to fight the devils".[434] Much further to the north at Tabennisi in the Thebaid in the Nile delta, Pachomius started a community of ascetics where much emphasis was placed on manual labour organised with almost military discipline together with communal prayer.[435]

In these early years of asceticism before the rules of Basil or Benedict, forms of asceticism could range from the unruly to the bizarre. There was an ideological tension between the life of a hermit and those gathered in a *Lavra*, an ascetic community, as in Palestine. There monks grouped together as hermits in a dispersed community in caves for cells but shared prayers and meals near an acknowledged leader. A more closely knit community was the *coenobium* where a closer common life was shared. Again almost vagrant peasant monks wandered the countryside and could form a kind of mob rule, used either in the destruction of pagan temples or to attack those considered heretical. Often Church Councils were intimidated by such rioting. Later, from the fifth century onwards, forms of asceticism would grow more bizarre with monks feeding on grass like animals, living on columns like Symeon the Stylite, or living in the open air with a minimum of clothing or shelter.

Amongst the fourth century Church the call to virginity was strong, with Gregory of Nyssa writing one of his early works *On Virginity*, and other literature on the subject, apocryphal or real, proving highly influential. In particular, the story of Thecla and St Paul, almost certainly apocryphal, proved highly influential. Guided by the Apostle to give up her fiancé, Thecla from Iconium in Pisidia (the neighbouring province to Cappadocia) was condemned to be burnt to death for her breach of contract, but miraculously escaped. Her shrine was at Meriemlik near Seleukia. Her story was influential, so much so that one of Gregory and Basil's sisters was called Thecla, perhaps in the expectation of a similar celibate calling.

In the midst of a rising tide of asceticism Basil set out, soon after his return from Athens and a brief spell of instructing at Caesarea, on a tour with Eustathius in 356 to Egypt and the near East looking at ascetic communities which had sprung up. On his return in 357/8 he started his own community on their estates at Annisa in Pontus, which he recalls a little wistfully after his break with Eustathius for his Sabellian views and his inadequate understanding of the divinity of the Holy Spirit. In letter 223, in which Basil publicly announces his break with Eusthathius, he writes of those early years together when all was fresh and new. Basil writes of those post-Athens days in which he seems to rue his time associating with what he then described as the worldly wisdom of the schools. He writes:

> And before all things my care was to make some amendment in my character, which had for a long time been perverted by association with the wicked (presumably in Athens). And accordingly, having

> read the Gospel, and having perceived therein that the greatest incentive to perfection is the selling of one's goods and the sharing of them with the needy of the brethren, and being entirely without thought of this life, and the soul should have no sympathetic concern with the things of this world, I prayed that I might find some one of the brethren who had taken this way of life, so as to traverse with him in life's brief flood.
>
> And indeed I found many men in Alexandria, and many throughout the rest of Egypt, and others in Palestine, and in Coele-Syria and Mesopotamia, at whose continence in living I marvelled, and I marvelled at their steadfast sufferings, I was amazed at the vigour in prayers, at how they gained mastery over sleep, being bowed down by no necessity of nature, ever persevering exalted and unshackled the purpose of their soul, in hunger and thirst, in coldness and nakedness, not concerning themselves with the body, nor deigning to waste a thought upon it, but as of passing their lives in alien flesh, they showed in deed what it is to sojourn here below, and what to have citizenship in heaven.... I prayed that I myself also, in so far as was attainable by me, might be an emulator of these men.

Despite some people's reluctance to support him in this ascetic venture and their questioning of the sincerity of some of these ascetics, Basil following the inner guidance bequeathed him by his grandmother Macrina and his mother Emmelia and set up a community near the river Iris in Annisa, Pontus for prayer. He recalls, "ask yourself (Eustathius): How often did you visit us in the monastery on the river Iris, when moreover, our most divinely-favoured brother Gregory was present with me, achieving the same purpose in life as myself?"[436]

It was on the banks of the Iris that one or more communities with members of the family began. Basil started his before the return of Grgegory of Nazianzus from Athens, but later, after his own ordination by his overbearing father, Gregory fled there "like a cow stung by a gadfly" to Basil's community where "he was practising communion with God concealed in a cloud like one of the wise men of old".[437] Not far away was Basil's brother Naucratius, a much loved, attractive, and able young man who also lived with a community of "old people living together in poverty and sickness" for five years, but was tragically killed by a boar while out hunting.[438] Another brother, Peter, was also there, as was Macrina, who had herself formed a community of women including her mother, where she lived in utmost simplicity and where her brother after his exile from Nyssa visited her and gained stimulus for his own spiritual writings. Macrina lived there until her death, receiving a healing for breast cancer. Too modest to show off her tumour, it was healed by the prayer of her mother who "when she put her hand inside Macrina's robe to make the sign of the cross on the affected spot, the sign of the cross worked and the affliction disappeared."[439] Here too they fed the hungry that came in large numbers during time of famine. One of her final prayers being:

> You who have on earth the power to forgive sins
> Forgive me, so that I may draw breath again
> And may be found before you
> In the stripping off of my body
> Without stain or blemish in the beauty of my soul,
> but may my soul be received
> Blameless and immaculate into your hands
> as an incense offering before your face."[440]

Here was an experiment in philosophic life which Basil would develop and organise in Casearea as a bishop. Here Gregory of Nazianzus would get a taste of what his temperament enjoyed, a life of letters, prayer, and seclusion, even if the conditions of life and company were not quite to his liking. And here Gregory of Nyssa would eventually return in his own exile for the life offered there.

The Philosophic Life and the Search for Virtue

What was it that drew this family and others beside into this type of existence? Undoubtedly the upsurge of ascetic life in communities or amongst solitaries in Egypt, the Holy Land, and their surroundings played its part. Already there was a well-worn tradition in classical life of withdrawal for study. But other more spiritual, theological, and scriptural reasons also played a significant role in establishing this way of life.

The teachings of Moses and Elijah in the Old Testament, and then principally John the Baptist and Jesus in the New Testament, together with those of the Apostles, about spiritual disciplines and asceticism proved formative. There was a kind of Arcadian bliss about the spot itself near the Iris River:

> ... even Kalyps's isle, which Homer seems to have admired above all others for its beauty, is insignificant compared with this ... Why need I mention the exhalations from the land, or the breezes from the river? Someone else might well marvel at the multitude of the flowers or of the song-birds; but I have not leisure to turn my thoughts to these. The highest praise, however, which I can give to this place is that, although it is well adapted by its admirable situation to producing fruits of every kind, for me the most pleasing fruit it nourishes is tranquillity.[441]

It was here then, in this place of great natural beauty and solitude that three things could be pursued: contemplation of God through the lens of scripture and in the context of prayer, the pursuit of virtue, and stretching oneself in pursuit of God. These were goals that were pursued in these early ascetic communities in Pontus and were invested with great significance by Basil's family.

For Basil, the process was clear: this solitary life was an "escape" from the "violent desires, rebellious impulses and morbid lusts" of those not yet married; from the "tumult of cares" of those already married and from the longing for or care of children of the married. Indeed, husbands with children are subject to "solicitude for their nature, by keeping watch over his wife, by the management of his household, the protection of his servants' rights, losses on contracts, quarrels with neighbours contests in the law-courts, risks of business, or labours of the farm. Every day brings with it some particular cloud to darken the soul".[442] By withdrawal, solitude:

> gives us the greatest help, since it calms our passions, and gives reason leisure to sever them completely from the soul. For just as animals are easily subdued by caresses: so desire, anger, fear, and grief, the venomous evils, which beset the soul, if they are lulled to sleep by solitude and are not exasperated by constant irritations, are also easily subdued by the influence of reason . . . The very beginning of the soul's purgation is tranquillity, in which the tongue is not given to discussing the affairs of men, nor the eyes to contemplating rosy cheeks or comely bodies, nor the ears to lowering the tone of soul by listening to the songs whose sole objects is to amuse, or to words spoken by wits or buffoons, a practice which above all things tends to relax the tone of the soul.[443]

Here scripture could be read in the context of prayer and God himself contemplated and sought without the distractions of worldly living. So he writes "a most important path to the discovery of duty (virtue) is also the study of the divinely-inspired Scriptures . . . Prayer again, following such reading finds the soul stirred by yearning towards God, fresher and more vigorous. Prayer is to be commended, for it engenders the soul a distinct conception of God". It is through prayer and this way of life that the often overwhelming human passions of desire, anger, fear, and grief can be ordered by reason and reworked as faith expressing itself in love for God, others, the earth, and self. Solitude, with this combination of contemplation of the scriptures, prayer, and simplicity, would always be, for Basil, the means of purging passion and preparing the soul to meet with God.

It is in Gregory of Nyssa's writings that this quest for the philosophic life or solitude would become the first step in a process of the unceasing quest for fulfilment. In contrast, for Basil, this would be the necessary preparation for a life lived in community and leadership of the Church in the heat of the furnace of doctrinal conflict and in need of godly leadership that dealt with the pressing social needs of the day. For Basil, this search for, and satisfaction in, solitude would be reflected in his own calling into a passion for social justice, expressed in very practical ways, as well as in passionate teaching about it. But it is Gregory of Nyssa who takes forward the spiritual progress of the soul and what that means into new elevations.

Gregory of Nyssa's Ideas on the Progress of the Soul

Gregory wrote extensively, passionately, philosophically, and vividly on the progress of the soul and what this entails. His works on the subject are wide ranging; in particular we will refer to his *On Virginity* (368; an early work), his commentaries or homilies on the *Song of Songs* (390–5), *Ecclesiastes* and the *Beatitudes*, *The life of Moses* (390–5), and his treatise *On Perfection*. Most of these works were written specifically on the subject of the spiritual journey; others, like his long work *Against Eunomius*, contain passages about the journey of the soul more incidental to the main purpose of the work. In that case he uses the example of Abraham as one who sought the "upward journey" and in so doing "set out upon an exodus, fitting for a prophet who was striving to arrive at the knowledge of God."[444] What was essential about Abraham was that he left behind the vain search of knowledge, made faith the rule of his life, and journeyed towards and into God.[445]

On Virginity was one of Gregory's earliest works, written probably in 368 before he was made Bishop of Nyssa by his brother Basil, possibly when he was a rhetor or public teacher of philosophy between 362–371,[446] a post he much enjoyed—too much according to Gregory of Nazianzus who said of him, "You had rather be thought of as a Rhetor than a Christian".[447]

On Virginity provides a fascinating insight into Gregory's mind: his reflection on how to conduct the spiritual journey; his attitude to marriage and everyday life (vexatious!); his personal reflections of the possibility of this life for him; his description of the virgin life which oscillates from being a physical condition but also an inner disposition of the soul, of purity and self-mastery.

At the outset there is a strong sense of leaving a previous life in which human passions dominated. "The real virginity", he says, "the real zeal for chastity, ends in no other goal than this, viz. the power thereby of seeing God".[448] But to achieve this, there must be a turning from what he calls a secular way of life, in which the vexations of family life, marriage, death, and sorrow too often dominate, to a deliberate search for God. Gregory himself seems a little wistful that he has not been able to pursue this life himself, presumably because of his marriage to Theosebeia.

He writes, "As it is, this my knowledge of the beauty of virginity is in some sort vain and useless to me, just as the corn is to the muzzled ox that treads the floor, or the water that streams from the precipice to a thirsty man when he cannot reach it. Happy they who have still the power of choosing the better way, and have not debarred themselves from it by the engagements of the secular life, as we have, whom the gulf now divides from glorious virginity: no one can climb up to that who has once planted his foot upon the secular life. We are but spectators of others blessings and witnesses to the happiness of others blessings and witnesses to the happiness of another class".[449]

Gregory bemoans that he cannot fully enter into this lifestyle since he is debarred by marriage, and he appears a little jaundiced at both the burdens and complexities of marriage. He lists the benefits of a well-balanced marriage: "let us sketch a marriage in every way most happy; illustrious birth, competent means, suitable ages, the very flower of the prime of life, deep affection, the very best that each can think of the other, that sweet rivalry of each wishing to surpass the other in loving; in addition, popularity, power, wide reputation, and everything else. But observe that even beneath this array of blessings the fire of an inevitable pain is smouldering".[450]

This pain is death, which must have been extremely prevalent in the fourth century, indeed as in any pre-modern setting, and which severed the bonds of love. For Gregory, the very sweetness of love in marriage is the spark that kindles pain; consequently, better to live a celibate, virgin life, and not invite the pain of death. Then the couple need not fear loss which can come suddenly as in childbirth when "still in love's fever . . . they (the couple) are suddenly torn away from all that they possessed"[451] when unexpected death comes!

Gregory speaks of "the freedom of virginity ... where there is no orphan state, no widowhood to mourn; and it is always in the presence of the undying bridegroom", and even freedom from family quarrels or the chain of sin in which the need to provide for a family, he says, drives ambition, greed, and sometimes hypocrisy.[452] In this way of seeing things, virginity is more like an escape from marriage and its costs and pains, rather than being a positive choice; nor does this attitude commend the state of marriage to his flock, which must have been the calling for most people. It all seems like a case of the ideals of an ascetic overtaking the calling of ordinary people who cannot aspire to the levels of virtue or contemplation which the virgin life may reach.

But having made a stark contrast between the snares of the marriage state and the possibilities of the virgin state, Gregory still leaves you with the sense that the virgin life is not simply an outward physical condition or the absence of marriage but is also regarded as a spiritual life in its own right—a symbol—which all may follow who set their heart on, virtue, piety, and prayer. "Virginity, the real zeal for chastity, ends in no other goal than this, viz. the power thereby of seeing God".[453] So all who aspire to become pure in heart (virginal) will see God in the image of their own cleansed and purified hearts, and in so doing will, metaphorically at least, chose the virgin life. Those who chose this way of life, whether literal or only spiritual, must find the help of a mentor in whose company he may pursue it. "A man cannot be instructed thoroughly unless he puts himself into the hands of one who has himself led it in perfection", and it seems one who has been long at it for "in any matter youth is generally a giddy guide" and "it would not be easy to find anything of importance succeeding, in which grey hairs have not been called in to share deliberations".[454] Having found such a guide, "look on him who has succeeded, and boldly launch upon the voyage with confidence that it will be prosperous, and sail on under the breeze of the Holy Spirit with Christ your pilot and with the oarage of good cheer".[455]

The virginal life in *On Virginity*, for the most part, is a deliberate choice to forego the distractions and burdens of marriage—not least the pain of death—but it is also a symbol for pursuing single-mindedly the virtuous life: a life of contemplation and prayer. This fits in with Gregory's general understanding of the nature of man. The pursuit of this virginal life, this life of separation for the purposes of virtue and closeness to God, was itself part of a deeper response to what Gregory elsewhere calls "the garment of skin". This corruptible nature given to man as a result of the fall was both a judgement and a medicine to humankind: a judgement since it opened the door to death and decay, but a medicine since so vile was our corrupt nature (vile bodies) that it brought about a choice in man to seek a path back from the abyss. In exercising his free will, the chief mark for Gregory of being made in the image of God, man chooses redemption.

As Jean Danielou writes, "In Gregory there are two aspects to be considered. In his work *On the Dead* he explains the *garment of skin* allows man to turn back freely to God: since man had despised the life of the spirit for carnal pleasure, God did not wish man 'to withdraw from sin unwillingly and be forced by necessity towards the good' for this would have destroyed man's freedom and the image of God within him. Hence He made use of man's tendency by giving him the *garment of skin*. This would cause man to experience a disgust with the things of the world, and thus he would desire to return to his former blessedness".[456] How different this is to Augustine of Hippo's later teaching about the necessity of grace to help man to turn back to God, without which such a choice to leave *the garment of skin* would be impossible. But, for Gregory, this free choice of man motivated by his disgust with his fallen and corrupt nature (the garment of skin), leading to unity with Christ in his incarnation/redemption which in turn is offered and made real through the sacraments, enabled our return to God and the restoration of all that had been lost in Adam.

Most of all the death of Jesus signalled a complete victory over the Devil who was deceived by, and took the bait of, the Cross only to find himself defeated. For as Gregory writes, "The Godhead hid under the covering of our human nature so as to offer an easy bait to him who sought to exchange us for a more precious prize. And the aim was that just like a greedy fish he would swallow the hook of divinity together with the bait of the flesh. Thus life would come to dwell in death (the cross), light would appear in darkness, and thus light and life would achieve the destruction of all that stood against them".[457]

Gregory's understanding of the devil and evil is never easy and to many appears unorthodox. For him, the devil appears to dwell, simply in the negative choices of humans to be disobedient to God,[458] so that once that negative principle is removed by the resurrection it seems that, for Gregory, everything is reconciled to God, even the devil. For Gregory, the solidarity of Jesus with human flesh by virtue of the incarnation meant that the effect of the resurrection spread to the whole of humanity in total.[459]

But, returning to the growth of the soul and its journey, once the decision has been taken to live a virginal life, either actually in the body or as a symbol of piety, the soul must then journey from this place of consecration by means of stretching through a state of ecstasy or sober inebriation into the darkness of his presence. It is time to explore what Gregory meant by these, his mystical, ideas.

Gregory's Doctrine of Perpetual Progress

Just as the story of Abraham provides a rich vein of allegory for the journey of the soul so does the life of Moses. This work of Gregory's is the nearest we get to a handbook to the mystical journey of the soul into the presence of God. At its heart is the concept of *epectasis*, stretching forward or expansion in the context of tension which is taken from Philippians 3:13. This concept is mentioned at the outset of the *Life of Moses*. So Gregory writes "But in the case of virtue we have learned from the Apostle that its one limit of perfection is the fact that it has no limit. For the divine Apostle, great and lofty in understanding, ever running the course of virtue, never ceased 'straining toward those things that are still to come'".[460] For Gregory, this stretching forward involved the idea of perpetual ascent, transformation, and change—but change which combined both movement and stability.

The tension of which *epectasis* is expressive is that of movement and stability, change and progress, participation and falling short. In the *Life of Moses* this is described as a paradox of motion and stability, so Gregory writes "a man advances farther on the path of perfection precisely insofar as he remains fixed and immovable in good . . . the more steadfast and unshakeable he becomes in good, so much more quickly will he accomplish his course. His very stability becomes as a wing in his flight towards heaven; his heart becomes winged because his stability is good".[461] Likewise, although for the Platonist the idea of change is often redolent of corruption and decay, the idea of change in Paul, and hence in Gregory, is both dynamic and fulfilling. As Paul's critical teaching to the Corinthians says, "And we who with unveiled faces all reflect the Lord's glory, are being transformed into his likeness with ever increasing glory which comes from the Lord, who is the Spirit."[462] Change may lead in the power of the Spirit to glory.

The last paradox expressed by the sense of tension in the word *epectasis* is the sense of participation and falling short. "On the one hand, there is a certain contact with God, a real participation, a divinisation (e.g. the *ep* part of the word denotes "at" or "towards"). The soul is, in a true sense, transformed into the divine; it truly participates in the Spirit, the *pneuma*. But God at the same time remains constantly beyond, and the soul must go out of itself (*ek*: "out of")—or, rather, it must continually go beyond the stage it has reached to make a further discovery."[463] Thus Gregory says of Abraham, another who journeyed away from what was familiar like Moses: "Relying on what he had already found *he stretched himself forth to the things that were before* . . . And as he disposed all these things in his heart, he kept constantly transcending what he had grasped by his own power, for this was far inferior to what he sought."[464] Abraham did stretch himself forth but he had still not arrived.

Of all scripture the piece to which mystic writers most return, and not least Gregory, is the Song of Songs. His commentary on the Song of Songs, along with his *Life of Moses*, carries most of his mystic and spiritual writing. Here the journey of the soul towards perfection and the presence of God passes through other stages, as illustrated by the search of the bride for her bridegroom and the passion each has for the other. This search or journey is further illustrative of the soul's ascent to God. The removal of garments exposing the beauty and nakedness of the bride is part of this unveiling of the soul in the presence of God. "Even after that complete stripping of herself she still finds something further to remove. So it is with our ascent towards God: each stage that we reach always reveals something heavy weighing on the soul. Thus in comparison with her new found purity, that very striping of her tunic now becomes a kind of garment which those who find her must once again remove".[465]

But not only is there unveiling in the presence of God making possible intimacy, self-knowledge, and purity, there is an ever increasing *desire*. Just as John Donne, in his Holy Sonnet 14 ("Batter my heart, three-personed God . . ."), writes "I . . . never shall be free, Nor ever chaste, except you ravish me", so with Gregory desire is illustrated by the Dove: the metaphor illustrating desire or love, purity and passion being present in the eyes. "Thus the beauty of the bride's eyes is praised because of the image of the Dove which appears in her pupils. For we receive within ourselves a likeness of what we look upon. Now the man who no longer looks toward flesh and blood, gazes rather on the life of the Spirit . . . This is the reason why the Bridegroom praises the soul that has been freed of all carnal passions by saying that the image of the Dove is in its eyes: for this means that the impression of the spiritual shines within the clarity of the soul. And when the purified eye of the soul has received the impression of the Dove, it turns to contemplate the Bridegroom's beauty. *For no man can say the Lord Jesus, but by the Holy Ghost*."[466] Doves in the eyes are an illustration of desire for God and the purifying of our earthly desire by the Spirit.

Furthermore, it is a picture of unsatisfied longing. The bride is told by the watchman that he whom she seeks is unattainable (Song of Songs 3:3).

> She calls on him, though he cannot be reached by any verbal symbol, and she is told by the watchman (the angels) that she is in love with the unattainable, and that the object of her longing cannot be apprehended. In this way she is, in a certain sense, wounded and beaten because of the frustration of what she desires, now that she thinks that her yearning for the Other cannot be fulfilled or satisfied. But the veil of her grief is removed when she learns that the true satisfaction of her desire consists in constantly going on with her quest and never ceasing in her ascent, seeing that every fulfilment of her desire continually generates further desire for the Transcendent. Thus the veil of despair is torn away and the bride realizes that she will always discover more and more of the incomprehensible and unhoped-for beauty of her

spouse throughout all eternity. Then she is torn by an even more urgent longing.[467]

This longing and desire is unwearying and unwavering, and as such it too presses on in a passionate expression of *epectasis* so the soul "that looks up towards God, and conceives that good desire for His eternal beauty, constantly experiences an ever new yearning for that which lies ahead, and her desire is never given its full satisfaction. Hence she never ceases to stretch herself forth to those things that are before, ever leaving the stage in which she is to enter more deeply into the interior, into the stage which lies ahead."[468]

But such yearning often takes the soul into darkness as well as "sober inebriation or ecstasy".

Darkness

In the *Life of Moses*, the high point of the journey, literally and spiritually, was the ascent of "the mountain of divine knowledge" which, in the original story, was Sinai. In the spiritual allegory which is Gregory's *Life of Moses*, the mountain is called "The mountain of divine knowledge"; it is there that Moses encounters God and does so in deep darkness. It marks the limits of the soul's search for God where only further revelation can penetrate the mystery symbolised by darkness. "Moses' vision of God began with Light: afterwards God spoke to him in a cloud. But when Moses rose higher and became more perfect, he saw God in darkness."[469]

Gregory, in a way which goes beyond Origen, shows the journey of the soul in mystic prayer as being one *into darkness*, rather than into ever increasing light. This darkness represents the "obscurity of mystical union".[470] Darkness for Gregory symbolises one of three things: the ignorance in which the Jews held the Messiah who were consequently in the dark both about the true identity of Jesus and the glory of God—a rather technical meaning of darkness; a second meaning is used of those doctrinal and spiritual truths which could *not* be known without revelation (hence they are shrouded in a kind of darkness); and thirdly, and most importantly in this context, darkness represents the limits of our knowing and the perception of the divine being. Hence, in his *Commentary on the Psalms*, Gregory speaks of Moses, "whose eyes sharply penetrated the divine darkness, and therein contemplated the invisible".[471] Or again in the *Life of Moses* we read, "the true vision and the true knowledge of what we seek consists precisely in *not* seeing, in an awareness that our goal transcends all knowledge and is everywhere cut off from us by the darkness of incomprehensibility."[472] This then is an *apophatic* theology in which the soul in union with God has advanced to a place where what is now known is how much we *cannot* know of God and of his essence, which defies our human knowledge. God remains incomprehensible, invisible, and inexplicable. In the *Life of Moses* this reaches a culmination when Moses ascends the mountain of Sinai to receive the Law, where he was to "come to know that what is divine is beyond all knowledge and comprehension, for the text says, 'Moses approached the dark cloud where God was'" (Exodus 20:21).[473]

What was illustrated by Gregory in the *Life of Moses* is also demonstrated in the Song of Songs. Using the symbols of a bride and bridegroom in love, Gregory shows the knowing and the unknowing of this mystical union. "All night long on my bed I looked for the one my heart loves: I looked for him but did not find him."[474] Gregory explains that the word "bed" suggests that the soul has become the spouse of the Word, and being united to Him by love, she has "received in his goods".[475] Gregory goes on to say:

> By the night she refers to the contemplation of the invisible, just as Moses, who entered into the darkness to the place where God was: and God, as the prophet says, made the darkness his cover round about him. Now she says that I have been deemed worthy of the nuptial rites I rest as it were upon the bed of all that I have hitherto understood. But I am suddenly introduced into the realm of the invisible, surrounded by diving darkness, searching for him who is hidden in the dark cloud. Then it was that I felt that love for him whom I desired, though the beloved himself resists the grasp of our thoughts ... Then at last she gives up all she has found; for she realizes that what she seeks can be found; for she

realizes that what she seeks can be understood only in that very inability to comprehend his essence, and that every intelligible attribute becomes merely a hindrance to those who seek to find him. . . And I will never let him go, now that I have found him, from the grasp of faith, until he comes within my chamber, for the heart is the chamber to be filled by the divine indwelling—that is, when it is restored to the state that it had in the beginning.[476]

Darkness, therefore, marks a final encounter of the soul's union with God, a darkness of unknowing which is virtually impenetrable but also creates a mystery which burnishes desire. Such thinking, so present with Gregory, became a benchmark for mystical prayer and theology. Why, virtually a straight line can be drawn from such an understanding of the soul's progress and union with God to *The Cloud of Unknowing* to Julian of Norwich's *Revelation of Divine Love* and, supremely, John of the Cross in the seventeenth century. "The image of darkness is merely a way of expressing the fact that the awesomeness of the divine essence is more than human nature can endure".[477]

Ecstasy or Sober Inebriation

The idea of *sober inebriation* originates from scripture recalling the day of Pentecost. The onlookers in Jerusalem that day thought that the disciples who were filled with the Spirit were drunk, so great was their joy and abandon.[478] The usual explanation for such behaviour was too much wine, but theirs was a sober inebriation.

Later in Alexandria, the Jewish mystic writer Philo uses this actual expression for the first time.[479] A paradox like *luminous darkness*, it serves to express the sense of ecstasy possible through union with God by his Spirit in which passivity is combined with an altered state of being through the presence of God. The experience is of God himself in which a person enters the reality of the Godhead by going out of herself, but then returning to their own fragile human nature. In such a way St John the

Divine received his Revelation on the Lord's day on Patmos, for he was in the Spirit. Or likewise when Paul was taken out of himself in order to experience things of which he could barely write.[480]

The soul is on such occasions over-powered. It is then marked by a degree of detachment (*apathia*) form the normal world around and a heightened degree of confidence (*parrhesia*) and trust in God. This is made possible only by faith (our response) to the initiative of grace (God's gift).

Abraham was one of the first examples of such "sober inebriation" according to Gregory. He writes of Abraham, "after this ecstasy which came upon him as a result of these lofty visions, Abraham returned once more to human frailty".[481] As Hausherr writes, "ecstasy is a going out of oneself, not by an unconsciousness involving the suspension of sense activity, but by a kind of projection of the soul beyond the laws of reason under the impulse of love".[482]

The experience is supremely of the love of God. It is given through the impulse of love, in which knowledge is replaced by love, "and it is this that distinguishes his (Gregory's) doctrine from the more intellectualistic approach of those great contemplative writers, Origen and Eavagrius. In Gregory knowledge becomes love".[483] Not surprisingly, the word used to describe such love is Eros. Gregory uses it because "it is more suggestive of the passivity of the soul as it is overpowered by the revelation of the infinite beauty of God".[484]

In turn this ecstasy leads to a kind of spiritual inebriation.[485] The effect of this was sleep, a symbol for Gregory of contemplation as well as a kind of spiritual vertigo in which the soul is also overwhelmed by the majesty of God: "Thus the soul, enjoying alone the contemplation of Being, will not awake for anything that arouses sensual pleasure. After lulling to sleep every body motion, it receives the vision of God in a divine wakefulness with pure and naked intuition. May we make ourselves worthy of this vision, achieving by this sleep the awakening of the soul!"[486] And likewise Gregory says his soul is seized "with dizziness" as it meditates on the word of God, in this case the beatitude—"Blessed are the pure in heart for they shall see God".[487]

The experience of the soul on this journey of ascent, and especially at its apex, is thus described by Gregory as both one of seeing the darkness, the unfathomable nature of his divine being, as well as one of ecstasy or "sober inebriation". Above all it is a journey in which the soul ascends to God, knowing him and yet being lost in him, extended but never finally finding, in constant stretching but always with the promise of his presence.

Gregory: Christian Platonist or Platonist Christian?

One of the age old questions in studying Gregory of Nyssa is how does he use Platonism. Is he a syncretist, blending Christianity and Platonism in a kind of amalgam which was acceptable in his day? Or did he use Platonism and some of its concepts in a discriminating way to describe the journey of a Christian soul in both re-discovering the buried image of God in each individual and charting its progress to an ecstasy of love in knowledge?

At the outset it is worth saying that there is a clear dissonance with Plato, and also close association with, and use of, his most celebrated vocabulary or metaphors about human destiny and fulfilment. The dissonance revolves around the reality of the Trinity, the divinity of Christ, and the absolute distinction between the Creator and the created order. The doctrine of the Trinity which Gregory so ably defended in his *On Not Three Gods* describes the unity of the three in the Trinity, just as there is unity of substance between three people although they also exist individually (the three men analogy). But, despite the three *hypostases* in the Trinity, there is complete unity so that "in the case of the Father we find no activity in which the Son does not work. Similarly, the Son has no special activity without the Spirit. The divine persons, thus do not simply act together, they function inseparably to constitute any and every divine activity towards creation."[488] In a word, they transcend creation, they are "other" to it, acting together in it, unknown in being *(ousia)* but knowable in action.[489]

By clearly teaching this, Gregory turns his back fully on any Platonic view of God in which there is hierarchy of being through which God operates in the world. As Balthasar argues, "what distinguishes Gregory at once from Philo and Plotinus (and Origen and Plato I might add) is the radical opposition between the triune God and the creature, an opposition that is not mitigated by any kind of intermediary zone. The fundamental dogma of Platonism is completely absent from his philosophy".[490] For Gregory there is no separation of *Idea* or *nous* between God and his creation, so to seek true knowledge is to seek God—and seek him fully and alone who is transcendent but immanent ,and thus knowable too. He is both the source of our being and the fulfilment of our desire. Gregory, in describing the Triune God in his more polemical volumes, sets out the ground work of our understanding of God as utterly transcendent but who in Christ has made himself known and, to a point, knowable. In this way Gregory is no Platonist but with the fundamental proviso that Gregory is still adept at using Platonic vocabulary to describe the growth or aspiration of the soul.

The main categories in which Gregory thinks and describes our Christian journey to restoration and transformation are familiarly Platonic. Again the point is whether in using these words he uses Platonic concepts as a Trojan horse for Christian truth or whether he tailors Christian truth to make a Platonic suit. This appears to be a much closer run thing. The vocabulary which Gregory uses, and which is familiar to any reader of Plato, is soul, image, progress, virtue, desire (*eros*), love (platonic), contemplation, becoming, and rest. The two works in which they are most clearly used in the context of change and progress in the spiritual life are the *Life of Moses* and his homilies on the Song of Songs.

Both works were written towards the end of Gregory's life, probably between 385 and 392.[491] As such they are a mature reflection on Gregory's mystical thinking after a lifetime's contemplation. Based as they are on two biblical accounts well used in ancient Christian times to chart the allegorical ascent of the soul, especially by Origen in relation to the Song of Songs, they have a biblical starting point but they use the well-known categories of Platonic thought as a means of interpretation or hermeneutic. Just as in Plato's Symposium, the human soul is driven by unsatisfied desire to behold ultimate beauty, so both in the *Life of Moses* and in his homilies on the Song of Songs, Gregory shows the unsatisfied longings of the soul to see God or the Bridegroom as a spiritual quest that brings greater perfection to the soul.

The Soul for Gregory is central to this quest. For Gregory, "Man is twofold, comprised of both body and soul. His life is also twofold".[492] The soul both relies on the senses in its ascent but at the same time must be freed from any heaviness or weight that they may instil, becoming free from passion. The senses "carry the soul on their back in a way and raise her toward the height".[493] For Gregory, senses and their attendant passions must be trained and qualified that they may help the ascent of the soul. Thus sex for Gregory was both negatively a punishment for abuse of our original freedom from which we fell and a necessity because of death and the consequent need to sustain the human race; but it also provides those senses that could be disciplined and trained with the function of fuelling our desire for both seeking and knowing God. Just as kingship in Israel was both a burden and a blessing so likewise death is both a supreme punishment for our sin but also a blessing—since it can detach us from our earthly life and prepares us for heaven, so these passions can both hold us back in our aspiration of becoming and drive us on in our ascent.[494] They must be trained for ascent. Not surprisingly in Gregory's Homilies on the Song of Songs and the bride-mysticism in it, it is the dart of love from Christ, the "archer of love", that provokes the soul's ascent to God.[495]

In the *Life of Moses* there appears to be a quest for virtue. "It marks the end as well as the high point of Gregory's re-working of the Platonic tradition."[496] Its subtitle is "On the perfection of virtue". Whereas in neo-Platonic thought, especially as developed by Plotinus, the goal of unity is the purpose of our ascent, there are parts of Plato's *Theaetetus* where there is a more moral imperative. In the *Life of Moses* the word virtue occurs over a hundred times and so expresses the aim of achieving likeness to God through a virtuous life, but the virtue is not gained by pulling up our moral socks but through a number of encounters or theophanies which transform Moses and the pilgrim following in his steps. It is through the blend of the ascetic, the moral and the contemplation of God that the perfection and transformation of the soul takes place.

The *Life of Moses* is an allegory of the spiritual life and a growth in virtue, and as such follows the tradition of Philo and Origen: both had written significant works on the *Life of Moses* and the Song of Songs. In one sense it was a well-worn path, but Gregory gave it fresh meaning. For Gregory, the pursuit of virtue was the dominant thought. "Certainly whoever pursues true virtue participates in nothing other than God, because he is himself true virtue".[497] Virtue, as it is explored by Gregory, is a paradox of standing still and forever stretching and moving forward, "it is a mixture of standing on a rock which is Christ and forever moving forward, a mixture of *dromos* (running) and *stasis* (standing still)."[498] For Gregory, virtue is linked to the idea of infinity, of never possessing or grasping the very goal of the search, of going forward but returning to the beginning, "or going forward to a perpetually recessive goal"[499]

It is a journey which takes Moses through three theophanies, to the Burning Bush, to the Mountain where he received the Law, and then further into the mountain to glimpse the back of God. Together they intermingle revelation about Christ, the identity of God, the morality of his existence, and the incomprehensibility of his presence. At the Burning Bush Moses confronts reality which is the very expression of truth. Here the Platonic reality of truth and reality is evident. As Plato asserts in *Timaeus*, "we must begin by distinguishing that which always is and never becomes from that which is always becoming and never is".[500] Indeed our existence of always becoming is predicated on God's existence which ever is. So, as Gregory says about this theophany, "In my view the definition of truth is this: not to have a mistaken apprehension of Being".[501]

The second theophany on the Mountain is an exegesis of Exodus 20:21: "The people remained at a distance, while Moses approached the thick darkness where God was".[502] This represents a progress towards greater truth. The man who has journeyed from Egypt, has been delivered from the plagues, escaped the armies of Pharaoh, "he it is who advances to the contemplation of the transcendent nature"[503] but at the same time moves into greater darkness or into God's unfathomable nature in which his essence cannot be grasped, even if his deeds or actions can be seen. Only the one who has purified himself and relies not on the irrational senses but on the intellect can approach the divine. Here he may reach the "tabernacle not made with hands" which is the incarnate Christ: "for the power which encompasses the universe in which the fullness of divinity, the common protector of all, who encompasses everything within himself, is rightly called 'tabernacle'".[504] Once again the journey reflects Plato, who says in *Timaeus*, "To discover the maker and father of the universe is indeed a hard task, and having found him it would be impossible to tell everyone about him".[505]

But a third theophany awaits (Exodus 33:17–23) in which God passes by Moses, revealing his glory but covering Moses with his hand until he has passed by so that he may only be seen from behind. Here the principle revelation is the infinity of God as a consequence of which God cannot be known or fully comprehended. He may be experienced as life-giving but he may not be grasped by knowledge or reason. This was novel in Hellenic thought for which everything was susceptible to reason, but here Gregory, siding with Plotinus, demonstrates the unfathomable nature of God. Indeed, for Gregory, such a quality in God only fans our desire, "for the true sight of God consists in this, that the one who looks up to God never ceases in that desire. For he says: 'You cannot see my face, for you cannot see me and live'".[506]

But the other great work of Gregory's which both emulates Plato but also transcends his thought are Gregory's homilies on the Song of Songs. If the driving force of the *Life of Moses* was the search for virtue then, not unexpectedly, the fulfilment of the ascent of the soul is the search for love and union driven by desire. The fifteen homilies on the Song of Songs were dedicated to Olympias and they "mark the high point of the literary and theological achievement of Gregory".[507] Just as there is the upward movement of the soul towards the ultimate beauty as in the Symposium, so in the Song of Songs there is unceasing desire by the bride for her beloved, the Christian for his Lord, the Church for her bridegroom. As Balthasar so succinctly puts it, "In order to understand love, it was necessary for our desire to become love. But our desire could become love only through the initiative of divine love. Indeed, knowledge through desire could only grasp God in his very incomprehensibility. This knowledge turned on this paradoxical limit: to understand is not to understand God (to know that the object is ungraspable): not to understand is to understand God (in the self negation of the intellect, to grasp the object)."[508] Equally, desire is never satiated it simply longs for more of the beloved by which to know him and know ourselves.

The Song of Songs traces the ascent of the bride in her love for the bridegroom in a progress of ever deepening love driven by desire. "Desire focused on God is 'the deepest and most true expression of humanity'".[509] "And desire properly trained and educated enables the bride to search for her Beloved through the transcendent realm into the realm of unknowing".[510] The Song of Songs is used as a biblical allegory for the ascent of the soul in love for God. Gregory defends the practice of allegory in the prologue to his commentary on the Song of Songs. The love about which he is writing is spiritual both in its source and in its object, generally using the word *agape*; though Gregory makes little distinction between *agape* and *eros*.[511] So Gregory tells us that "the bride refers to the soul; God is called the Spouse, Whom she loves with all her heart and soul and strength. And consequently, having come as, to the height of her hopes, and thinking that she is already united with her beloved, she speaks of her more perfect participation in good as *a bed*, referring to the *night*, the time of darkness. By the *night* she refers to the contemplation of the invisible, just as Moses, who entered into the darkness to the place where God was: and God as the prophet says made *the darkness his covert round about him*."[512] In the course of this journey of love or desire in which this love is never fully satisfied, Gregory uses two important metaphors, one unfamiliar, one familiar, to explain the progress of the soul. The first daring metaphor is the *wound of love* and the second is he more familiar metaphor of *darkness*.

The wound of love occurs in Homilies Four, Twelve, and Thirteen. The archer is Love (God), the arrow itself is Christ, the tip of the arrow (faith) is triple pointed, dipped and moistened by the Spirit and made powerful by the Word. The wounds created by the arrow are beautiful, desirable, and inflame yet more vehement desire. The Bride cries out, "I am wounded by love" and is immediately immersed in an apophatic context indicated by oxymoron expressions and images of union.[513] Gregory tells us the bride cries out, "O beautiful wound and sweet blow by which life penetrates within! The arrows penetration opens up, as it were a door and entrance for love. As soon as the bride receives the arrow of love, the imagery shifts from archery to nuptial delight."[514]

The other metaphor is more familiar from the *Life of Moses* and this is *darkness*. Just as Moses entered the darkness on the mountain side and his eyes were covered as the glory of God passed him by in the cleft of the rock, so the bride, in finding union with the Beloved and being brought to his chamber (Song of Songs 1:4), also finds an ungraspable infinity of love construed as darkness, because it is beyond comprehension. Through the purification of the Spirit, "she searches the depths of God within the inner Sanctuary of paradise and, and as the great Paul said, sees things unseen and words unspoken".[515] "Gregory sees the Song of Songs using powerfully erotic images to bring one to the imageless space of the Holy of Holies, where union with God beyond all image and concept take place".[516]

Both the *Life of Moses* and the Song of Songs use the Platonic motif of the ascent of the soul towards Beauty and perfection, but in Gregory's use, it is only a motif, familiar certainly from Platonic thought but now dis-associated from the philosophy from which it sprang. It is now tethered firmly to the Trinity and the Incarnation. For not only is the One to whom we ascend the Holy Trinity who is separate and distinct from all creation, but the basis for this opportunity of knowledge through desire or pursuit of virtue is the Incarnation. It is the Incarnation, with its sequel in the resurrection, which provides the basis for our hope and transformation, and the restoration of Man to his first nature and being in paradise. The Cross is mostly portrayed by Gregory as the defeat of the devil by whose devilish schemes man has become ensnared.[517] But, for Gregory, the heart of his theology is the Johannine idea of Incarnation: "we are thus aware of a twofold nature, the first by which we were formed, and a second, by which we were re-formed ... Of old God fashioned man ... now he clothes himself with him; of old he created, at present he is created. Of old the Word made flesh, now he is made flesh".[518] Gregory goes on to speak of "a new man who has been brought on the scene by the favour of God".[519] If, therefore, humanity, through sin, has lost the true image of God, and if sin has entered into the new humanity as a condition of nature, only the presence of a "true" and pure man effects in humanity as a whole a "change in our very nature".[520] This is pure Pauline theology, reflecting the significance of the Incarnation in the remaking of man (Romans 8:3–4).

Gregory may be a Platonist Christian in his description of change and the ascent of the soul, in the categories, he uses and the allusions he recalls from Plato and his followers, but he is certainly not a Christian Platonist. He loved paradox, the mystery of the Godhead, the unfathomableness of the Trinity, but he was a focus for orthodoxy, for the most part, both in his teaching and as a senior bishop in the Church.

CHAPTER 9

The Work of a Bishop

The office of Bishop (*episkopos* or overseer) seems to have been established by the end of the first century. In Antioch, where the believers were first called Christians, Ignatius (c.35–107) was the second (or maybe the third) Bishop of Antioch following the Apostle Peter. To be bishop simply meant that he had the oversight (the literal meaning of the Greek word *episkopos*) of the flock of God in that place. Since then the office of Bishop has become familiar in the Church. Each of the Cappadocians was to become one.

In the following two hundred and fifty years from the end of the first century until the arrival of the Cappadocians in the life of the Church in Asia, the office and work of a bishop was to develop dramatically—especially with the conversion of Constantine. From the earliest days the life of the Church was organised around towns from which the surrounding rural areas were evangelised.[521] Bishops were appointed in each town of any size and, except in the larger ones such as Antioch, Rome, Alexandria, and Constantinople, bishops could be known by most of the population.[522] A bishop was chosen by the church itself; the people gave their consent, but increasingly the bishops from surrounding towns were involved both in their selection and then the consecration of a new bishop. So Hippolytus wrote, "Let the bishop be ordained who is elected by *all the people* . . . With the agreement of all let the bishops lay hands on him and the presbyters stand in silence."[523] The resulting appointment was a consensus of the local and the catholic, the communal and the regional. "No small part of the aura attaching to the local bishop depended upon this catholicity of recognition".[524] It was then the custom for the country bishops (*chorepiskopos*) to be appointed by the city bishops. City bishops were suspicious that without their involvement nepotism and faction could too easily corrupt the appointment of bishops in more closed communities of the countryside.[525]

That each city should have one bishop was always the ideal. This gave unity to the Church, cohesion to its local structure, and the possibility of teaching clearly and refuting heresy. "The conflict with heresy made it a practical necessity to make one presiding figure the personal focus of ecclesial unity in the local congregation".[526] But the autonomy of the individual city bishop diminished with the passing of time and especially following the conversion of Constantine. Once the Church became the official religion of the Roman Empire, a number of new aspects to the office and role of a bishop quickly followed. Whereas in former days persecuting the Church often meant beginning with the bishop ("strike the shepherd and the flock will be scattered"; see Mark 14:27 quoting Zechariah 13:7), from Constantine onwards the bishop became an instrument of the state as much as an overseer of the church. Suddenly their function, if not changed, was greatly extended.

In a number of respects the role of the bishop changed. They were placed into an ecclesiastical hierarchy aping the Roman Imperial system. Just as the Empire was divided into dioceses and provinces by the emporer Diocletian, so now city bishoprics fell into metropolitan areas shadowing Roman Provinces, with Metropolitans or Archbishops residing in the provincial capitals. The size of the Church greatly increased. By the sixth century Justinian was ordering the manpower of *Hagia Sophia* alone in Constantinople to be reduced to a total of 485, with a total of sixty priests and 100 deacons.[527] In Carthage there were over 500 clergy in one city.[528]

The Church increased in size and wealth because of the special privileges that it was given, although in the years between 325 and 380 these privileges depended somewhat on agreement with the doctrines held by the Emperor. But some almost irreversible changes had been made. The bishop became a legal officer, capable of resolving domestic, land, and family disputes. This became an onerous burden which Augustine of Hippo came to dislike as it distracted him from other, more rewarding, spiritual work. "In his (Augustine's) experience those who brought cases before the bishop were not good faithful members of his congregation, but persons with a consistent record of being tiresome and contentious".[529] Augustine only discovered what many have experienced since. The bishop's tariff of punishment was restricted: he could fine and possibly inflict corporal punishment, and in some cases imprison, but he could do no more.

The bishop was expected, in the Roman Empire, to be not only a spiritual leader but also a public one who would deal, on behalf of the flock of God, with the Roman administration. Episcopal appointments themselves and the scope of a bishop's work reflected this. In 335, during Constantine's reign, an appointment of a new Bishop of Constantinople needed to be made. The present bishop was nearing his end and asked his clergy what kind of a man should succeed him. If a teacher was required they should elect Paul, but if they wanted someone good at public affairs and negotiating with the authorities then the right man was Macedonius. Paul was so eager to be elected that he got himself consecrated by some of the bishops without the consent of the Metropolitan of Heracla, or the approval of Constantine, so that it was easy for his opponents to have him expelled synodically.[530] The deposition of Gregory of Nazianzus as Archbishop of Constantinople in 381 was followed by the appointment of an ex-Senator, Nectarius, as the new Archbishop, a swift change from a teacher of the faith and theologian to a man well used to public affairs. Likewise in Milan, Ambrose—also a Roman official, governor, and aristocrat—was literally marched by the crowd to the bishop's throne and installed. Bishops had to tread a fine line between being able to deal with the Roman authorities and the court without being corrupted. While some wore purple as a symbol of the ruling class, others generally wore black, no doubt as a sign of identifying with the poor.[531] Gregory of Nazianzus, whilst living very simply himself ("My conversation is with beasts in rocky places, where in solitude, apart from all others, I inhabit a miserable and stony little dwelling. I own one coat, no shoes, have no hearth. I live only on hope"),[532] was able nonetheless to square with Roman tax officials like Julian and win important concessions for the townspeople and church in Nazianzus.[533]

Whereas in some parts of the Roman world monks and bishops were distinctly suspicious of one another, in Cappadocia, and largely as a result of the contribution of the Cappadocian Fathers themselves, there was much less tension between them. Famously John Cassian, himself an acute observer and interpreter of monasticism, wrote in his conferences, "A monk should by all means flee women and bishops".[534] Both were means of temptation, the latter temptation to power, prominence, and pride. Indeed some monks like Jerome were caustic in their condemnation of bishops and their traits of self-importance. In his commentary on St Matthew, Jerome comments adversely (and with some tongue in cheek) on the practice of saluting bishops with the acclamation, "Blessed is he that comes in the name of the Lord, Hosanna the highest".[535] It was not that this practise was widespread but it was more a piece of ironic criticism about how Jerome saw things. However, it does show that in some places there was more than a hint of underlying hostility between monks and bishops. Monks found the power, prestige, and the very presence of the bishops irksome, while the bishops found the independence, ecclesial unruliness, and sometimes anarchic quality of the monk hard to take. But in Cappadocia such tensions were bridged by monk-bishops and none more so than by Basil, Gregory, and Gregory.

Basil of Caesarea

We have already seen the development of Basil's monastic life. Its origins at Annisa, its links with Eusthathius, its rigours questioned by Gregory of Nazianzus, and its later development in Caesaera into a full blown institution of care (the *Basiliad*) for the hungry, diseased, and dying which was staffed by brothers under a developing monastic rule. Basil was never to depart from this kind of model of the monk-bishop and nor were the two Gregorys, although their scope for action was more restricted by their much more uneven tenures of episcopal oversight. Gregory of Nazianzus never lived in Sasima (his diocese), which he detested, only briefly acting as bishop in Nazianzus in the final years of his father's life and was quickly forced to resign as Archbishop of Constantinople. Gregory of Nyssa was forced into exile in 376 by the Emperor Valens for his Nicene teaching and although he returned to office in 378 on the death of Valens. He then attended the Councils of Antioch and Constantinople before being appointed as Bishop of Sebaste, from where he undertook extensive peripatetic teaching on behalf of the Emperor Theodosius, as an advocate of the Creed of Constantinople. It was Basil's tenure of office in Caesarea from 370–379 which provided a solid opportunity to develop a style of episcopacy which was to have lasting impact. "Basil saw no opposition between asceticism and church office . . . In fact given the turmoil of the church in his day, Basil saw all the more need to hold monastic life and ecclesiastical authority in tandem . . . For him, leadership of the church as a whole encompassed oversight and care of the monastic communities."[536]

The general features of Basil's episcopal ministry were defending orthodoxy (although he was criticised by some for dallying with an homoiousios position in the hope of building a central consensus and for insufficient robustness in declaring the divinity of the Spirit by Gregory of Nazianzus), giving support to the *Basiliad*, dealing with issues relating to Imperial government, seeking support from the West for Nicene appointments, encouraging good character in leadership, mentoring particular bishops who were amenable to his instruction like Amphilochius of Iconium, and resolving conflict where possible for the good of the Church, as in the almost unending episcopal wars in Antioch. The best source for his vision and labouring for the well ordering of the Church are his letters.[537] As a collection of classical letters they are only bettered in quantity and importance by those of Cicero in classical literature. To have found time to write or dictate this correspondence, travel, write longer theological works like *On the Holy Spirit*, and generally order the Church at a time of schism was a prodigious feat of dogged perseverance and effort, often in the face of great personal weakness and ill health. The letters are a testimony to an extremely diligent bishop who, on more than a few occasions, spoke in them movingly of his ill health. The letters and the *Moralia* together describe the kind of leadership Basil offered and can be divided across at least six main themes.

The Business of Orthodoxy

Not surprisingly, the greatest bulk of his writing, mostly because it tended to generate the longest letters, was about orthodoxy and the struggle for it. Some of the letters stem from his time in Caesarea before he was a bishop but when he was already fully immersed in this struggle. In a letter written in 360 (not 380 as ascribed by Deferrari, as Basil had died by then!), when Basil withdrew from Caesarea to stay with Gregory of Nazianzus and when Dianius, the bishop who baptised him, subscribed to the Arian Creed of Ariminium, Basil robustly condemned the Arian position, writing, "For he who introduces 'unbegotten' and 'begotten' into our faith, and declares that he who always was, at one time was not, and that He who naturally and always was Father became Father, and that the Holy Spirit is not eternal, is he not an out-and-out Philistine? He goes on to say that those who teach such things have 'forsaken me, the fountain of living water, and have digged to themselves cisterns, that can hold no water?' (Jeremiah 2:13). They ought to confess that the Father is God, that the Son is God, and that the Holy Ghost is God, as the divine words and those who have had the highest conception of them have taught us".[538]

If later on Basil seemed shy to Gregory of Nazianzus in proclaiming the full divinity of the Spirit, there is no such shyness here; later in this same letter he writes: "The Son is not a creature. And if He is not a creature, He is consubstantial with the Father . . . The Holy Spirit is not a creature, he is consubstantial with God".[539]

In a slightly later letter to Maximus the Philosopher, written before Basil became a bishop, he explains his willingness to use the word *homoiousios* (like in substance). In criticising Dionysius, a former Bishop of Alexandria (from 247) and pupil of Origen, for being a forerunner doctrinally of Arius, Basil says that he Basil accepts the phrase, "like in substance" provided the qualification invariably is added to it, on the grounds that it comes to the same thing as "identity of substance", according, be it understood, to the sound conception of the term. In other words, Basil was prepared to accept at this stage the use of the word *"homoiousios"* provided it was qualified with another term "invariably" as this caught the sense of the Nicene Creed.[540]

But the difficulty of building a consensus around the Nicene Creed was made problematic on two counts: those who were suspicious of *homoousios* because of its perceived materialism,[541] and, from the other extreme, the Sabellianists who stressed the monarchy of God and an unwillingness to accredit the distinct *hypostasis* of the Son and the Spirit. Basil sought to maintain their unity of substance but also their distinctiveness of existence. Hence, in Letter 189 on the Trinity, also attributed to Gregory of Nyssa, written in 374/5 ensuring the individuated existence of each member of the Trinity, Basil or Gregory wrote, "If we see that the activities manifested by the Father and the Son and the Holy Spirit are different, from the diversity of their activities, we shall conjecture that the acting natures also are different".[542] Here the goal was to ensure the distinctiveness of the members of the Trinity, whereas earlier Basil was arguing for the common substance of the members of the Trinity.

The constant need to fight the extreme positions of both Arianism and Sabellianism—in its modalist form—was a continual and wearing challenge for Basil and the Cappaodcians in contending for orthodoxy. The additional difficulty of dealing with Eustathius of Sebaste, one time friend and monastic companion, but whose lack of adherence to the divinity of the Spirit had to be smoked out, made public, and then disassociated from, was a further deeply wounding skirmish on behalf of orthodoxy which Basil suffered.[543] The letters certainly bear witness to the long and tiring struggle for orthodoxy, but they also show a developing epistolary network of support for Nicene orthodoxy, as well as a growing place of significance for Basil within that network.

The defence of orthodoxy, which Basil saw as one of his chief callings as a Church leader and bishop, was re-enforced and fortified by the creation of networks of episcopal support. Basil was not slow in writing to the leading contenders of Nicene orthodoxy, showing his concerns and asking for the support of Church leaders in the West and in Egypt. With the imperial support for the *Homoians* and its consequent ascendancy in Constantinople, as well as appointments to the episcopacy by the Emperor Valens of Arian sympathisers *and* the exiling of many who were loyal to Nicaea—such as Gregory of Nyssa—Basil was in need of such a network.

Epistolary Networking

Basil was effective in creating a circle of support, or at the very least awareness, amongst many of the Church leaders committed to Nicaea. If some of the correspondence with principal Church leaders, such as with Athanasius and Ambrose, was thin and more formal, with others who were closer at hand, like Eusebius of Samosata and Amphilochius of Iconium, a much closer relationship was forged. It seems that Basil's objective was both to gather support for orthodoxy amongst more local bishops in Asia whilst making sure influential voices in Egypt and in the West (see Letter 263) were kept fully briefed as to the difficulties he faced in promoting orthodoxy. No one could have envisaged then that Valens would perish in battle at Adrianople against the Goths and that a young Emperor, Theodosius, who was committed to Nicaea, would succeed him and would intervene actively in the affairs of the Church to ensure the victory of Nicaea, as he did in Constantinople in 380/381. In letters written to Athanasius c.371, when Athanasius was in his final years of his episcopate and unusually secure in his office, Basil sought Athanasius' support in two ways: to encourage the bishops in the West to support Basil and his cause in Asia as well as intervening in the Church in Antioch to bring to an end to its divisions. Basil wrote, "verily the ills of that city (Antioch) stand in need of your wisdom and evangelical sympathy; for it has not only been completely divided by heretics, but it is also being torn asunder by those who affirm that they hold identical opinions with one another".[544] But Athanasius was to die two years later on 2 May 373), and divisions in Antioch would rumble on for nearly another ten years with both Gregory of Nazianzus and Peter of Alexandria becoming embroiled in them. If by now Athanasius' star was setting in Alexandria and he was not able to do much to help Basil, Ambrose, on the other hand, was the rising episcopal star in the West. Appointed by popular demand to the See of Milan in 374 (literally dragged by the crowds to the episcopal throne), he was to herald the new age of Augustinian orthodoxy in the West. Basil wrote to him in answer to a not unusual request that the relics of St Dionysius, a previous Bishop of Milan, be returned to the city. Basil expressed the hope that these remains interred in Cappadocia might be "received with joy as great as the grief with which their guardians have sent them on",[545] and, since they are relics of a man who "shared in the contest along with other blessed departed souls", Basil hoped that their eventual presence in Milan would nerve their fight against Arianism.

Closer to Caesarea, Basil sought the friendship of other bishops who, like him, struggled for the Nicene cause. Among them was a bishop who, like Basil, had suffered long for the Nicene cause, Eusebius of Samosata, and a younger bishop for whom Basil acted as a mentor, Amphilochius of Iconium. Eusebius is almost entirely known through Basil's and Gregory of Nazianzus' correspondence with him. A bishop of Samosata from 361, he made common cause with Basil of Ancyra and later Basil of Caesarea against Arianism. In one letter written by Basil in 373 shortly before Eusebius' own exile, Basil strengthens Eusebius' nerve against Eustathius of Sebaste urging that that there cannot be fellowship with those "who do not accept the Nicene creed" and those "who dare to call the Holy Spirit a creature".[546] So fierce was the opposition against him that Eusebius, who was exiled by Valens in 374 to Thrace, travelled across his diocese in disguise. But on his recall in 378 to Samosata he was killed by an Arian woman who hurled a brick at his head.

Basil's letters to Amphilochius were much lengthier and had much of the older bishop instructing and confiding in a younger man whose life and ministry he sought to shape as a future leader of the Nicene cause. Much of the teaching we have about Church discipline was first given to Amphilochius and to some of it we shall return. It was also to Amphilochius that Basil dedicated his work *On the Holy Spirit*.

The Pastoral Care of a Bishop

Much more common to a bishop's oversight was the administration of pastoral care and Church discipline. Basil spent a good deal of his time in ordering the Church and many of his letters were concerned with these matters. He wrote about the right tariff of penances for misdemeanours. In the Eastern Church, public penitents were divided into four groups: the Weepers or Mourners, the Hearers, the Prostrates, and the Standers.

"The Weepers were not permitted to enter the church at all. They took their station in the courtyard outside the church building, and besought the faithful as they entered the church to pray for them. The Hearers were permitted to enter and to remain at mass until after the instruction but were dismissed together with the catechumens before the Eucharist. The Prostrates were permitted to remain prostrated during the prayers at which the faithful stood. The Standers were permitted with the faithful during the entire mass, but were prohibited from receiving Holy Communion".[547]

In a long letter to his mentoree Amphilochius, Basil lays down a tariff of penance for voluntary or involuntary murder. For voluntary murder the tariff is twenty years penance, for involuntary (unintended killing or manslaughter) ten years. A person who hurls an axe or uses a sword in a fight and kills will serve twenty years penance, while one who uses a stone or heavy club will be liable to involuntary murder and serve ten years, for "in his anger he dealt such a blow as to kill his victim, although his purpose, was perhaps, to thrash him soundly but not to kill him outright."[548] A person who in self-defence "directs his blow unsparingly to the vital parts so as to injure him" but who subsequently dies will be subject to the penitential tariff of an involuntary death.[549] A woman who aborts a child *and* the person who supplies poison to her will both be subject to a penance in keeping with voluntary death. Laws of adultery and fornication were equally severe: if a woman left her husband because of being beaten and lived with another she would still be guilty of adultery.[550]

Sexual misdemeanours were also closely scrutinised: a reader who has intercourse with his betrothed shall only be re-admitted after a year's inactivity as a reader, while a person who has illicit intercourse where there is no betrothal should cease from ministry.[551] It is possible that these penalties were handed down by Church courts which, in Asia, came to replace civil ones, so replacing civil punishment with penance with its strong element of public disgrace being the retributive part. If so—and it may be that this was the case only in Asia—the replacement of civil punishment by ecclesiastical punishment, in some cases, was much more marked at this point in the East than in the West.

Alongside the letters on Church discipline, and all the myriad circumstances of life and church life that they sought to cover, was further correspondence and teaching on pastoral care. Such care was found not only in Basil's letters but also in works like *Moralia*, about Christian character, and the homilies, such as the one on *Anger* which is as relevant today as it was then. Basil's pastoral letters cover a wide range of activities, some expressing consolation on bereavement, others to monks or virgins who had "fallen", another about eunuchs, others about the right use of relics, and many about the need for perseverance and endurance in the pursuit of mission or Church work.

Basil's letters following bereavement were both touching and bracing; you often get the impression that, having had to forego much of the comfort and intimacy of human friendship, he was in a position to nerve others who were facing such loss for the first time. Writing to Nectarius and his wife on the loss of their son, and like so many pastors before and since, he wrestles with the issues of loss and God's providence: "I exhort you, as a noble contestant, to stand firm against the blow. However great, and not to fall under the weight of your grief, nor yet lose your courage, having assurance that even if reasons for God's ordinance elude us, yet surely that which is ordained by him who is wise and who loves us must be accepted, even if it be painful... For there exists a reason, incomprehensible to man, why some are sooner taken hence, while others are left behind to *persevere* for a longer time in this life of sorrows." He goes on, "We have not been bereft of the boy, but we have given him back to the lender; nor has his life been destroyed, but merely transformed for the better; earth has not covered our beloved one, but heaven has received him ... Nor will the period of separation be great, since in this life, as on a journey, we are all hastening to the same caravansary ... The same hospice awaits us all."[552] No evasion of the issues here, not just tea and sympathy but a grasping of the realities of life and faith in the mystery of human incomprehension of God's will.

Other letters of consolation strike similar notes, such as that to Maximus on the loss of his wife. Basil begins by praising their marriage: "As for us we had experienced even from our first intercourse together a certain feeling of kinship towards your Reverence, and we were won over by your virtue that every hour we had you on our tongue; and when we came into intimacy with that blessed soul also, truly we were convinced that the saying of the Proverb (19:14; A prudent wife is from the Lord) was confirmed in you: that woman is joined unto man by God—so congenial were you to one another, each revealing in himself, as in a mirror, the character of the other. Even if one should speak at length about her one could not attain a fractional part of her worth."[553] Basil goes on to say that to be so blessed in marriage is the lot of only a few and "for a husband to grieve over his separation from his wife is itself no small gift among the gifts of God, to those who look at the matter reasonably: for many have we known who accepted the dissolution of an incompatible marriage as a relief from a burden!"[554] Basil is nothing if not straight-talking and free of encouraging any self-pity.

To those whose loss was not through bereavement but through their own failure or misdemeanour, Basil could be severe but not, I suspect, out of keeping with his times. To a monk accused of adultery, Basil begins his letter with words pregnant with impending reproach: "Even as I set out to write this letter though by reasoning I can nerve my benumbed hand, yet my countenance, distressed by the dejection I feel for your sake, I have not the strength to alter, as great is the feeling of shame that overwhelms me on your account—so great indeed, that the portals of my mouth straightway fall apart, and my lips are turned to sobbing. Alas!" He goes on to recall this monk's ascetic life: "You rid your flesh of all its fat, nobly drained the channels of your abdomen dry, and by compressing your stomach itself with fastings, you caused your outstanding ribs, like the eaves of a house, to cast a shadow about the region of your navel. Thus with your whole body contracted, you spent hours of night making your confessions to God, and with the streams of your tears smoothed out the curls of your drenched beard".[555] But Basil goes on, where has it all led: "What sorcerer's art was so subtle as to drive you into so deadly a snare? What tortuous meshes of the devil got their coils about you, and exposed the true character of that unswerving practice of virtue of yours?"[556] He judges the effects of his action: "You have therefore at once become liable for a deadly perjury, and by casting disparagement upon the character of asceticism you have carried your disgrace back even to the Apostles and the Lord himself. You have put our boast of purity to shame, you have mocked the vow of chastity; we have become a tragedy of captives, and our lives are placed on the stage for Jews and Greeks. You have cut the pride of all monks asunder."[557] The only recourse says Basil is to return to God and to the community: "The tower of our strength has not fallen, brother; the remedies of amendment have not been mocked; the city of refuge has not been closed. Do not abide in the depths of iniquity; do not give yourself over to the slayer of men. The Lord knows how to raise up those who have been dashed down. Flee to no distant place, but hasten back to us."[558] The pastoral care was severe but nonetheless hopeful.

The counsel to a fallen virgin was similar: "What had become of that dignified bearing of yours, that decorous character, that simple dress befitting a virgin, that beautiful blush of modesty and that comely pallor, which blooms through temperance and vigils and has a radiance more charming than any ruddiness of complexion".[559] But now "you have been seduced by the serpent, a more biter seduction than Eve's. And not only your mind has been corrupted but your very body". Then, summoning all his feelings of revulsion, Basil says he must make mention "of a crime I hesitate to name, and yet cannot pass over in silence (for it is a burning and flaming fire in my bones, and my strength is altogether gone,and I cannot bear under it): 'You took the members of Christ, and made them the members of a harlot' (2 Corinthians 11:3). Basil urges her to think of her last day, her time of death, the judgement of her soul, and then says, "The Lord wishes you to purge you of the pain of the wound, and to show you the light after darkness. The good Shepherd, who has left those which have not strayed, seeks you. If you give yourself over to Him, He will not delay, nor in his kindness will disdain to carry you on his shoulders, rejoicing that He has found his sheep which was lost."[560] Severity is thus combined with hope and mercy.

Basil took care not only to order, discipline, and encourage the Church with his pastoral letters and teaching but, in addition, he was one of the chief advocates of the Church in its relations with the Imperial administration. With his background and education he was at ease in dealing with officials and rulers in Cappadocia and beyond. Part of his responsibility in society was to represent the Church to the Emperor and the administration and the decrees of the Emperor to the Church. After the Constantinian settlement of Church and state, bishops were appointed with Imperial permission: they could be exiled from their sees, as many were at the decree of the Emperor, and likewise could be summoned by the Emperor through the *cursus publicus*, as some 400 bishops in 359 were by Constantius for a Council at Rimini and where they were to remain for over six months to agree that the "Son was like the Father as the scriptures say and teach" (i.e. a *homoian* Creed that rejected Nicaea). All the powers of the Emperor were deployed by Constantius to get the doctrinal result he wanted.[561]

In Basil's correspondence, he often wrote to officials on behalf of others. He wrote to Sophronios, a high official in the civil service whom Basil had met in Athens, on behalf of Gregory of Nazianzus whose brother Caesarius' will had been frustrated by certain slaves getting hold of his estate and giving it away so that Gregory of Nazianzus, received little or nothing. Sophronios was asked to look into it and settle the matter justly.[562] Of Callisthenes he asks for clemency on behalf of some slaves who were liable for punishment.[563] On a number of occasions Basil writes about the taxation of the Church. He wrote to Modestus, a Prefect, in 372 and on a further five occasions. Modestus had previously relied on Basil's intercession for his own healing from severe sickness and so was well disposed to grant his requests. In Letter 104 Basil asks for exemption from taxation for all presbyters and deacons, and does so not without a little hyperbolae writing, "This (exemption) will not only keep the glory of the good deeds of your great lordship immortal, but it will also increase the number of those who pray for the Imperial house, and will confer a great benefit even upon the public revenues, since our immunity from taxation, is not altogether for the clergy, but for those who are at any time in distress".[564] In other words, exemption would increase prayer for the government and stimulate charitable acts which in turn would bring relief: it was in the interests of the Imperial administration to treat the Church so. The synergy of Church and state, first conceived by Constantine, was now being well advanced and advocated by Basil as it was by Gregory of Nazianzus. Letters to prefects, governors, taxation officials, and even generals like Trajan, who was possibly the Commander in Chief under Valens, were frequent. Basil had written to Trajan in order to plead for the restoration of a certain Maximus, formerly the Governor of Cappadocia, who appears to have been unjustly stripped of office and livelihood. The work of a bishop was to seek support from the administration, use his position to gain favours for the distressed or dispossessed, and plead for the establishment of the Church in society. With such a task on his shoulders, it is not surprising that Basil felt at times pitifully weak and ill, occasionally isolated and friendless, and overwhelmed by the task before him. Often he complained of illness and weakness in his letters, as he did with some vividness in his letter to Eusebius, Bishop of Samosata in 374: "The reason why I am not already present with you is not easy to explain in words, not only because I am hampered by my present infirmity, but also because I never gained a command of the language sufficient to enable me to describe clearly my varied and complex sickness. But the truth is that from the day of Easter until now, fevers, dysenteries, and the rebellion of my bowels, drenching me like recurring waves, have not permitted me to emerge".[565]

Gregory of Nazianzus as Bishop

Gregory's experience of episcopacy could not have been more different to Basil's. Whereas Basil served as Archbishop of Caesarea continuously for nearly nine years, Gregory never settled into any of his episcopal appointments. Appointed by Basil against his will to Sasima in Cappadocia, he remained adamantly hostile to the place for the rest of his life. He resented the appointment which he felt had been stitched up by Basil and his father, and, as far as we know, he hardly ever visited it, referring to it as an "utterly dreadful and cramped little settlement".[566] In fact he had little aspiration to episcopal office wanting, it appears, to pursue a philosophic or ascetical life, and had felt betrayed when Basil had sought election to Caesarea as Archbishop and gave up on the life of withdrawal which they had both talked about and aspired to in Athens.[567] When Gregory was expected to campaign for Basil's election, insult seems to have been added to injury,[568] and a virtual breach seems to have occurred in their relationship, though there was a rapprochement in the interests of orthodoxy when the Emperor Valens came to Caesarea.

It was nevertheless a *virtual* rather than absolute breach, for whatever personal difficulties they encountered and whatever bruising Gregory felt he suffered, from the more commanding side of Basil's nature (which was also unhelpfully reminiscent of his own father), Gregory always had a deep respect for Basil and his model of ministry. This was made clear, that is the ambivalence of respect and criticism, in his panegyric on Basil which is Oration 43—delivered after Basil's funeral which Gregory did not attend for reasons of illness.[569]

The oration tells, amongst other things, of Basil's election to the Archbishopric supported by Gregory's father who went to the election synod in Caesarea—armed with a persuasive speech in favour of Basil's election written by his son—virtually a dead man, so old and weak was he; but surprisingly he returned triumphant: "In short he was placed in his carriage like a corpse onto a bier, but came back home in vigour of youth, head held high, eyes shining brightly".[570]

After Basil's election, Gregory refused to go and congratulate him and was wary of the new found authority that Basil had gained.[571] It took the arrival of the Emperor Valens in Caesarea at Epiphany 372 to bring Gregory to the city where he appeared as rhetor in defence of the Nicene party in opposition to the Arianising tendencies of Valens' court which was committed to the *homoian* settlement of the Synod of Rimini of 360. During the imperial visit Basil himself bravely stood trial before the Imperial Prefect for the East, Modestus, and boldly withstood his interrogation.[572] At a subsequent meeting with Demosthenes, an Imperial eunuch and theoretician and later opponent of Gregory of Nyssa, Gregory argued convincingly for the Nicene position, though not in a way to change imperial policy. Basil was affirmed in his office. The Emperor personally attended Eucharist in the cathedral celebrated by Basil whilst his son, Prince Galates, fought for his life and subsequently died. Nonetheless the province, and hence the diocese, of Cappadocia was divided by the Emperor and this was seized upon by Basil's enemies, principally Anthimos of Tyana, as an opportunity to rest *Cappadocia Secunda* away from the authority of Basil. It was his antipathy especially which made Basil seize the moment to strengthen his province against them by creating the Sees of Sasima and Nyssa and installing his friend and brother respectively in them. Gregory was caught in the midst of diocesan power play.

Gregory's experience of appointment to the office of a bishop was therefore tied up with the underlying issues of his relationship with Basil. The two became indistinguishable in his mind. Furthermore his work as a kind of un-appointed assistant bishop to his ageing father in

Nazianzus, after his appointment to Sasima, was equally tied up with the other most formative relationship in his life, his relationship with his father. So, for Gregory, episcopal oversight was made more problematic by the way in which it came about. In the case of Sasima it came to nothing because of Basil's overweening use of patronage, in Gregory's eyes, and the problems of the place itself. Indeed it produced a negative effect in his later appointment to Constantinople, as we have seen. But in the case of Nazianzus where Gregory acted as an assistant-bishop (but un-consecrated) to his father, who was not far off 100 years old, there was a much more positive outcome in terms of ministry.

Gregory's response to his various episcopal appointments takes us to the heart of the man himself: loyal in friendship but ambitious as a theologian, dutiful as a son but wanting to be independent in the spiritual journey he sought to follow. It would be too easy simply to say that Gregory was guilty of a being a "vacillating dilettante"[573] in spurning the appointment to Sasima. Rousseau, in his biography of Basil, says of Gregory's response that it was illustrative of his "muddled thinking".[574] But the appointment, and Gregory's response, was probably the result of several things: his father's hope to see his son settled in a post worthy of his education and standing; Basil's persuasion of Gregory that he was needed in the Church at this episcopal level to rebut the ideas and actions of an Arianising Emperor,[575] and Gregory's own desire to please them and be of use. But looking back on his appointment in the light of later events and especially his appointment to Constantinople—an appointment however difficult and problematic—he thought that Basil used him and his father colluded with Basil so that Gregory was sold, in effect, an episcopal pup. He wrote scathingly of this episode and especially of Basil's use of him: "So what happened to you? How could you cast me off so suddenly? May the kind of friendship which treats its friends in such a way be banished from this life. We were lions yesterday but today I am an ape. But to you even a lion is of little worth. Even if you have regarded all your friends in this way, (for I will make a proud claim) you should not have regarded me so. I whom you once preferred to all your friends before you were raised above the clouds and considered beneath you."[576] Gregory felt his friendship with Basil deserved better. This appointment was not worthy of their friendship, was "dishonourable" and a slight on Gregory's family honour.[577] For all these reasons, and the subsequent one of preventing him from enjoying the See of Constantinople because he was supposedly wedded to the See of Sasima, made this appointment a bitter pill.

Gregory was determined to use his new office not just for the *mystagogy* of his episcopal oversight, whereby he was a focus for unity in the sacraments and rites of the Church, but he also would speak boldly, *parrhesia*, for the Nicene truths of the Trinity—indeed in relation to the godhead of the Spirit he would even surpass Nicaea.[578] At his consecration as Bishop of Sasima, in fact in Nazianzus in the presence of his father and Basil, Gregory shared in public his reluctance, his sense of being compelled and even betrayed. He questioned his own ability to deliver effective care given the tempest inside him: "This is the pastoral duty I would have you teach me, my dear ones, whom I shall henceforth call pastors and fellow-pastors. The insignia of this vocation bestow upon me, both you, our common father (Gregory the Elder) who has trained and out stripped many a pastor in years gone by and you righteous arbiter of my life in grace (Basil). And yet—graciously hear what I have to say—can we really provide pastoral care and nurture in a conscientious way when we are being pulled hither and yon by a roaring tempest?"[579] His premonitions of pastoral difficulties were only confirmed when, upon seeking entry to Sasima, he was prevented access by Anthimos who had placed agents in the neighbouring village to prevent Gregory from taking control of his diocese, thereby frustrating his enemy Basil. Lying as it did on the border of the two newly created dioceses,[580] Sasima was like a border town in the ensuing episcopal wars between Basil and Anthimos, until eventually a measure of peace broke out.

As was often the case, Gregory took himself off for a period of exile or retreat, most probably to Seleukia. On his return he delivered what would become Orations 10 and 11. Oration 10 seems composed and calm: "I look kindly upon the hand that played the tyrant (Basil)", but with the rider, "Never again will I put my trust in friendship".[581] Gregory seems to have come through whatever despair he had felt. Oration 11 is a summary of Gregory of Nyssa's address; he had come to Nazianzus to reconcile Gregory with Basil. We can see from Gregory's own panegyric on Basil that it was not entirely successful. There seems to have been a lasting ambivalence in his relationship: respect for all that Basil achieved but genuine hurt at his treatment. Following Gregory of Nyssa's visit, Gregory of Nazianzus settled into his home town, but now as acting bishop since his aged father, well into nineties, required help.

Here he was to preach, no doubt amongst many other sermons not recorded or passed on to us by Gregory, six Orations, including his panegyric on his father (Orations 12, 13, 16, 17, 18—which was on the death of his father—and 19). In a very real sense they show Gregory fulfilling the role of a bishop in a way he never could in the more volatile circumstances in which he would later find himself in Constantinople. In Oration 12 he dedicates his ministry to the Spirit: "I opened my mouth and drew down the Spirit. To that Spirit I dedicate my entirety, and my very self. Only let him have me, and lead me and move me—hand, mind and voice. Take them wherever he wishes, whatever is right, and stop them moving wherever is unfitting."[582] It is a moving opening to his episcopal ministry, but more than that it shows his theology of the Spirit whom Gregory was soon to show as being of the same substance (*homoousios*) as the Father and Son, which itself was a challenge to Basil.[583] In Orations 16, 17 and 19, Gregory brings consolation to the town. In Oration 16, entitled *On his Father's silence because of the plague of hail*, Gregory outlines a fitting response in the light of the calamities that have affected the harvest in the area. Gregory does not believe in the inevitability of hardship as some sophists did nor did he think they were simply judgement. Nevertheless, a response of confession and prayer may avert worse disaster and provide a way for future blessing: "Let us anticipate his anger by confession; let us desire to see him appeased, after He was wrath. Who knoweth, he says, if he will not turn and repent, and leave a blessing behind him? This I know certainly, I the sponsor of the loving-kindness of God. And when he has laid aside that which is unnatural to him, his anger, he will betake himself to that which is natural, his mercy".[584] Hope for the future was firmly fixed by Gregory in the unchanging, merciful character of God.

If one part of a bishop's work was speaking in times of crisis and theological conflict with *parrhesia*, bold speech, another part was representing the needs of the community to the government. If storms and cruel weather was one challenge to deal with, taxes and the imperial administration were another. In Orations 17 and 19, Gregory deals with such issues. Gregory calls for the submission of his people to the imperial powers and to leave off suicidal political protests, but equally he calls upon the imperial power to act in a Christian and responsible way: "You rule with Christ and you govern with Christ; it is from him that you receive your sword, not to use, but to brandish. May you preserve it as an unstained offering to him who conferred it upon you".[585] A further, less compelling, letter to Julian, written after his father's death and after a period of mourning, around Christmas 374, sought more favourable taxation treatment for Nazianzus, and Gregory seems to have gained an effective hearing.

Another Oration that stems from this time is 13, on the occasion of an election to Doara, edited by Eulalios.[586] This Oration was made by Gregory to the new Bishop of Doara in the newly formed Diocese of Cappadocia Secunda, still led by the troublesome but now reconciled Bishop Anthimos, and is a call to fight for the orthodoxy of the Nicene faith as well as living a life of simplicity, humility, poverty, and contemplation. "Help us to learn", says Gregory, "to worship God the Father, God the Son, and God the Holy Spirit as three in their individual realities (hypostasis), one in glory and splendour".[587] The fact that Gregory was both a consecrating bishop and gave the homily at the consecration shows the measure of independence he now felt from Basil.

The final Oration from this time was his panegyric for his father, Oration 18. For Ullman, this Oration "will be read and admired as long as Greek literature remains".[588] Gregory senior was much praised for his simplicity, sincerity, generosity, and orthodoxy—his earlier lapse from orthodoxy being mostly overlooked or explained away as a piece of overzealous discipleship created by unusual local influences.[589] Basil, who was also at the funeral, had only to endure one sideswipe at both himself and Gregory's father for their treatment of Gregory in making him firstly a priest and then bishop against his will.[590] But after the death of both his parents—his mother Nonna died soon afterwards—Gregory went into decline. Unable to persuade his diocesan, Anthimos, that he had not taken on a permanent role as Bishop of Nazianzus, he typically retreated to a convent at Seleukia in 375. From there he would be summoned to Constantinople.

Gregory's tumultuous time in Constantinople has already been discussed. Summoned to shore up the Nicene position in the chapel of

Anastasia, where he delivered his seminal Theological Orations (Nos. 27–31) in a city which had largely gone "*homoian*" he would always be vulnerable. He suffered the duplicity of Maximus, the attacks of the *homoian* mob, illness, and finally the factions in the Council of Bishops with its fissures over episcopal succession in Antioch and the intrigues of the Egyptian contingent controlled by Bishop Peter of Alexandria. It needed a more commanding presence than Gregory could supply with a stronger support base than a faraway community in provincial Nazianzus. Nevertheless, in his brief time as an unconfirmed Archbishop of Constantinople, from 380, Gregory spoke passionately for the orthodox faith he believed in and which would eventually triumph. In the series of Orations, 38–40, from Christmas 380 to 6 January 381, the Feast of Christ's Baptism, his teaching and bold-speaking, *parrhesia*, continued. At Christmas he proclaimed, "Christ in the Flesh, rejoice with trembling and joy; with trembling because of your sins, with joy because of your hope".[591]

In his Orations on the Feast of the Holy Lights, on the eve of Epiphany (6 January), when those to be baptised the following day—the neophytes—carried lights to the baptistery, Gregory proclaimed the Trinity in whose name they would be baptised: "And when I speak of God you must be illumined at once by one flash of light and by three. Three in Individualities or Hypostases, if any prefer so to call them, persons, for we will not quarrel about names so long as the syllables amount to the same meaning; but One in respect of substance—that is the Godhead. For they are divided without division, if I may so say; and they are united in division. For the Godhead is one in three, and the three are one, in whom the Godhead is, or to speak more accurately, Who are the Godhead".[592]

And on the following day, on the occasion of their baptism, Gregory gave a further Oration, mostly to encourage people in general not to defer baptism (as was the fashion with many, in case they committed mortal sin following the baptism and could not be restored again), but also, once again, to uphold the Trinity. In a cascade of phrases that extol the illumination that baptism brings he says, "Let us discourse upon the second birth—(the first being natural birth: the second being Illumination representing conversion and baptism, and the third being Resurrection), which is now necessary for us, and which gives its name to the Feast of the Lights. Illumination is the splendour of the souls, the conversion of the life, the question put to the Godward conscience. It is the aid to our weakness, the renunciation of the flesh, the following of the Spirit, the fellowship of the Word, the improvement of the creature, the overwhelming of sin, the participation of light, the dissolution of darkness. It is the carriage to God, the dying with Christ, the perfecting of the mind, the bulwark of Faith, the key of the Kingdom of heaven, the change of life, the removal of slavery, the losing of chains, the remodelling of the whole man".[593] Such an oration about Baptism must have lifted the significance of the occasion and heightened the sense of drama.

Gregory had only two further Orations to deliver in Constantinople and those were his Oration at Pentecost and his Farewell Oration (42). After the withdrawal of support by the Emperor Theodosius as well as by the Antiochene bishops over the issue of succession at Antioch and further meddling by the Egyptian bishops in the appointment of an Archbishop of Constantinople, Gregory could no longer chair the Council of Constantinople effectively. Seeing the writing on the wall he resigned, but not without making a final address to the Council. Disappointed by their lack of boldness in describing the Spirit as *Homoousios* with Father and Son, he tersely stated in his address that "Now, the name of that which has no beginning is the Father, and of the Beginning the Son, and of that which is with the Beginning, the Holy Ghost, and the three have one nature—God".[594] What could be plainer! Then he took his leave: "Farewell Anastasia, whose name is redolent of piety: for thou has raised up for us the doctrine which was in contempt" and, "Farewell, mighty Christ-loving city . . . Approach the Truth: be converted at this late hour. . . . Farewell ye Angels, guardians of this church, and of my presence and pilgrimage, since our affairs are in the hands of God. Farewell, O Trinity, my meditation, and my glory. Mayest Thou be preserved by those who are here, and preserve them my people. May I learn that Thou (the Trinity) art ever extolled and glorified in word and conduct. My children keep, I pray you, what is committed to your trust. Remember my stoning. The Grace of our Lord Jesus Christ be with you all. Amen".[595] And with that he left all episcopal ministry in the great city and went home to write up his life and Orations in Nazianzus.

Gregory of Nyssa

By contrast, Gregory of Nyssa's episcopal ministry was more straightforward, unencumbered by the complex relationship with father and friend which so affected Nazianzen's career. Appointed to the see of Nyssa in 371 by his brother Basil, there appears to have been no such sensitivities as Gregory of Nazianzus experienced. Exiled by Valens in 376, he returned to his see on the Emperor's death. Attending the Council of Antioch, which subsequently moved to Constantinople, and able there to witness first-hand the drama of those years in the company of Jerome and others, Gregory must have experienced an unforgettable melting pot of theology, politics, and ecclesiastical manoeuvrings that make the novels of Trollope look very tame by comparison. He championed the Nicene cause and was elected Bishop of Sebaste in succession to Eustathius with whom Basil had broken over the doctrine of the Holy Spirit. Appointed by the Emperor as one of eleven bishops to advocate the resolutions of the Council of Constantinople, he was used in the district of Pontus to uphold orthodoxy, negotiate settlements where there were disputes, and appoint new bishops to sees when vacant. In addition, he maintained close contact with monastic communities by whom he was held in high regard.[596] Much in demand as a preacher and teacher, he remained at Sebaste—though he often went on tour—until his death in c.394.

Gregory espoused the ministry of the monk-bishop. The model for Gregory of Nyssa's episcopal life was more clearly defined and more easily followed than by his friend Gregory of Nazianzus. His dispute with the Imperial authorities as a result of his support of the Nicene position, which led to his exile from Nyssa, afforded him the opportunity for writing, monastic life, and contemplation. As such, it was not unproductive, and in some ways it allowed time for what otherwise would have been squeezed out. His older sister, Macrina, encouraged him in these things. But, for Gregory, the path of episcopal ministry was clear. He "simultaneously engaged in pastoring his flock and pursuing spiritual perfection and knowledge of God" as, for him, the monk-bishop was the model for leadership in the Church. "This *typos* of episcopal authority, Gregory implied, was foreshadowed by Moses and fulfilled by the bishop of Caesarea".[597]

Both Moses and Basil were lodestars in Gregory's understanding of ministry. He pursued the "mixed life", combining the contemplative life of the philosopher or monk and the active vocation of civic or ecclesiastical service.[598] Basil was, in this respect, a follower of Moses. So Gregory said of him, "many times we perceived that he (Basil) also was in a dark cloud wherein God was. For what was invisible to others, to him the initiation into the mysteries of the Spirit made visible, so that he seemed to be within the compass of the dark cloud in which the knowledge of God was concealed".[599] Like Moses, both Basil and Gregory went through a kind of three stage development of spiritual life: training in the general education of the day—for Moses it was all the learning of the Egyptians, but for Basil and Gregory it was the philosophy of the Greeks—the abandonment of that learning in order to lead a life of virtue and contemplation of God, which in turn would lead onto the final stage of sacrifice, in which a life of solitude was exchanged for leading the Church of God. This threefold progression could also be found in Gregory's Oration on the life of Gregory Thaumaturgus[600] who likewise gave up the pursuit of knowledge through the classics in order to study under Origen and then return to Cappadocia to "perfect his soul in virtue",[601] and then lead the Church. Although some of the details of this life of the Wonderworker by Gregory were spurious, a general pattern of preparation for leadership has emerged, and supreme in Gregory's understanding of leadership was the pursuit of virtue in the context of contemplation. Contemplative prayer and study leading to action, whilst upholding orthodoxy, was a touchstone for the Cappadocians.

CHAPTER 10

The Cappadocians and the Struggle for Orthodoxy

When Constantine died in 337, twelve years after the Council of Nicaea, it was by no means apparent that orthodoxy would triumph. Indeed it would be nearly fifty years, and not until the Council of Constantinople under the patronage of Theodosius and the brief presidency of Gregory of Nazianzus, before Nicene orthodoxy would seemingly succeed. Moreover other battles, especially over the nature of Christ, were looming for, if we do not understand who God is, how can we understand our own identity, predicament, and destiny? The settling of the question of the Trinity was the essential starting point for all else. By orthodoxy we mean the faith taught in the scriptures and in particular in relation to, in this case, the Trinity. Orthodoxy is simply another word for truth, and for something to be true it must accurately represent reality, for what is true is real and what is real is true. The onslaught of Arianism, taken forward by Aetuis and Eunomius in Cappadocia, was a powerful attack on orthodoxy as expressed in Nicaea. Undoubtedly the advocacy of the Trinitarian faith by Athanasius, from Nicaea onwards, was foundational to its eventual establishment. But from 360–380 the Cappadocians played a critical role in the struggle for orthodoxy, especially in the Eastern part of the Empire.

The Cappadocians themselves did not approach this struggle in an especially co-ordinated or strategic manner. Indeed a lot of energy was spent in dealing with peripheral issues, not least their own personal agendas as bishops (Basil), or an aspiring theologian and teacher (Gregory of Nazianzus), or speculative mystic (Gregory of Nyssa). Not that any of these definitions was a water-tight description of their role or function, for each was so diverse that none could, or would, pursue a single agenda. But what did unify them, although once again in a real diversity, was the struggle for the Trinity; the three *hypostases* in a single *ousia*. Seemingly the position that Basil came to hold, that Father and Son were *homoousios*, was not always what he advocated because of the need to build alliances with a wider circle of leaders who held to the *homoiousios* position (i.e. like in substance). But the two Gregorys were adamant that to shift from *homoousios* was to sell scripture short and invite confusion.

Words

It was in *Alice through the Looking Glass* that Humpty Dumpty famously said "When I use a word it means just what I chose it to mean—neither more nor less".[602] Sometimes in Church history we find that a whole debate turns on the significance or meaning of a single word. Such was the time that the Cappadocians lived in and the word was *homoousios* (of the same substance). In fact it is not a biblical word but a word that existed in the theologian's Greek lexicon before Nicaea, but was used as the defining term for the unity of Father and Son (the Spirit's unity of substance with Father and Son came later especially because of the work of Gregory of Nazianzus). In later centuries, such words as *grace* and *justification* became the turning points for complete movements within the Church. These words would figure largely in the vocabulary of the Reformers in their struggle with the Papacy. Today the word might be *marriage*: for the Church, not least the Orthodox Church, describes marriage as between a man and a woman whereas others speak of same sex marriage as if it were the same thing. It raises questions of by what authority do we give meaning to words: is it simply the consensus of society or do words which represent so fundamental a thing as marriage have an inalienable meaning and significance given by God, and that its very meaning is wrapped with the very created order itself?

Basil started out with the word which Nicaea had used to describe the relationship of Father and Son, *homoousios,* but he found it necessary to build alliances with like-minded Church leaders against rampant Arianism. So he sought to build a middle course between polytheism or tritheism (three gods) and Judaism or Sabellian Monarchism or Marcellanism which stressed the unity of the Godhead at the expense of their individuate persons. In the 360s, to strengthen the anti-Arian alliance, he made common cause with Eustathius of Sebaste and Basil of Ancyra and the *homoiousians* but was never wholly comfortable, especially when Eusthathius came out in his true colours of not admitting the divinity of the Spirit. Having been shy of using the word *homoousios* in his work *Against Eunomius* in 364, once he became a bishop in 370, Basil stuck firmly to his interpretation of *homoousios* which emphasised community of essence (*ousia*) but distinction of person (*hypostasis*). For Basil, the Trinity should be thought of as a union of the common divine nature (*ousia*) with each individual person (*hypostasis*).[603]

It is instructive that the foray into an alliance with the slighter, "softer" *homoiousios* position was short lived. It blurred the truth, gave hostages to fortune, and made him vulnerable to further weakening of his position in the light of the pursuance of the *Homoian* policy by the Emperor. Even non-biblical words are worth sticking with if they make the reality which they are describing unmistakeable. And that is the point of words, especially in the context of a struggle for what is true.

But it was not as though the Cappadocians got everything right. We have seen the influence of Platonism on their theology, in part through Origen, but also through its appeal as the dominant world view in the Greek world, reworked through Plotinus. If Basil was tempted into theological alliances which at one point may have compromised what he held most dear, the Trinity, Gregory of Nyssa also compromised his orthodoxy—as far as many of the early Fathers were concerned including Augustine—through the influence of Plato and his understanding of evil. Gregory of Nyssa thought that even the devil himself would be reconciled to God. "For Plato there was no form of evil. It had no eternal significance. He identified *being* with goodness and *non-being* with evil".[604] The teaching of *apocatastasis* or the restoration of all things (Acts 3:21), including the devil to God, was part of Gregory's teaching. In effect this denied the final reality of hell, and for Gregory the purpose of hell fires were not so much punishment as the means of cleansing the soul as it passes on to perfection; in other words, it was akin to purgatory. At the

Council of Constantinople of 553, Origen's teaching on the restoration of all things was posthumously anathematised. "If anyone asserts the fabulous pre-existence of souls, and shall assert the monstrous restoration which follows from it: let him be anathema". Simply put, the truth that Orthodoxy sought to establish was that evil would be judged for what it was. It did not exist *per se* in matter (Plotinus' view) nor was it simply a wrong choice which would no longer exist once the restoration of all things occurred, it was rather a violation of human freedom and dignity which, if not forgiven, would bear punishment. In other words, responsibility was not swallowed up by grace.

The Cappadocians: The Bridge to the Augustine

In broad terms the Cappadocians could be seen as the theological bridge between Athanasius and Augustine, and in particular Gregory of Nazianzus, in terms of his benchmark expression of the Trinity in his *Five Theological Orations*, and Gregory of Nyssa, in terms of his teaching on spirituality. When Basil died before the Council of Constantinople and before the preaching of Gregory's *Five Theological Orations* in the chapel of the Anastasia in Constantinople this bridge had not been finally secured. But by the time the Council had finished, however incomplete it would prove to be, a point of no turning back for Trinitarian orthodoxy had been reached. It was as if a set of theological foundations had been firmly laid in the statute book from which the Church would never turn back. Admittedly more work had to be done on the Holy Spirit's place in the Trinity, for which Gregory of Nazianzus was impatient. And likewise there was yet to be a further costly schism over the nature of Christ with the Nestorian controversy, this time with Cyril of Alexandria, but by and large East and West were now singing from the same Trinitarian hymn sheet which they had not been for many years. And if in the East the Cappadocians had prevailed thus upholding Athanasius' teaching, then in the West Ambrose likewise held the torch for orthodoxy, and later Augustine.

Ambrose, as Bishop of Milan, was the man most responsible for the conversion of Augustine in 386. Ambrose had been in correspondence with Basil and knew of his struggles against Arianism. On Easter eve in 387 after seclusion in a philosophic community in Cassiciacum, not unlike the retreats which the Cappadocians had become accustomed to, Augustine was baptised. Returning to North Africa, Augustine set up a comparable philosophic community in Thagaste using experiences of Cassiciacum and earlier ones of ascetic communities in Rome where Jerome, fresh from Constantinople, in 382-5 gave these philosophic communities rather uneven patronage.[605] It is speculation, but since Jerome had attended Gregory's *Five Theological Orations* in the Anastasia chapel,[606] he may well have conveyed the flavour or indeed the substance of Gregory's teaching to these communities.

Although Augustine may have been indirectly influenced by the Cappadocians, he had little direct knowledge of them, mainly because Augustine had limited understanding of Greek, itself an important point in grasping the separate development of East and West in their theological trajectories. Ambrose, on the other hand, knew Greek and incorporated the Geek Fathers into his teaching. Nevertheless, there was still much in common between Augustine and the Cappadocians: the influence of neo-Platonism, especially Plotinus—although at the same time resisting his hierarchical structure of reality;[607] the love of the philosophic life and contemplation; the centrality of the bible; the commitment to prayer, and the love of the Trinity. But, on the Trinity, Augustine would teach the procession of the Spirit from the Father *and* the Son, so laying the groundwork for the later split between East and West around the use of the *filioque* clause in the creed. What was unique in Augustine was that he made his own personal experience the laboratory in which to test the doctrines of sin and grace. To this end his Confessions bear witness. "The Confessions are a manifesto of the inner world: 'Men go to gape at mountain peaks, at the boundless tides of the sea, the broad sweep of rives, the encircling ocean and the motions of the stars; and yet they leave themselves unnoticed; they do not marvel at themselves.'"[608]

But both the Cappadocians and Augustine agreed that, for Gregory of Nyssa, *desire* and, for Augustine, *delight* are the main spring of contemplation, gazing upon God and becoming like him. "For Augustine delight is the only possible source of action, nothing else can move the will. Therefore a man can only act if he mobilizes his feelings, only if he is 'affected by an object of delight'".[609] And for Gregory of Nyssa, according to Meredith, "desire, *eros* or *pathos*, lie at the root of human craving for God. It is a theme which finds expression in all his ascetic writings".[610] Naturally for Gregory, as for so many of the Fathers, this idea found its fullest biblical expression in the Song of Songs. Augustine famously summarised the moral outcome of such a love or desire with the words, "love God and do you what you like" or "We become what we love".[611]

The Cappadocians, therefore, were the theological bridge between Alexandria and Hippo, not only in terms of their defence of the Trinity and the beginnings of their theology of the Spirit but also in terms of the values that underpinned their spirituality and ascetic life. Both would have agreed that "to contemplate God is the life of the soul"[612] and that *desire for* and *delight in* God was the trigger for this contemplation with the result of becoming like him.

Imperial Power

In the context of the struggle for orthodoxy, imperial power was critical. In the first instance, it was Constantine who brought the bishops together at Nicaea under the leadership of Hosios of Cordoba and Eustathius of Antioch to hammer out a creed which would isolate Arianism and unite the Church in orthodoxy. With the Emperor present, or not far away, agreement was reached with only two dissenting voices: Theonas of Marmarcia and Secundus of Ptolemais. Even Eusebius of Nicomedia signed his assent, although later, as we have seen, he weakened the meaning of the text in his explanations and resiled from his commitment. But Constantine himself seemed to weaken in his commitment to the Creed, by 334 recalling Arius from exile and commanding Athanasius to receive him back into communion, which Athanasius understandably refused to do. Under both Constantius and Valens, the Nicene party was opposed by both Emperors who were committed to a more or less Arian or *homoian* policy. For his part Julian the Apostate reinstated paganism and in 362 prevented Christians from holding office or teaching in the universities. His reign was short lived but it served to show how strong imperial power was in quickly turning the tables on the Constantinian settlement of Church and state. Following Julian, Valens returned to a generally *homoian* position deposing or exiling bishops of Nicene orthodoxy, like Gregory of Nyssa. His death at the hands of the Goths at Adrianople ushered in Theodosius, the young Spanish general who not only saw off the Goths, securing Constantinople, but sought to return the Church in the East to its apostolic fundamentals and to Nicene orthodoxy. The point is that Imperial power was now needed to establish orthodoxy ever since the Empire under Constantine had got in the position of ruling the bishops as other Imperial officials. The bishops may not have been appointed by the Emperor but they could be *easily* removed by him. And although, as in the famous case of Athanasius, he might resist the will of the Emperor, nevertheless for theological settlements to be accepted across a broad front in the Empire the Emperor's support was needed. Strained relations between Church and state would rumble on for centuries to come with the spiritual power sometimes gaining the upper hand as Ambrose did with Theodosius, insisting on his repentance for needlessly massacring Goths in an amphitheatre in Thessalonica (what today we might call a war crime) or the Pope did at Canova. After the Enlightenment—and successive revolutions in individual European countries—the Church in Europe become subservient to the secular or temporal state. During the time of the Cappadocians, relations with the Emperor were critical in the struggle for orthodoxy.

The Path to Orthodoxy

A study of the Cappadocians' struggle for orthodoxy shows that they were far from "single club" ecclesiastics. Their very humanity and diversity make them at once attractive and difficult, exasperating and inspiring, speculative and systematic in their theology, demanding and wide ranging in their leadership. No assessment of their achievement can neglect their family influences, their relationship with Hellenism, their commitment to the monk-bishop model of contemplative leadership, their care for the poor and advocacy of their interests. In a word, their espousing of these things, which might be called "orthopraxy", enhanced their campaigning for orthodoxy with all its twists and turns. In the vocabulary of the Greek Orthodox Church, such a combination of *othodoxia* and *orthopraxis* led to a right state of mind (*phronema*—a biblically-used Greek word which denoted a mind-set which, in this context, was the first step to *theosis* or glorification or even becoming like God). The notion of *becoming* and *restoration of image* were key concepts in Gregory of Nyssa's pathway of contemplation and prayer.

For all the Cappadocians, family and the relationships within their families were of critical importance to their development. We have noted earlier the especial influence of the women in their families. For Basil, his background as an aristocratically trained young man with a future in public life was formed by his family background. The influence of Gregory Thaumaturgus on his grandmother, Macrina, was imbibed from an early age. "What indeed could be clearer proof of our faith than that we were brought up by a grandmother, a blessed woman who came from amongst you. I mean the illustrious Macrina, by whom we were taught the sayings of the blessed Gregory".[613] Another Macrina was of equal influence on Gregory of Nyssa, and it is in conversation with her in Platonic dialogue that his *On the Soul and the Resurrection* was born. Equally the nurture and example of his mother, Nonna, and the expectations of his father and his friend, Basil, were the polarities within which Gregory of Nazianzus had to develop his own pathway: a pathway as much formed by positive formation as by negative reaction. Alongside the atmosphere of these deeply spiritual, Christian, and almost ascetic households set in the midst of privileged and well-educated surroundings, the Cappadocians had to filter their education with its classical training and integrate it with the ascetic Christian traditions that shaped them. Like cattle that chew the cud, the Cappadocians had to regurgitate their classical learning, breaking it down into digestible form which would be able to nourish their Christian vocation.

The Cappadocians showed us the limits of classical knowledge: its value and its pitfalls. By the fourth century "the majority of cultivated Christians took it for granted that the marriage between the Gospel and the Greeks was advantageous to the church".[614] However, this alliance was often questioned from both sides of the intellectual divide. In the West,

Tertullian had seriously questioned the benefit of this alliance. Origen had been deeply suspicious of pagan literature: "Pagan literature was for Origen an indissoluble part of the tradition of pagan society, to which as a member of the persecuted church he felt himself to be implacably opposed".[615] Nevertheless, Origen, as well as the whole Alexandrian and Antiochian schools, was deeply influenced by Plato. And from the pagan side, the Emperor Julian in the School Law of 362 sought to banish Christians from teaching in the philosophic schools.

The reactions of the Cappadocians to this law which sought to divorce Christianity from Hellenic studies were varied. Gregory of Nazianzus, who in some ways had most to lose from this, since his oratory was often a sophisticated interweaving of Christian teaching using Greek allusion, wrote a long and at times bitter polemic against it in his Oration 4. Meredith writes of this Oration that "the bitterness of the invective reveals that Gregory regarded Julian's law and actions as an attack not only upon the Christian community but also upon all that he, Gregory, held dear—above all the marriage between Hellenism and Christianity, which had informed his own life".[616]

Contrastingly, Basil wrote a long treatise to "Young men, on how they might derive profit from pagan literature",[617] a work long held, even in the middle ages, as a guide to students about both the benefits and pitfalls of non-biblical knowledge. In it Basil looks for eternal benefit from education,[618] appreciates anything which will train the mind in its preparation for understanding the scriptures, and draws encouragement for the discerning study of Hellenic literature in the same way as Moses and Daniel learnt from the Egyptian and Babylonian teachers in their times.[619]

In his case, Gregory of Nyssa, though well versed in the study of the ancients, was for the most part influenced by Plato and his successors. This influence was especially strong in the case of his concept of evil, his belief in the universal victory of God's love over all, the emancipation of the soul from the body as expressed in "the image of God" concept, and, finally, in the movement or ascent of the soul towards likeness with God through contemplation and meditation. Gregory's world view was an amalgam of the biblical and the Platonic; he even used Platonic forms of dialogue to teach Christian doctrine as in *On the soul and Resurrection*. Julian's separation of Hellenic studies from Christian understanding was not going to affect the deeper impregnation of Platonism into the Christian faith. No School Law could unpick this synthesis. It would take almost a thousand years and the coming of Thomas Aquinas for that to happen in the West, and in the East the synthesis would be even more enduring.

Another part of the legacy of the Cappadocians, apart from their response to Hellenism, was their model of contemplative leadership based on an ascetic model. There are three parts to this: their care of the poor and, when necessary, advocacy of their needs; their own personal choice of the ascetic or monastic path; and their spirituality which included the notions of *epectasis*, change, and contemplation of the unknowable nature of God in the apophatic tradition.

Both Gregory of Nazianzus and Basil made the care of the poor a foundation stone in their spirituality. For both of them it meant teaching about its importance: Gregory, in his Oration 14, wrote, "we must regard charity as the greatest of the commandments since it is the very sum of the Law and the Prophets, its most vital part is the love of the poor along with compassion and sympathy for our fellowman".[620] Likewise Basil taught similarly in addresses about social justice including, *To the rich* and *I will tear down my barns*. But they did not leave it at teaching alone. They lived ascetic lives, dressed in the simplest clothes, lived in community, forewent marriage, and extolled the virtue of virginity in both their words and lifestyle. During his lifetime Basil gave away his inheritance in the founding or development of the *Basileiados*, a foundation of buildings given over for the care of the sick, the dying, and the destitute within the care of a community. Likewise Gregory at his death gave over all his property to the church in Nazianzus. But they also were prepared to be advocates on behalf of their communities to the Emperor and his officials, seeking redress from inspectors of taxes or relief from the devastation of famine from the Emperor. They used their position, their confidence as men from local landowning families and as such part of the *hesiarchs* of the community to bring the causes of the needy to the ear of the imperial administration, often with real success.

If asceticism and care of the poor were part of the "weapons of their spiritual warfare", the other most important and long lasting effect of their leadership was their gift of contemplative leadership. No one was more influential in this respect than Gregory of Nyssa. In a real way the Cappadocians' struggle for orthodoxy led them, and especially Gregory of Nyssa, to a deeper appreciation of negative theology or the mystery of God as expressed in darkness. This truth discovered by Moses in his approach to God on Sinai who was not able to see God's face but only his "back" conveys the truth that "to man's natural powers the knowledge of the divine essence is impossible. Such knowledge only becomes possible by the grace of Christ, which elevates man's mind above itself; by it the invisible becomes visible. And this illumination of the human spirit is the grace of contemplation".[621] Contemplation is possible through the stripping away of the fallen human *skin* so that the tarnished image of God may be both cleansed and freed to ascend to God in prayerful communion and at times in ecstasy or sober inebriation. The model for this ascent of the soul is found particularly in the *Life of Moses* and in Gregory's commentary on the Song of Songs. The effect of contemplation together with the idea of *epectasis* is the transformation of the soul. The soul "is transformed into something divine, and it is transformed from the glory in which it exists to a higher glory by a perfect kind of alteration".[622] As Rowan Williams says, "to be contemplative as Christ is contemplative is to be open to all the fullness that the Father wishes to pour into our hearts".[623] For the Cappadocians, such contemplation was also the basis of leadership: they sought it, they retreated into it, and they recognised that it enabled them to hold the mystery of their faith with a firm expression of orthodoxy: by encountering the Trinity they were able to defend the Trinity with *parrhesia*.

Unfinished Business

Some forty to fifty years after the death of Gregory of Nyssa (c.395) the final great dispute in early Church history broke, this time about the nature of Christ or Christology, between the teaching of Nestorious and Cyril of Alexandria. It was essentially about the nature of Christ and the way the divine and the human in Jesus intermingled or remained distinct in his person and will. Once again the Greek desire to define what remains a mystery led different schools, whether at Antioch or Alexandria, to emphasise different facets of Christ's being. At Antioch, the emphasis was that Christ was fully human and became united with the Word at his birth, baptism, or resurrection (the so called *logos-anthropos* school) as a result of Jesus' perfect obedience. In contrast, Alexandria, the theological trajectory was more that the divine took on flesh (the *logos-sarx* school). Here the ascendancy was with the divine word. This was true of Athanasius' teaching and his successor Cyril who used the word *theotokos* (God-bearer) as a slogan much as in the same way *homoousios* was used in the Trinitarian disputes of the fourth century. *Theotokos* is not so much a statement about Mary as about the divinity of her child. However, in the transliteration to Latin, *dei genitrix*—which meant Mother of God, there were obvious allusions about Mary which became highly influential. But the origins of this dispute were, in part, to be found in the Cappadocians' contemporary Apollinarius.

The tendency in Apollinarius' theology was to a monarchical position stressing the unity of the Trinity at the expense of their individual persons. However, when it came to his Christology, Apollinarius taught that the *logos* element replaced the human spirit in Jesus making no need for moral development or epistemological growth in his life. In a word, the human was subsumed in the divine logos. You could argue therefore that Apollinarius' Christological position was a forerunner to the *monophysite* position which stressed the single divine will of Jesus (rather than a double nature fused together as one) and which was later to define the Coptic, Syrian, Jacobite, and Armenian Churches. But since Apollinarius was contemporary with the Cappadocians, they formed the beginning but incomplete response to this growing heretical tendency. But their work was very much unfinished business in the light of what was to follow.

Basil's own relationship with Apollinarius was problematic, with Basil rebutting Eustathius' charge that Apollinarius had some influence over him. In Letter 261, written to the people of Sozopolis, Basil makes plain that Jesus had a human soul capable of development and that he took on human feelings or passions "yet without sin".[624] Basil rejects Apollinarius' teaching because it leads to a denial of Christ's full humanity. Equally, Gregory of Nazianzus expressed his Christology in his *Letters to Cledonius*. It was in these letters that Gregory came up with the famous statement that, "Whoever has set his hope on a human being without mind (Apollinarius' position) is actually mindless himself and unworthy of being saved in his entirety. The unassumed is the unhealed, but what is united with God is also being saved".[625] In other words, only if Jesus took on our human nature *entirely* would he be able to save our nature *altogether*. It was a piece of Greek and Pauline parallelism (see also Romans 5) which was also strongly present in Athanasius, who himself makes the point in *De incarnatione* that only if Christ is fully God and man can he save us, lifting our humanity into his divine life through his redemptive sufferings and resurrection.

Lastly, of the three Cappadocians, Gregory of Nyssa, perhaps not surprisingly, has the most complex Christology. Gregory's Christology is so capable of various interpretations that he has been accused of being both a proto-Nestorian and a crypto-Monophysite![626] Gregory appears to have a two-stage Christology. In Gregory's thought, in his earthly life, Jesus was both man and God, "held together in a loose unity, after a Nestorian model".[627] But, following the resurrection, the humanity of Jesus is swallowed up by his divinity now in a resurrected form. A glimpse of this is seen in John's Gospel when Jesus is held by the weeping Mary Magdalene. Her relationship with him appears to change now that he is risen (John 20:17). Thus, in his pre-resurrection description of Jesus, Gregory is akin to a Nestorian but in his post-resurrection description "he is a pronounced Monophysite".[628] But more than that there is rightly a strong soteriological side to Gregory's understanding of the incarnation and the nature of Christ. So Balthasar says, "If, therefore, humanity through sin, has lost its image, and if sin has entered into humanity as a condition of its nature, only the presence of a 'true' and pure *man* effects in humanity as a whole a 'change in our very nature'",[629] and that only "by a simple and incomprehensible coming of life, by the presence of light".[630] He goes on, "without excluding the Incarnation or the life of the Lord in its entirety, which was necessary for the transformation of all human life, the Resurrection denotes, however that precise point which the deepest roots of sin are extirpated".[631] Gregory's answer to an incipient Nestorianism in Apollinarius is to show the necessity of Christ's coming as fully human to bring about the possibility of our transformation and then completing this transformation by the power of his resurrection. His was a twofold Christology.

These views as expressed by the Cappadocians were the opening shots of a Christological controversy which would go on to the Council of Chalcedon in 451. They first became involved in it through their refutation of Apollinarius, but the controversy would continue long beyond their deaths. Like the controversy over the Trinity, it would engulf Christendom for a further seventy years.

Conclusion

The legacy of the Cappadocians is considerable. Like the orthodoxy of the Trinity for which they struggled, they too were joined by a common cause or substance, but each one too was distinct in their gifting and calling. Sometimes rubbing each other in the wrong way, they nevertheless remained loyal to each other even if sometimes with deeply felt complaint. Through their writings, voluminous at times, in defence of the Trinity they established a deeper understanding on the Nicene position: not only holding that the Godhead was one in substance but was also three in their individuated hypostasis, using fresh analogies to make this clear. In particular, by degrees, they ensured that the Holy Spirit was attributed full divinity. They commonly asserted that:

> All that the Father is, we see revealed in the Son; all that is the Son's is the Father's also; for the whole Son dwells in the Father, and he has the whole Father dwelling in himself... The Son who exists always in the Father can never be separated from him, nor can the Spirit ever be divided from the Son who through the Spirit works all things. He who receives the Father also receives at the same time the Son and the Spirit. There is between the three a sharing and a differentiation that are beyond words and understanding.[632]

Although they made common cause in both the defence and exposition of the Trinity, as far as was possible in words despite their inadequacy, they also brought unique gifts of insight and action. Action following contemplation was fundamental to their discipleship and the resulting ministry was different for each of them. For Basil, it would lead him to administer a large and strategic diocese as an ascetic bishop deeply committed to helping the poor, to social action, and to the Trinity. We imagine him moving around the *Basiliad*, washing the feet of the lepers and serving in the hospice he founded: for such acts of charity he is still remembered in Cappadocia today. It is a case in point that orthopraxy may speak longer than orthodoxy, not that there ever should be a choice between the two: orthodoxy should always lead to orthopraxy, right understanding to right action.

Likewise, we may recall Gregory Nazianzus in the chapel of Anastasia in Constantinople teaching the doctrine of the Trinity to a deeply suspicious city whom Gregory says resented his presence: "they found it intolerable that a man of such abject poverty, withered bent and shabbily dressed, wasted by the restraints imposed on the stomach and by tears as well as by fear of what was to come and by the wickedness of others, not possessed of a handsome appearance, a stranger, a vagrant, buried in the darkness of the earth should have much more success than fine, strong men".[633] Yet his Orations preached there became an elegant and classic description of the Holy Trinity for the Church thereafter. His brief tenure as Archbishop of Constantinople was defining in its significance.

And lastly, Gregory of Nyssa bids us continually search for a union with God himself which is inspired by a pursuit of virtue and a consummation of love provoked by desire. To him we will give the final word:

> Let us suppose that someone is standing up close to a wellspring ... he will admire that endless gush of water that is always rising from within and spilling out. He will never say, though, that he has seen the water entirely. For how could he see that which is still hidden in the bosom of the earth? And even if he remained a very long time beside the bubbling waters, he would always be at the outset of his view of the water. For the water never becomes weary of flowing, and it is constantly beginning to gush forth again. The same applies to the one who looks to this divine and infinite beauty. Since what he finds at each moment is always newer more paradoxical than what his sight had already grasped. He can only admire what at each moment is presented to him. But his desire to look never tires, for the revelations he awaits will always be more magnificent and more divine than all he has already seen.[634]

Brief chronologies of the Cappadocian Fathers

Basil of Caesarea, Archbishop

329/30: Born
337: Death of Constantine
351: Basil at Athens
357: Basil is baptised
358: Monastic tour with Eustathius; monastic retreat
364: Ordained priest; writes long work *Against Eunomius*
370: Consecrated Archbishop of Caesarea; founds the Basiliad Monastic Hospice; writes *Long and shorter Rules*
372: Consecrates Gregory of Nazianzus Bishop, and likewise his brother Gregory of Nyssa
374: Writes *On the Holy Spirit*
379: Dies, aged 49

Gregory of Nazianzus, Theologian

326/30: Born on the family estate at Arianzus
346: Secondary education in Caesarea
348: Alexandria; sea voyage and conversion
349: Athens
357: Returns to Arianzus and Nazianzus

361/2: Ordained priest by his father; Oration 2, *On defence of his flight to Pontus*
369/70: Writes *On loving the poor*
372: Consecrated Bishop of Sasima, but returns to Nazianzus
374/5: Pastoral work in Nazianzus, and retreat in Seleukia
379: Called to Constantinople to minister to the Nicene Community at the Chapel of Anastasia
379: *The Five Theological Orations* Nos. 27–31
379: Defeat of Valens at Adrianople; appointment of Theodosius, emperor in the East
380/1: President of the Council of Constantinople; Bishop of Constantinople; Orations 38-40
381: Retreat to Nazianzus and Arianzus, the family estate: life of a hermit, writer and poet
390: Dies, aged *c*.60

Gregory of Nyssa, Bishop

c.**334:** Born; educated at home
362: Shares his brothers' monastic life in Annisa, the family estate
368: Writes *On virginity*
372: Consecrated Bishop of Nyssa
374: Exiled by Valens for his Nicene views
375: Writes *Not three Gods*
380: Writes *On the Soul and the Resurrection, On the Making of Man, On the Holy Trinity*
380/1: Present at the Council of Constantinople
382: Writes *Against Eunomius, The life of Moses, The life of Macrina*
382/386: Preaches the Council of Constantinople's findings in the East
395: Dies, aged c60

Glossary

Some terms used in the fourth-century Trinitarian Controversy

Anomoios: the Greek word to say that the Son (and Holy Spirit) are unlike the Father. The position of Eunomius which was categorically rejected by the Nicene Orthodoxy, Athanasius and the Cappadocians.

Apollinarianism: after Apollinaris of Laodociea who believed that Christ was of the same substance as the Father but that his human mind was replaced by divine intelligence, so compromising his full humanity.

Homoian: the Greek word which drops the use of the root word *ousia* (substance) and suggests the Son is like the Father but not the same substance. Their tag was "like in will; but unlike in substance"; this was also rejected by the Cappadocians.

Homoiousios: the Greek word used to say that the Son is like the Father and likewise the Spirit. It did not deliver the same certainty as *homoousios*, so was rejected by the Cappaocians in relation to the Son and the Spirit.

Homoousios: the Greek word used at Nicaea and beyond to denote that the Son is of the same substance or essence as the Father or from the substance of the Father; approved by Athanasius and the Cappadocian Fathers. The benchmark of the Trinity later extended to the Holy Spirit.

Hypostasis: the Greek word used to distinguish each individual in the Trinity. It means that which exists in its own right, and emphasises the distinctive role and being of each member of the Trinity.

Ousia: the Greek word meaning essence and substance; that which is the very defining essence or substance of God's being.

Sabellian: from Servetus who taught that God had three ways of being God, often called Modalist (three modes). It fails to do justice to the three *hypostases* in the Trinity. Emphasising the unity of the Godhead at the expense of their individuated being.

Some terms commonly used in the description of the contemplation of God and the development of our understanding

Apophatic: the understanding of God being beyond knowledge. It means speaking of God in the negative: incomprehensible, unknowable, unseen, indescribable, etc. This is symbolised by his presence being wrapped in thick darkness (e.g. Exodus 20:21).

Epectasis: stretching forward of the soul to hold onto what is not yet grasped, based on Philippians 3:13.

Epinoia: the discipline of reflecting on the person and qualities of God in order to understand them.

Eros: a truly ecstatic love as seen in the Song of Songs, sometimes described as the *agape* (God's self offering love) of the Gospels.

Idiomata: the properties of God on which we may reflect; e.g. Christ being the door, the way, the bread, the light.

Parrhesia: speaking with boldness and confidence. In public speaking, forthright; in private seeking of God, confident.

Notes

1. David Hunt, "The successors of Constantine" in *The Cambridge Ancient History*, ed. Averil Cameron and Peter Garnsey, vol. 13, The Late Empire, AD 337–425 (hereafter *TCAH*) (Cambridge University Press, 1997), p. 1.
2. Eusebius, *Life of Constantine*, tr. Averil Cameron and Stuart Hall (Clarendon Press, 1999), p. 61.
3. Ibid., p. 62.
4. Ibid.
5. Ibid., p. 65–72.
6. *TCAH*, op. cit., p. 20.
7. Ibid.
8. Peter Heather, *The Fall of the Roman Empire: A New History* (Pan, 2005), p. 15.
9. Ibid., p. 16.
10. Ibid., p. 20.
11. Ibid., p. 28.
12. Ammanius, quoted in ibid., p. 155.
13. Ibid., p. 182.
14. Ibid., pp. 164–165.
15. Ibid., p. 182.
16. Acts 20:29–30.
17. Acts 4.
18. Acts 26:31.
19. Henry Chadwick, *The Early Church* (Penguin, 1993), p. 29.
20. Ibid., p. 123.
21. Peter Brown, *Augustine of Hippo* (University of California Press, 1969), p. 334.
22. See Acts 5:17, 24:5, 24:15, 26:5; 1 Corinthians 11:19.
23. Chadwick, op. cit., p. 561.
24. See Romans 7:4.
25. See Galatians 1:6, 3:1–9.
26. John 1:14.
27. 1 John 4:2.
28. Chadwick, op. cit., p. 74.
29. Ibid., p. 35.
30. Ibid., p. 80.
31. Ibid., p. 86.
32. Ibid., p. 88.
33. Ibid., p. 91.
34. Tacitus, *Annals*, 2:42.
35. Acts 2:9.
36. See Acts 13 and 14.
37. 1 Peter 1:1.
38. Oration 43.9, 505A in Philip Rousseau, *Basil of Caesarea* (University of California Press, 1998), p. 4.
39. See Gregory of Nyssa, *The Life of Saint Macrina*, tr. Kevin Corrigan (Wipf & Stock, 2005), p. 27.
40. See Anthony Meredith, *Gregory of Nyssa* (Routledge, 1999), p. 2.
41. See Oration 43 in Rousseau, op. cit., p. 4.
42. Lewis Ayres, *Nicaea and its Legacy: An Approach to*

Fourth-Century Trinitarian Theology (Oxford University Press, 2009), p. 188.
43. Oration 43.4 in Rousseau, op. cit., p. 4.
44. Brian Daley, *Gregory of Nazianzus* (Routledge, 2006), p. 3.
45. Ibid., p. 3.
46. "Concerning his own Affairs" in Gregory of Nazianzus, *Three Poems*, tr. Denis Molaise Meehan (The Catholic University of America Press, 2001); see also "Letter 30 to Philagrius grieving the loss of Caesarius" in Daley, op. cit., p. 175.
47. Oration 8 in Daley, op. cit., p. 68.
48. Rousseau, op. cit., p. 6.
49. Daley, op. cit., p. 7.
50. Gregory of Nazianzus, Oration 4 "Adversus Julianin imperatorem" in *Sources chrétiennes* (hereafter *SC*); see also Daley, op. cit., pp. 6–8.
51. Daley, op. cit., p. 4.
52. Gregory of Nazianzusm, Epitaph 5 on Thespesios, *PG* 38:12-13; Daley, op. cit., p. 5
53. Daley, op. cit., p. 4.
54. "Concerning his own Life" in Gregory of Nazianzus, *Autobiographical Poems*, tr. and ed. Caroline White (Cambridge University Press, 1996) p. 25.
55. Rousseau, op. cit., p. 30.
56. See Eunapius, *Lives*, B475.
57. Daley, op. cit., p. 7.
58. "Oration on Basil" in Philip Schaff, *The Nicene and Post Nicene Fathers*, Series II (hereafter *NPNF*) (T. & T. Clark, 1886–1900; page numbers refer to Cosimo Classics, 2007), vol. VII, p. 400.
59. Homily 358.8 in ibid, p. 401.
60. Ibid.; he called Athens an empty happiness.
61. Acts 17:21.
62. Rousseau, op. cit., p. 45.
63. An example of his use of classical literature may be found in Basil's letter to Eusthathius the Philosopher, Letter 1 in Basil the Great, *Letters*, tr. Roy J. Deferrari (Loeb, 1926), vol. I, p. 5.
64. Rousseau, op. cit., p. 52.
65. Daley, op. cit., p. 8; see especially Gregory's Oration II, *In his Defence of his Flight to Pontus*, when Gregory tells why he fled to Pontus for three months following his Ordination in 361 to a rather sceptical congregation in Nazianzus on his return; *NPNF*, vol. VII, p. 204.
66. Daley, op. cit., p. 34.
67. Oration 38:7 in Daley, op. cit., p. 36.
68. Gregory of Nazianzus, "Letter 47 to Basil on the division of his Diocese" in *SC*.
69. Oration 8 in Daley, op. cit., p. 66.
70. Daley, op. cit., p. 28.
71. Ibid., p. 28.
72. "Carm. de Vita Sua" l.221 in *NPNF*, vol. VIII, p. 190.

73. See "Letter 11 to Gregory of Nyssa" in Meredith, op. cit., pp. 3–4.
74. See 2 Timothy 1:10.
75. John 1:1.
76. Bertrand Russell, A *History of Western Philosophy* (Routledge, 2007), p. 109.
77. Ibid.
78. Ibid.
79. Meredith, op. cit., p. 11.
80. Russell, op. cit., p. 123.
81. Ibid., p. 134.
82. Ibid., p. 136.
83. Meredith, op. cit., p. 11.
84. Russell, op. cit., p. 145.
85. See Chadwick, op. cit., p. 76.
86. Exodus 3:14.
87. Plotinus, *Enneads*, tr. McKenna, v. 3.14, available at <http://classics.mit.edu/Plotinus/enneads.html>. See also Bertrand Russell, *History of Western Philosophy* (Routledge, 20016), p. 274.
88. Russell, op. cit., p. 273.
89. Ibid., pp. 273–274.
90. Porphyry, *Life of Plotinus*, 3, 14, 20.
91. Chadwick, op. cit., p. 100.
92. See Walter Bauer's *Orthodoxy and Heresy in Earliest Christianity*, pp. 44–60; quoted in Joseph Trigg, *Origen* (Routledge, 1998), p. 16.
93. Trigg, op. cit., p. 24.
94. Chadwick, op. cit., p. 105.
95. *Periarchon*, quoted in Morwenna Ludlow, *The Early Church* (I. B. Tauris and Co. Ltd., 2009), p. 79.
96. *Periarchon*, op. cit., 2.11.6; see also Trigg, op. cit., p. 26ff.
97. *Periarchon*, op. cit., 1.6.2 or 3.6.3; Trigg, op. cit., p. 30.
98. See T. H. L. Parker, *John Calvin: A Biography* (Westminster John Knox Press, 2007).
99. Trigg, op. cit., p. 39.
100. Ibid., p. 45.
101. Robin Lane Fox, *The Classical World* (Penguin, 2005), p. 66.
102. Ibid., p. 197.
103. Tom Holland, *Rubicon* (Abacus, 2010), p. 324.
104. William Shakespeare, *Anthony and Cleopatra*, Act II, Scene 2.
105. Luke 2:1.
106. Eusebius, *Historia*, II.17.
107. Ludlow, op. cit., p. 76.
108. Ayres, op. cit., p. 16.
109. Basil Studer, *Trinity and Incarnation: The Faith of the Early Church* (T. & T. Clark, 1993).
110. Ayres, op. cit., p. 21.
111. Ibid., p. 22.
112. See Ayres, op. cit., p. 23, quoting Alastair H. B. Logan, "Origen and Alexandrian Wisdom Christology" in *Origeniana Tertia: The Third International Colloquium for Origen Studies*, eds. Richard Hanson and Henri Crouzel (edizioni Dell'Ateneo, 1985), pp. 123–129.
113. Ibid., p. 24.
114. Ibid.
115. Trigg, op. cit., p. 24.
116. Ayres, op. cit., p. 25.

117. Ibid., p. 25.
118. Ibid., footnote to p. 25.
119. Rowan Williams, *Arius: Heresy and Tradition* (Darton, Longman and Todd, 1987; second edn. SCM Press, 2001), p. 29.
120. Ibid., p. 30.
121. Ibid., p. 31.
122. Ibid., p. 32.
123. Chadwick, op. cit., p. 124.
124. Ibid.
125. Williams, op. cit., p. 30. Many scholars put Arius' birth in the 250s, e.g. *Oxford Dictionary of the Christian Church*, eds. F. L. Cross and E. A. Livingstone (Oxford University Press, 2005).
126. Differing timetables have been suggested by Opitz, Hanson and others—see the suggested table of dates in Williams, op. cit., p. 58.
127. Ibid., p. 96.
128. Ibid., p. 97.
129. Ibid., p. 95ff.
130. Ibid., p. 231–232.
131. Urkunde 14:11.
132. Williams, op. cit., p. 43ff; see his discussion of the *he philarchos* document.
133. Ayres, op. cit., p. 89, quoting Thoedoret *Ecc. Hist.* 1.743-4 and *Ep. Caes.* 4–6.
134. Ayres, op. cit., p. 90–91.
135. J. N. D. Kelly, *Early Christian Doctrines* (A. & C. Black Ltd, 1960), p. 232.
136. Ibid., p. 232.
137. Ayres, op. cit., p. 92.
138. See Barnes, "A Note on the Term Homoiousios" in *Zeitschrift fur Antike Christentums* 10 (2006).
139. Ayres, op. cit., p. 93.
140. A heresy which confused the permanent distinction of each member of the Trinity.
141. Ibid., p. 98.
142. Kelly, op. cit., p. 234.
143. Ibid., p. 236.
144. Ayres, op. cit., p. 97.
145. Williams, op. cit., p. 81.
146. Ibid., p. 81.
147. "The Arabic History of the Patriarchs", quoted by Khaled Anatolios, *A New Eusebius* (SPCK, 2004), p. 3.
148. Oration 21:6 in *NPNF*, vol. VII, p. 269.
149. Anatolios, op. cit., p. 4.
150. Ibid., p. 14.
151. Ibid., p. 17.
152. Ibid., p. 19.
153. Ayres, op. cit., p. 106.
154. Ibid., pp. 118–119.
155. Ibid., p. 107.
156. Ibid., p. 111.
157. Ibid., p. 114.
158. Barnes, op. cit., p. 82; cf. Festal Index 18, quoted in Anatolios, op. cit., p. 25.
159. "Defence of his Flight 24", quoted in Anatolios, op. cit., p. 26–7.
160. See Athanasius' work *De Decretis*, on the decrees of Nicaea.
161. Athanasius, 3rd Oration AD 34 in Ayres, op. cit., p. 115.
162. Ayres, op. cit., p. 91.
163. See Ayres, op. cit., p. 140.

164. See Theodoret, *Haer. Fab.* 4, 3 and J. N. D. Kelly, op. cit., p. 249.
165. Epiphanius, *Panarion* 73.4.4 and Ayres, op. cit., p. 152.
166. See *De synodis* 41—written from the desert during his third exile.
167. Ayres, op. cit., p. 155.
168. Cyril, *Catechetical Lectures* 11:4 (Patrologia Series Graeca 33).
169. Ayres, op. cit., p. 160.
170. Ibid., footnote to p. 145.
171. Ibid., p. 145.
172. Ibid., p. 146.
173. Ibid., footnote to p. 146.
174. See John 14:28.
175. See Ayres, op. cit., p. 152.
176. See Simonetti, *La Crisi*, p. 234ff.
177. See *TCAH*, pp. 2–3.
178. Ayres, op. cit., p. 188.
179. Letter 2 in Deferrari, op. cit., pp. 13–15.
180. The Arian slogan: "There was a time when he was not".
181. Letter 7 in ibid., p. 51.
182. Ayres, op. cit., p. 188.
183. Letter 242 in Deferrari, op. cit., vol. III, p. 433.
184. Ayres, op. cit., p. 189.
185. On the debate surrounding this, see G. L. Prestige, *St Basil the Great and Apollinaris of Laodicea* (SPCK, 1956).
186. See "Contra Eunomium" in *SC*, 299, 305.
187. Ibid., 1:5.
188. Ayres, op. cit., p. 191.
189. Origen, "Comm. John" in *SC* 0.37.246.
190. Ayres, op. cit., p. 192.
191. Ibid., p. 197.
192. See Letter 16, "Against Eunomius, the heretic" in Defarrari, op. cit., p. 117.
193. See especially Basil's Letter to his brother Gregory of Nyssa, Letter 38 written probably in 369/70 where he writes, "if you transfer to divine dogmas the principle of differentiation which you recognise as applying to substance and person in human affairs you will not go astray. In the Trinity there is "no variation of life-giving nature" and "each is apprehended separately"; Defarrari, op. cit., p. 209.
194. Meredith, op. cit., p. 3.
195. Ibid., p. 5.
196. Ibid., p. 6.
197. Deferrari, op. cit., p. 357ff.
198. *NPNF*, vol. V, chronology of Gregory's writings.
199. *NPNF*, vol. V, p. 332.
200. Ibid.
201. See "Contra Eunomium" i.227 in *SC*.
202. *NPNF*, vol. V, p. 334.
203. Ibid., p. 335.
204. Ayres, op. cit., p. 352.
205. Ibid., p. 352.
206. Ibid., p. 355.
207. See "Contra Eunomium" 1:37 in *SC*.
208. See Eunomius, *The Extant Works*, tr. Richard Vagionne

(Oxford University Press, 1987).
209. The best translation of which is to be found in Werner Jaeger, *Gregorii Nysseni Opera* (hereafter *GNO*) (Brill, 1986), 1, 2.
210. Book 1:15 in *NPNF*, vol. V, p. 51.
211. Meredith, op. cit., p. 64.
212. Ibid., p. 65.
213. Ibid., p. 65.
214. Gregory of Nazianzus, "De vita sua" in *Autobiographical Poems*, tr. Caroline White (Cambridge University Press, 1996), 350–356.
215. Ibid., 440–450.
216. Oration 43:59, "Oration at Basil's Funeral" in *Sources Chrétiennes* 384.
217. See Daley, op. cit., p. 9.
218. A phrase of Origen's included by Gregory in his letter to Cledonius, Ep. 101.
219. Gregory of Nazianzus, *On God and Christ: The Five Theological Orations and Two Letters to Cledonius*, tr. Lionel Wickham and Frederick Williams (St Vladimir's Seminary Press, 2002), p. 156.
220. Ibid., p. 113.
221. Ayres, op. cit., p. 169.
222. C.Th XVI.1.2.; see André Piganiol, *L'Empire Chretien (325–395)* (Presses Universitaires De France, 1972), pp. 237–8, quoted in *TCAH*, p. 103.
223. John McGuckin, *St Gregory of Nazianzus: An Intellectual Biography* (St Vladimir's Seminary Press, 2001), p. 240.
224. *TCAH*, p. 102.
225. "De Deitate Filii et Spiritus Sancti" in *Patrologia Graeca*, ed. J. P. Migne (hereafter *PG*) (Paris, 1886), XLVI.557–8; also *TCAH*, p. 103.
226. Daley, op. cit., p. 15.
227. Especially Orations 20–42, including those against Eunomians and on the Trinity, especially Orations 27–31; see especially McGuckin, op. cit., in which McGuckin weaves together the events in 379/380 whilst Gregory conducted his theological campaign at Anastasia with the theology of his Orations 27–31.
228. Daley, op. cit., p. 15.
229. White, op. cit., 1312–1324.
230. Ibid., 1532–1559.
231. Gregory of Nazianzus, *The Fathers of the Church: Select Orations*, tr. Martha Vinson (Catholic University of America Press, 2003), p. 181.
232. Orations 27–31 in Williams and Wickham, op. cit.
233. Orations 39, 40, and 38 respectively, in *NPNF* vol. VII, pp. 352ff, 360ff, and 345ff respectively.
234. Oration 42 in ibid, pp. 385ff.
235. "Farewell Oration" section 15, in ibid., p. 385–395.
236. Oration 29 "On the Son" in Williams and Wickham, op. cit., pp. 87–88.
237. Ayres, op. cit., p. 253.

238. Ibid., p. 236.
239. For greater discussion of these issues read Ayres, op. cit., pp. 236–240.
240. See Letter 361 to Apollinarius, Deferrari, op. cit., vol. IV, p. 331.
241. See Chadwick, op. cit., p. 89.
242. Ibid., p. 113.
243. See Khaled Anatolios, *Athanasius* (Routledge, 2004), p. 27, quoting *Athanasius' defence before Constantius* 30, ed. M. Tetz (Kirchenvater-Kommission der Preussichen Akademie der Wissenschaften Berlin, 1934–2000), Athanasius Werke 1/1.
244. Anatolios, op. cit., p. 30.
245. Ibid., p. 212.
246. Ibid., p. 213.
247. "Letters to Serapion", 16 in *PG* 568C, quoted by Anatolios, op. cit., p. 215.
248. Anatolios, op. cit., p. 215.
249. Ibid., p. 213.
250. Ibid., pp. 220–221.
251. Ibid., p. 223.
252. Ibid., p. 230.
253. Ibid., p. 229.
254. Ibid., p. 232, para. 33.
255. See ibid., pp. 225–227. N.B. this is the only instance of Athanasius's direct application of the term *homoousios* to the Holy Spirit. It is sometimes claimed that the designation is repeated in *PG* 2:6 (see R. P. C. Hanson, *The Search for the Christian Doctrine of God: The Arian Controversy* (T. & T. Clark, 1988), p. 752, note 70) or *PG* 3:1 (see C. R. B. Shapland, *The Letters of Saint Athanasius Concerning the Holy Spirit* (Epworth Press, 1951), p. 133, note 7), but in both these cases the term is applied to the Son's relation to the Father (Anatolios, op. cit., p. 277).
256. Anatolios, op. cit., p. 232.
257. Rousseau, op. cit., p. 245.
258. "Letter to the Westerners" 268 in Deferrari, op. cit., vol. IV, p. 98.
259. Ibid., pp. 99–100.
260. Ibid., p. 95.
261. *NPNF*, vol. VIII, p. xxvii.
262. Rousseau, op. cit., p. 239.
263. Ibid., p. 240.
264. Letter 119, Deferrari, op. cit., p. 243.
265. Deferrari, op. cit., p. 259ff.
266. For example, the use of the term "like without a difference" in speaking about Father and Son, Basil says, is to be preferred to "consubstantial"; see "Letter to Apollinarius" 361, Ibid, vol. IV, p. 335).
267. Ibid., pp. 252–253.
268. See Letter 223 in Deferrari, op. cit., vol. III, p. 287.
269. Basil of Caesarea, *On the Holy Spirit*, tr. Stephen Hildebrand, ed. John Behr (St Vladimir's Seminary Press, 2011), ch. 1, p. 22.
270. Ibid., ch. 2, p. 30.
271. Ibid., ch. 9:22, p. 53.
272. Ibid., ch. 16:37, p. 69.

273. Ibid., ch. 16:38, p. 71.
274. Ibid., ch. 16:39, p. 73.
275. Ibid., ch. 16:40, p. 74.
276. Ibid., ch. 16:39, p. 74.
277. Ibid., ch. 30:79, p. 121.
278. Ayres, op. cit., p. 209.
279. Ibid., p. 217.
280. Ibid.
281. Hildebrand, op. cit., p. 90.
282. Williams and Wickham, op. cit., p. 13.
283. Ibid., p. 117.
284. Ibid., p. 118.
285. Ibid., p. 119.
286. Ibid.
287. Ibid., p. 120.
288. Ibid., p. 121.
289. See John 15:26, "The Holy Spirit which proceeds from the Father".
290. Williams and Wickham, op. cit., p. 123.
291. See Oration 5:11 in ibid., p. 124.
292. Oration 5:14 in ibid. p. 127.
293. Oration 5:19 in ibid., p. 131.
294. Oration 5:29 in ibid., p. 139; and see 1 Corinthians 2:11, Romans 8:9, 1 Corinthians 2:14–16, 2 Corinthians 3:17, and 1 Corinthians 2:14–16.
295. Oration 5:33 in Williams and Wickham, op. cit., p. 143.
296. See Meredith, op. cit., p. 38.
297. Ibid.
298. *NPNF*, vol. V, pp. 315–6.
299. "We say nothing different from what the scriptures says"; ibid., p. 316.
300. Ibid., p. 317.
301. Ibid., p. 320.
302. Ibid., p. 322.
303. Ibid., p. 321.
304. Ibid.
305. *SC* 160 and Basil the Great, *On the Human Condition*, tr. Nonna Vera Harrison (St Vladimir's Seminary Press, 2005)—sometimes classified as homilies 10 and 11 of the *Hexaemeron*—and his nine homilies *On the Six Days of Creation* or *Hexaemeron* delivered probably extemporaneously as a Lent series but both where and when is uncertain (although some think it is near the end of his episcopacy during a period of heightening confidence and optimism before the imminent defeat of Valens and his replacement by Theodosius as Emperor—see Rousseau, op. cit., p. 319).
306. Russell, op. cit., p. 131.
307. Ibid., p. 146.
308. *NPNF*, vol. VIII, p. 52.
309. Homily 1:1 in *NPNF*, vol. VIII, p. 5.
310. For example Plato arguing for a progressive creation but not *ex nihilo*, whilst Aristotle argued for creation *ex nihilo*.
311. Homily 1:5 in ibid., p. 54.
312. Colossians 1:5.
313. Homily 1:5. in *NPNF*, op. cit.
314. Ibid.
315. Homily 8:4 in Basil the Great, *Exegetic Homilies*, tr. Agnes Clare Way (Catholic University of America Press, 2003), p. 124.

316. Homily 7:4 in ibid., pp. 112–113.
317. Homily 4:4 in ibid., pp. 44, 60.
318. Homily 4:1 in ibid., p. 55.
319. Homily 2:5 in ibid., p. 28.
320. Homily 6:7 in ibid., pp. 94–95.
321. Homily 5:1 in ibid., p. 67.
322. Isaiah 40.6.
323. Homily 5:2 in Way, op. cit., p. 69.
324. Homily 5:5 in ibid., p. 69.
325. Homily 7:3 in ibid., pp. 109–110.
326. Ibid.
327. Homily 8:8 in ibid., p. 133.
328. Ibid.
329. Ibid.
330. See "On the Making of Man" I:5 in *NPNF*, vol. V, pp. 389–390
331. "Introduction" in Harrison, op. cit., p. 21.
332. "On the Making of Man", VI:3 in *NPNF*, vol. V, p. 392.
333. Discourse 1:4 in Harrison, op. cit., p. 33.
334. Discourse 1:5 in ibid., p. 34.
335. Discourse 1:6 in ibid., p. 35.
336. Discourse 1:7 in ibid., p. 36.
337. Discourse 1:9 in ibid., p. 37.
338. "Introduction" in ibid., p. 21.
339. 1:18 in ibid., p. 45; and Hildebrand, op. cit.
340. Genesis 2:7.
341. Discourse 2:3 in Harrison, op. cit., p. 50.
342. Discourse 2:15 in ibid., p. 60.
343. Discourse 2:15–16 in ibid., pp. 61–62.
344. Discourse 2:4–5 in ibid., p. 51.
345. Ibid.; Emphasis is mine.
346. Discourse 2:5 in ibid., p. 52.
347. Discourse 2:11 in ibid., p. 57–58.
348. "On the Making of Man" XVII:1 in *NPNF*, vol. V, p. 406.
349. Ibid., p. 407.
350. Meredith, op. cit., p. 57.
351. *NPNF*, op. cit., p. 407.
352. XVI:11 in ibid., p. 405.
353. XVI:10 in ibid., p. 405.
354. VII:1 in ibid., p. 392.
355. XI:4 in ibid., pp. 396–7.
356. See XXX in ibid., p. 422ff.
357. See XXI-XXIX in ibid.
358. See Gregory of Nyssa, *On the Soul and the Resurrection*, tr. Catharine P. Roth (St Vladimir's Seminary Press, 1993), p. 11.
359. Ibid., p. 38.
360. Ibid., p. 37.
361. Ibid., p. 100.
362. Ibid.
363. Ibid., p. 51.
364. Ibid., p. 53.
365. Ibid., pp. 61–62.
366. Ibid., p. 118.
367. See ibid., p. 65ff.
368. Ibid., p. 68.
369. Ibid., p. 84.
370. Ibid., p. 85.
371. Gregory of Nazianzus, Oration 43 "Panegynic on St Basil" in *NPNF*, vol. VII, p. 395.
372. Basil the Great, *On Social Justice*, tr. C. Paul Schroeder (St Vladimir's Seminary Press, 2009), p. 74.
373. Ibid., p. 84.
374. See Rousseau, op. cit., p. 137.
375. Ibid., p. 80.
376. Ibid., p. 76.

377. Ibid. How many pastors have echoed Basil down the ages!
378. Ibid., p. 86.
379. Ibid., pp. 76–87.
380. Luke 12:16–21.
381. "I will tear down my barns" in Rousseau, op. cit., p. 68.
382. Ibid.
383. "To the Rich" in ibid., p. 46.
384. "Against those who lend at interest" in ibid., p. 90.
385. Ibid., p. 92.
386. Ibid., p. 96.
387. Ibid., p. 98.
388. Peter Brown, "The Rise and function of the Holy Man in Late Antiquity" in *The Journal of Roman Studies* 61 (1971), 80–101, p. 110, quoted in Sterk, *Renouncing the World, Yet Leading the Church: The Monk-Bishop in Late Antiquity* (Harvard University Press, 2004), p. 19.
389. Sterk, op. cit., p. 26, and Sozomen, *Historia ecclesiastica* (fifth-century), 6.34.
390. Sterk, op. cit.
391. Ibid., p. 40.
392. Oration 63 in *NPNF*, vol. VII, p. 416.
393. Oration 43:35 in ibid., p. 407.
394. Oration 63:36 in ibid., p. 407.
395. See Rousseau, op. cit., pp. 191–2.
396. Sterk, op. cit., pp. 28–29.
397. Canons 1, 9, 10 in ibid., p. 29.
398. Canons 14, 17, 13 in ibid.
399. See Canon 15 in ibid.
400. "On Renunciation of the World" in Basil the Great, *Ascetical Works*, tr. Sister Monica Wagner (New York, 1950), pp. 17–18.
401. Deferrari, op. cit., vol. I, pp. 135–139.
402. Ibid., pp. 451, 453.
403. Ibid., p. 21.
404. Ibid., p. 29.
405. Ibid., pp. 23–24.
406. McGuckin, op. cit., p. 94.
407. Ep. 4, *PG* 37.24–25.
408. Ep. 5, *PG* 37.24–25.
409. McGuckin, op. cit., p. 93.
410. Ibid., p. 96.
411. See ibid., p. 145.
412. Ibid., p. 146.
413. Ibid., p. 147.
414. Ibid., p. 148.
415. Oration 14:10–11 in Vinson, op. cit., pp. 45–46.
416. Oration 14:16 in ibid.
417. Oration 14:30 in ibid.
418. Oration 15:31 in ibid.
419. Oration 15:32 in ibid.
420. Oration 14:27–28 in ibid.
421. Oration 14:25 in ibid.
422. Oration 14:26 in ibid.
423. Edward Champlin, *Final Judgments: Duty and Emotion in Roman Wills, 200 B.C.–A.D. 250* (University of California Press, 1991), p. 29; quoted in Daley, op. cit., p. 184.
424. Oration 14:28 in Vinson, op. cit.
425. The Neocaseareans, some of whom were influenced by Sabellius who stressed the monarchy of the godhead at the cost of the distinctiveness of three persons, accused

Basil of not sufficiently defending Nicaea.
426. Letter 204 in Deferrari, op. cit., vol. III, p. 171. Also, see Rousseau, op. cit., p. 12.
427. Letter 204 in Deferrari, op. cit.
428. See Rousseau, op. cit., p. 13.
429. Oration 43:9 in *NPNF*, vol. VII, p. 398.
430. Oration 18 in *GNO*, vol. IX.
431. Corrigan, op. cit., p. 26.
432. See Ludlow, op. cit., p. 145.
433. "The Life of Paul the Hermit" in *Early Christian Lives*, tr. Caroline White (Penguin, 1998), p. 78.
434. Chadwick, op. cit., p. 178.
435. Ibid., p. 78.
436. Letter 223 in Deferrari, op. cit., pp. 295, 303.
437. Chistoph Jungck, *Sua vita* (Heidelberg, 1974), p. 37 l; Caroline White, op. cit., pp. 353–354.
438. Corrigan, op. cit., pp. 2, 28.
439. Ibid., p. 48.
440. Ibid., p. 42.
441. Letter 14 in Defarrari, op. cit., vol. I, pp. 110–111.
442. Letter 2 in ibid., vol. I, p. 11.
443. Ibid., p. 13.
444. "Against Eunomius" 2:85 in *PG* 44–46, quoted in Meredith, op. cit., p. 89.
445. Ibid., p. 90.
446. Ibid., p. 3.
447. Letter 11 in ibid. p. 3–4.
448. "On Virginity" ch. XI in *NPNF*, vol. V, p. 357.
449. Ibid., ch. II, p. 345.
450. Ibid., p. 345.
451. Ibid., p. 346.
452. Ibid., pp. 347–350.
453. Ibid., p. 357.
454. Ibid., ch. XXIII, pp. 368–9.
455. Ibid., ch. XXIV, p. 371.
456. Jean Daniélou, *From Glory to Glory: Texts from Gregory of Nyssa's Mystical Writings* (St Vladimir's Seminary Press, 1979), p. 12.
457. "Great Catechetical Discourse" 24 in *PG* 45.64–65a.
458. See Gregory of Nyssa, *Gregory of Nyssa: The Life of Moses*, tr. Abraham J. Malherbe and Everett Ferguson (Harper Collins, 2006), p. 56: "nothing evil can come into existence apart from our own free choice".
459. "Great Catechetical Discourse" ch. XXXII in *NPNF*, vol. V, p. 498.
460. Philippians 3:13.
461. Daniélou, op. cit., p. 53.
462. 2 Corinthians 3:18.
463. Daniélou, op. cit., p. 59.
464. "Against Eunomius" 12 in *PG* 45.940d–941d.
465. "Comm. on Canticle of Canticles" in *PG* 44.1029b-c.
466. Ibid., 44.833d–836a.
467. Ibid., 44.1037b-c.
468. Ibid., 44.1033d–1038a.
469. Ibid., 44.1000c.
470. Daniélou, op. cit., p. 23.
471. "On the Psalms" in *PG* 44.457a and Danielou, op. cit., p. 28.
472. Daniélou, op. cit., quoting from "Life of Moses" in *PG* 44.376c–377a.

473. Gregory of Nyssa, The Life of Moses, tr. Abraham J. Malherbe and Everett Ferguson (HarperOne, 2006), p. 81.
474. Song of Songs 3:1 (NIV).
475. Daniélou, op. cit., p. 30.
476. "Comm. on the Canticle" in *PG* 44892c-d.
477. Daniélou, op. cit., p. 32.
478. See Acts 2:15.
479. Daniélou, op. cit., p. 36, and Hans Lewy, *Sober Ebrietas* (Giessen, 1929).
480. See Revelation 1:9–10 and 2 Corinthians 12:1–6.
481. "Against Eunomius" in *PG* 45.94a-941b.
482. Song of Songs, and Daniélou, op. cit., p. 33 quoting I. Hausherr, *Ignorance infinite*, Orientalia Christiana periodica, 1936) p. 356.
483. Daniélou, op. cit., p. 46.
484. Ibid., p. 44.
485. See Song of Songs 5:1b: "I have drunk my wine and my milk".
486. "Commentary on the Canticles of Canticles" in *PG* 44.993 a-c.
487. Daniélou, op. cit., p. 43.
488. Lewes, *Re-Thinking Nyssa*, ed. Sarah Coakley (Blackwell Publishing, 2003), p. 31.
489. Ibid., p. 33.
490. Hans Urs von Balthasar, *Presence and Thought: Essay on the Religious Philosophy of Gregory of Nyssa* (Ignatius Press, 1995) pp. 18–20.
491. Meredith, op. cit., p. 54.
492. Gregory of Nyssa, "In Ecclesiastes" 8.1 in *GNO* 736B; quoted in Balthasar, op. cit., p. 47.
493. Gregory of Nyssa, "In Psalm" 8.1 in *GNO* 478C; quoted in Balthasar, op. cit., p. 60.
494. Ibid., pp. 78–79.
495. Homily V "Song of Songs" in *GNO* VI.138.4; XIII *GNO* VI.383.9.
496. Meredith, op. cit., p. 60.
497. Gregory of Nyssa, *Gregory of Nyssa: The Life of Moses*, tr. Abraham J. Malherbe and Everett Ferguson (Harper Collins, 2006), p. 4.
498. Meredith, op. cit., p. 69.
499. Ibid., p. 71.
500. Plato, *Timmaeus*, 27d.
501. Malherbe, op. cit., p. 38.
502. Exodus 20:21 (NIV).
503. Gregory of Nyssa, op. cit., p. 77.
504. Ibid., p. 85.
505. Plato, *Timaeus*, 28E.
506. Exodus 33:20; Malherbe, op. cit., pp. 104–105.
507. Meredith, op. cit., p. 78.
508. Balthasar, op. cit., p. 152.
509. Morwenna Ludlow, *Universal Salvation: Eschatology in the Thought of Gregory of Nyssa and Karl Rahner* (Oxford University Press, 2000), p. 63; quoted in Martin Laird, "Under Soloman's Tutelage: The Education Of Desire In The *Homilles On The Song Of Songs*" in *Re-thinking Gregory of Nyssa*, ed. Sarah Coakley (Wiley-Blackwell, 2003), p. 79.

510. Laird, op. cit., p. 80.
511. Meredith, op. cit., p. 80.
512. Psalm 17:12; Danielou, op. cit., p. 20; Homily 6.888C–893C.
513. Laird, op. cit., p. 88.
514. Canticle 4:28, 2–7 in Laird, op. cit., p. 89.
515. Canticle 1.40.9–12 in Laird, op. cit., p. 87.
516. Laird, op. cit., p. 86.
517. Meredith, op. cit., p. 94.
518. *Contra Eunomoius* 4:II, 637AB; quoted in Balthasar, op. cit., p. 136.
519. *Contra Eunomoius* 12:II, 637AB; quoted in ibid.
520. Ibid., p. 137.
521. See Acts 19:10. Paul evangelised the surrounding areas at Ephesus through his preaching in the Hall of Tyrannus, presumably people came in from outlying areas for goods and services and were evangelised in the process then taking the faith back to their rural communities where churches began.
522. Henry Chadwick, *The Role of the Christian Bishop in Ancient Society: Protocol of the Thirty-Fifth Colloquy, 25 February 1979* (Wipf & Stock, 2012), p. 1.
523. Hippolytus, *Apostolic Tradition*; quoted by Chadwick, op. cit., p. 2.
524. Ibid., p. 1.
525. Ibid., p. 2; Basil's letters nos. 53 and 54.
526. Ibid., p. 3.
527. "The Church as Institution" in *TCAH*, p. 263.
528. Ibid.
529. Chadwick, op. cit., p. 6.
530. See Sozomen, op. cit., vol. III, 3–4, and Chadwick, op. cit., p. 9.
531. Chadwick, op. cit., p. 11.
532. Carmen Lugubre 2.1.45 vv. 125–128, 139–146; quoted by McGuckin, op. cit., p. 220.
533. Ibid., p. 221.
534. See John Cassian, *De coenobuiorum institutis* XI.17; quoted in Sterk, op. cit., p. 13.
535. Chadwick, op. cit., p. 12.
536. Sterk, op. cit., p. 43.
537. Vols. I–IV in Deferrari, op. cit.
538. Letter 8 in Deferrari, op. cit., vol. I, p. 51.
539. Ibid., p. 81.
540. Ibid., p. 97.
541. Ayres, op. cit., p. 24ff.
542. Deferrari, op. cit., Ibid., vol. III p. 63, see also Letter 210.
543. See Letter 125 in Deferrari, op. cit., vol. II, p. 259; Basil's attempt at gaining eusthathius' signature to Nicene Orthodoxy in 373 for the benefit of fellow bishop Theodotus of Nicopolis whose support Basil wanted in making episcopal appointments in Armenia for the Emperor proved fruitless. Theodotus would not give his support even after Eusthathius' signature and in the end Basil broke with

Eustathiuis because of his Apollinarianism; see Letter 223, ibid., vol. III p. 287.
544. Ibid., vol. II, p. 33.
545. Ibid., vol. III, p. 95.
546. Ibid., vol. II, p. 279.
547. Ibid., vol. IV, pp. XIII and XIV.
548. Ibid., vol. III, p. 33.
549. Ibid., vol. III, p. 33.
550. Letter 188 section IX in ibid., vol. III, p. 35.
551. Letter 217 section LXIX in ibid., vol. III, p. 255.
552. Letter 5 in ibid., vol. I, pp. 37–38.
553. Letter 301 in ibid., vol. IV, p. 227.
554. Ibid., p. 229.
555. Letter 45 in ibid., vol. I, pp. 278–283.
556. Ibid., p. 279.
557. Ibid., p. 281.
558. Ibid., p. 283.
559. Ibid., p. 291.
560. Letter 46 in ibid., p. 309.
561. See *TCAH*, p. 35.
562. See Letter 33 in ibid., vol. I, p. 185.
563. Letter 73 in ibid., vol. II, p. 61.
564. Letter 104 in ibid., vol. II, p. 197.
565. Letter 162, Deferrari, vol. II, p. 419.
566. White, op. cit., p. 443.
567. Gregory's scathing letter to Basil, Ep. 40 in *PG* 37.81–84; P. Gallay, *Langue et style de S. Gregoire de Nazianze dans sacorrespondence* (Paris, 1933) pp. 49–50, quoted in McGuckin, op. cit., p. 172.
568. McGuckin, op. cit., p. 171.
569. Ibid, p. 373.
570. Oration 43:37 in *PG* 36.545–548; McGuckin, op. cit., p. 175.
571. McGuckin, op. cit., p. 177.
572. Oration 43:49–50 in *PG* 36.560–561.
573. McGuckin, op. cit., p. 189.
574. Rousseau, op. cit., p. 235.
575. McGuckin, op. cit., p. 190, and Basil's Letters 74–76.
576. White, op. cit., II.405–414, p. 41.
577. See McGuckin, op. cit., p. 201.
578. Ibid., p. 192.
579. Oration 9 in Vinson, op. cit., p. 23.
580. See McGuckin, op. cit., p. 198.
581. Vinson, op. cit., p. 27.
582. *PG* 35.845, p. 204.
583. McGuckin, op. cit., p. 206.
584. Oration 16:14 in *NPNF*, vol. VII, p. 252.
585. Oration 17:9 in Vinson, op. cit., p. 91.
586. McGuckin, op. cit., p. 215.
587. Oration 13:4 in Vinson, op. cit., p. 38.
588. C. Ullman, *Gregorius von Nazianz der Theologe* (Gotha, 1967), p. 147; quoted by McGuckin, op. cit., p. 223.
589. See Oration 18:18 in *NPNF*, vol. VII, p. 260.
590. Oration 18:37 in Ibid., p. 267.
591. Oration 38:1 in ibid., vol. VII, p. 34.
592. Oration 39.11 in ibid., p. 356.
593. Oration 40:3 in ibid., p. 361.
594. Oration 42:14 in ibid., p. 390.
595. Oration 42:26–27 in ibid., p. 394.

596. Sterk, op. cit., p. 115.
597. Ibid., p. 104.
598. Ibid., p. 103.
599. Quoted in Sterk, op. cit., p. 104; *GNO* X.129.5-9; Stein, op. cit., pp. 47-49.
600. Sterk, op. cit., p. 106.
601. Ibid., p. 107.
602. Lewis Carroll, *Alice through the Looking Glass* (OUP Classics, 2009), ch. 6, p. 190.
603. Meredith, op. cit., pp. 104-5.
604. Ibid., p. 122.
605. Henry Chadwick, *Augustine of Hippo: A Life* (Oxford University Press, 2010), p. 42.
606. McGuckin, op. cit., pp. 264-265.
607. Meredith, op. cit., p. 13.
608. *Confessions*, X, viii, 15; quoted by Brown, op. cit., p. 168.
609. Ibid., pp. 154-155.
610. Meredith, op. cit., p. 55.
611. Ep. 122.1; Chadwick, op. cit., p. 96.
612. Gregory of Nyssa, *De infantibus* 3.176; quoted in Balthasar, op. cit., p. 11.
613. Ep. 204, Deferrari, op. cit., vol. III, p. 155ff.
614. Meredith, op. cit., p. 114.
615. Henry Chadwick, *The Early Church* (Penguin, 1993), p. 100.
616. Meredith, op. cit., p. 115.
617. See Deferrari, op. cit., vol. IV, p. 379ff.
618. Ibid., *Young Men* II, p. 381.
619. Ibid., *Young Men* III, p. 387.
620. Oration 14:5 in Vinson, op. cit., p. 42.
621. Danielou, op. cit., pp. 26-27.
622. "Commentary on the Song of Songs" in *PG* 44.945D-948A.
623. Quoted by Richard Harries, *The Times* (20 November 2012).
624. Letter 261 in Deferrari, op. cit., vol. III, p. 83.
625. Letter 101, Wickham, op. cit., p. 158.
626. Meredith, op. cit., p. 113.
627. Ibid.
628. Ibid.
629. Gregory of Nyssa, "In Pascha" in *GNO* 1:III, 604C; quoted in Balthasar, op. cit., p. 137.
630. Ibid, 1:609B.
631. Balthasar, op. cit., p. 137.
632. Letter 38 by Basil, commonly attributed to Gregory of Nyssa, in Deferrari, op. cit., vol. I, p. 226.
633. White, op. cit., pp. 696-702.
634. Gregory of Nyssa, "In Cant" 11, I000 AB in *GNO* 1:III, 604C; quoted in Balthasar, op. cit., p. 154-155.

Bibliography

Ayres, Lewis, *Nicaea and its Legacy: An Approach to Fourth-Century Trinitarian Theology* (Oxford University Press, 2009).

Balthasar, Hans Urs von, *Presence and Thought: Essay on the Religious Philosophy of Gregory of Nyssa* (Ignatius Press, 1995).

Basil the Great, *Ascetical Works*, tr. Sister Monica Wagner (New York, 1950).

Basil the Great, *Exegetic Homilies*, tr. Agnus Clare Way (Catholic University of America Press, 2003).

Basil the Great, *Letters*, vols. I–IV, tr. Roy J. Deferrari (Loeb, 1926).

Basil the Great, *On the Holy Spirit*, tr. Stephen Hildebrand, ed. John Behr (St Vladimir's Seminary Press, 2011).

Basil the Great, *On the Human Condition*, tr. Nonna Vera Harrison (St Vladimir's Seminary Press, 2005).

Basil the Great, *On Social Justice*, tr. C. Paul Schroeder (St Vladimir's Seminary Press, 2009).

Brown, Peter, *Augustine of Hippo* (University of California Press, 1969).

Chadwick, Henry, *Augustine: A Very Short Introduction* (Oxford University Press, 2001).

Chadwick, Henry, *Augustine of Hippo: A Life* (Oxford University Press, 2010).

Chadwick, Henry, *The Early Church* (Penguin, 1993).

Chadwick, Henry, *East and West: The Making of a Rift in the Church: From Apostolic Times until the Council of Florence* (Oxford University Press, 2005).

Coakley, Sarah, *Re-thinking Gregory of Nyssa* (Blackwell Publishing, 2003).

Daley, Brian, *Gregory of Nazianzus* (Routledge, 2006).

Daniélou, Dawn, *From Glory to Glory: Texts from Gregory of Nyssa's Mystical Writings* (St Vladimir's Seminary Press, 1979).

Fox, Robin Lane, *The Classical World: An Epic History of Greece and Rome* (Penguin, 2005).

Fry, Timothy (ed.), *The Rule of St Benedict in English* (The Liturgical Press, 1982).
Gregory of Nazianzus and Amrose, *Funeral Orations by Saint Gregory Nazianzen and Saint Ambrose* (New York, 1953).
Gregory of Nazianzus, *Three Poems*, tr. Denis Molaise Meehan (The Catholic University of America Press, 2001)
Gregory of Nazianzus, *On God and Christ*, tr. Lionel Wickham and Frederick Williams (St Vladimir's Seminary Press, 2002).
Gregory of Nazianzus, *Autobiographical Poems*, tr. and ed. Caroline White (Cambridge University Press, 1996).
Gregory of Nazianzus, *The Fathers of the Church: Select Orations*, tr. Martha Vinson (Catholic University of America Press, 2003).
Gregory of Nyssa, *Gregory of Nyssa: The Life of Moses*, tr. Abraham J. Malherbe and Everett Ferguson (Harper Collins, 2006).
Gregory of Nyssa, *On the Soul and the Resurrection*, tr. Catharine P. Roth (St Vladimir's Seminary Press, 1993).
Gregory of Nyssa, *The Lord's Prayer, The Beatitudes*, tr. Hilda C. Graef (Paulist Press, 1954).
Hardy, Edward R., *Christology of the Later Fathers* (Westminster John Knox Press, 1954).
Heather, Peter, *The Fall of the Roman Empire: A New History* (Pan, 2005).
Hilborn, David (ed.), *Evangelicalism and the Orthodox Church: A Report by the Evangelical Alliance Commission on Unity and Truth Among Evangelicals (Acute)* (Paternoster Publishing, 2001).
Holland, Tom, *Rubicon: The Last Years of the Roman Republic* (Anchor, 2005).
Hunt, David, "The successors of Constantine" in *The Cambridge Ancient History*, eds. Averil Cameron and Peter Garnsey (vol. 13: The Late Empire, AD 337–425) [TCAH] (Cambridge University Press, 1997).
Jerome, *Select Letters of St Jerome*, tr. F. A. Wright (William Heinemann/Harvard University Press, 1975).
Kelly, J. N. D., *Early Christian Doctrines* (A. & C. Black, 1960).
Khaled, Anatolius, *Athanasius* (Routledge, 2004).
Ludlow, Morwenna, *The Early Church* (I. B. Tauris and Co. Ltd., 2009).

McGuckin, John, *Saint Gregory of Nazianzus: An Intellectual Biography* (St Vladimir's Seminary Press, 2001).

Meredith, Anthony, *Gregory of Nyssa* (Routledge, 1999).

Meredith, Anthony, *The Cappadocians* (St Vladimir's Seminary Press, 2000).

Ramsey, Boniface, *Ambrose* (Routledge, 2005).

Rousseau, Philip, *Basil of Caesarea* (University of California Press, 1998).

Russell, Bertrand, *A History of Western Philosophy* (Routledge, 2007).

Sterk, Andrea, *Renouncing the World Yet Leading the Church: The Monk-Bishop in Late Antiquity* (Harvard University Press, 2004).

Stevenson, J. (ed.), *A New Eusebius: Documents illustrative of the history of the Church to A.D. 337* (SPCK, 1975).

Schaff, Philip, *The Nicene and Post Nicene Fathers* [NPNF], Series II, vols. V, VII, VIII (T. & T. Clark, 1886–1900; page numbers refer to Cosimo Classics, 2007). Available at <http://www.tertullian.org/fathers2/>.

Trigg, Joseph W., *Origen* (Routledge, 1998).

Ware, Kallistos, *The Orthodox Way* (St Vladimir's Seminary Press, 1979).

Williams, Rowan, *Arius: Heresy and Tradition* (Darton, Longman, and Todd, 1987; second edn. SCM Press, 2001).

Williams, Rowan, *The Wound of Knowledge: Christian Spirituality from the New Testament to St. John of the Cross* (Darton, Longman, and Todd, 1990).

Wright, Tom, *Virtue Reborn* (SPCK, 2010).

Index

Ablabius 69, 70
Abraham 148, 153, 158
Acacius of Caesarea 57, 58
Achillas 43, 45
Actium, Battle of 37
Adrianople, Battle of 5, 173, 196
Aetius 59–60, 85, 90, 94, 190
agape 28, 164
   see also love
Agrippa 6
Alamani 4
Alexander of Alexandria 39, 46, 50
   and Arius 43–5, 50
Alexander of Byzantium 45
Alexander the Great 36
Alexandria 12, 20, 31, 36–40, 85
   Athanasius in 51
   Church in 37, 38–9
   episcopacy 38–9
   Jewish Diaspora 38
   logos-sarx school 201
   and Origen 31–4, 35
   Plotinus in 30
   synod condemning Arius 45
Alypiane 138
Alypius of Iconium 15
Ambrose 168, 193–4
   and Basil of Caesarea 173–4, 194
Ambrosius 34
Ammianus Marcellinus 4
Ammon oracle 36
Ammonius Saccas 30, 31, 38
Amphilochius, Bishop of Iconium 14, 89, 93, 97, 170, 173, 174, 175
Amphilochius the Elder 14, 20
Anastasia chapel, Constantinople 77, 78, 80, 82, 97, 101, 185–6, 187, 193, 194, 204

Anatolis of Laodicaea 42
Annisa, Pontus 14, 61, 73, 91, 124, 134, 143, 144, 169
anomian party see *heterousian* party
Anthimos of Tyana 181, 183, 185
Anthony, St viii, 51, 142
Antioch 12, 75, 139, 166, 173
   Council of (AD 339) 51
   Council of, later moved
      to Constantinople *see*
      Constantinople: Council of (AD 381)
   Dedication creed 52, 60
   episcopal wars 170
   fourth Antioch creed 56
   logos-anthropos school 200–201
Antony, Mark 37
apathia 158
apocatastasis 192–3
Apollinarius of Laodicea 64, 75, 90
   and Basil of Caesarea 64, 88, 89, 90–91, 92, 201
   Christology 75, 201
   and Eustathius of Sebaste 90
   and the *logos* 75, 90, 201
apophatic theology/spirituality 66–7, 68, 69, 70
Aquileia 2
Aquinas, Thomas 28, 199
Arian controversy 8–9, 12–13, 43–84, 190
   Arian/semi-Arian Creeds 55, 61, 171
   and Athanasius 44, 45, 49–50, 52–3, 55, 56, 195
   and Basil of Caesarea 63–8, 171–2, 173–4, 181, 191–2
   and the Council of Constantinople 5, 65, 68, 187

227

and creation 30
developments following First
    Council of Sirmium 55
documents at root of 44
and Eunomius *see* Eunomius
and Gregory of Nazianzus 181
Gregory of Nyssa and the
    neo-Arians 69–73
and the *heterousian* party 59–60 *see
    also* Aetius; Eunomius
and the *homoian* party and
    creed 57–9, 60, 61, 172, 179, 181,
    192, 195–6
homoousios 46, 48, 49, 52, 55–7, 65,
    67, 84, 172, 187, 191–2
hypostasis 42, 44, 47, 48, 191
logos 30
and neo-platonism 40–42, 44, 64
and Nicaea 43–50 *see also* Nicene
    Creed and orthodoxy
and Origen 40, 44
ousia 42, 44, 47–8, 49, 55, 56, 191
roots of 39–40
and Sirmium *see* Sirmium
Ariminum, Council of (AD 359, Western
    Council) 55, 58, 178–9
Creed from 60, 61, 171
Aristarchus of Samos 108
Aristotelianism 28, 66
Aristotle 108
Arius 12, 39–40, 42–3, 49–50
    and Alexander of Alexandria 43–5,
        50
    and Constantine 195
    letter to Eusebius of Nicomedia 42,
        44
    and Marcellus of Ancyra 89
    ordination as deacon 39
    ordination as priest 43
    Thalia 44, 52
    theological controversy *see* Arian
        controversy
Arles, Council of (AD 353) 54, 55
asceticism 12, 28
    and Athanasius 55

and Basil of Caesarea 124–5,
    129–33, 143–4, 146–8 *see also*
    Basiliad/Basileiados
and Gregory of Nazianzus 74, 75,
    134–8, 145, 168
origins of ascetic life in
    Cappadocia 142–5
the philosophic life and the search
    for virtue 146–8
and renunciation viii, ix, 132–3,
    134–5, 136–8
solitude *see* solitude
see also contemplation and the
    contemplative life; monasticism
Athanasius viii, 20, 39, 50–54, 173
    in Alexandria 51
    and Anthony 142
    and the Arian controversy 44, 45,
        49–50, 52–3, 55, 56, 195
    and Basil of Caesarea 139, 140, 173
    Cappadocians as bridge between
        Athanasius and Augustine 193–5
    and Constantius 54, 85–6
    at Council of Tyre 51
    De incarnatione 202
    De Synodis 57
    Defence before Constantius 86
    Defence of his Flight 86
    education 51
    exile in Egyptian desert 55, 56, 85,
        86–8, 142
    exile in Rome 51–2, 56
    exile in Tyre 51
    Festal Letter 51
    *Against the Greeks—On the
        Incarnation* 51
    Gregory of Nazianzus's oration
        on 50–51
    History of the Arians 53, 86
    and the Holy Spirit 86–8
    hypostasis 52
    Letters to Serapion 86, 88
    Life of Anthony 86
    Melitian accusation against 51
    and Nicaea 20, 46, 52
    Orations against the Arians 52, 56

Athanasius (*cont.*)
  rise of 50–54
  and the Trinity 52–3, 56, 57, 86–8, 96, 190
  and the Tropici 86
Athens 20–22
  Basil in 21–2
  Gregory of Nazianzus in 20–22, 24
Augustine of Hippo 7, 151, 167–8, 194–5
  Cappadocians as bridge between Athanasius and 193–5
Augustus (Octavian) 37
Autun 2

Balthasar, Hans Urs von 159–60, 202
baptism 1, 80, 87, 93, 102, 186–7
Basil of Ancyra 56–7, 58, 60, 85, 174, 192
Basil of Caesarea (St Basil the Great) 12, 61–8
  Ad adulescentes 22
  and Ambrose 173–4, 194
  and Amphilochius 14, 89, 93, 170, 173, 174, 175
  at Annisa 14, 61, 91, 124, 134, 143, 144, 169
  and Apollinarius 64, 88, 89, 90–91, 92, 201
  and the Arian controversy 63–8, 171–2, 173–4, 181, 191–2
  asceticism 124–5, 129–33, 143–4, 146–8 see also *Basiliad/Basileiados*
  Asceticon 130, 132–3
  and Athanasius 139, 140, 173
  in Athens 21–2
  baptism 61
  and Basil of Ancyra 174, 192
  and the *Basiliad* ix, 125, 128–30, 134–5, 170, 199
  care of the poor 199, 204
  and Church discipline 175, 177–8
  compared with Moses 189
  contemplation 61–2, 67, 96–7, 124, 189
  Contra Eunomius 63–7, 84, 192
  correspondence 61, 170–80
  creation of dioceses at Sasima and Nyssa 13, 181
  education 14, 15–16, 19, 21–2, 61
  episcopal ministry 170–80, 203–4
  epistolary networking 173–4
  and Eunomius 63–8, 84
  and Eusebius of Caesarea 124
  and Eusebius of Samosata 173, 174, 180
  and Eustathius of Sebaste 54, 62, 88, 89, 90, 91–3, 143, 172, 174, 192
  family background 13–14, 15, 197
  feast day vii, 124
  Gregory of Nazianzus's correspondence with 61
  Gregory of Nazianzus's oration on 21, 74, 125, 140, 181
  and Gregory Thaumaturgus 13, 197
  Hexaemeron 109–19
  and the Holy Spirit 62, 67, 88–97, 174
  On the Holy Spirit 67, 92–7, 170, 174
  and human life 108, 109–19
  illnesses 180
  letters 170–80
  and Marcellus of Ancyra 84, 88, 91
  and marriage 114, 176–7
  Moralia 130, 132, 170, 176
  and Nectarius 176
  and Nicene theological development and orthodoxy 63–8, 83–4, 124, 171–2, 173–4
  ordination as deacon 54, 61
  ordination as priest 62, 125
  pastoral care 174–80
  penalty instructions for sexual misdemeanours 175
  Philocalia (with Gregory of Nazianzus) 35, 62
  relations with Gregory, his brother 68–9
  relations with Gregory of Nazianzus 13, 35, 61, 62, 73–4, 134–5, 171, 180–81, 182–4

and Sabellianism 172
and solitude 146–8
and the Spirit-fighters 88, 89, 93
spiritual formation, pedigree and development 139–40, 189, 197
and taxation of the Church 179
treatise on reading pagan literature 198
trial before Modestus 181
and the Trinity 63–8, 93–4, 171–2, 191–2
and Valens 13, 68, 172, 181
and virtue 21, 22, 127, 130, 132, 134, 147
Basil the Elder 14, 15
Basil (priest) 92
Basiliad/Basileiados ix, 125, 128–30, 135, 170, 199
and Gregory of Nazianzus 129–30, 134–5
Benedict 28
rule of 132, 142
Bishop, office of *see* episcopacy
Bithynia 15
synod in 45
Bright, Paul vii

Caecilian 7
Caesar, Julius 37
Caesarea, Cappadocia 12, 20
and Basil 63, 124, 125–7, 129, 134, 136, 143, 170, 171, 180–81 see also *Basiliad/Basileiados*
Basiliad see *Basiliad/Basileiados*
famine 125–7
monasticism 128–30, 135 see also *Basiliad/Basileiados*
Caesarea, Palestine 6, 12, 13, 20, 34, 45, 62, 65, 140
Caesarion 37
Caesarius of Nazianzus 15–16, 20
will of 179
Calcidius 29
Callisthenes (correspondent of Basil) 179
Callisthenes of Olynthus 36

Callistus 11
Cappadocia vii, 12–13
Caesarea *see* Caesarea, Cappadocia
Church in 13
division under Valens 181
famine 125–7
origins of ascetic life in 142–5
relations between monks and bishops 168–9
Cappadocian Fathers
apophatic theology 66–7, 68, 69, 70
as bridge between Athanasius and Augustine 193–5
and contemplation *see* contemplation and the contemplative life
education 14, 15–16, 19–20, 21–2, 197
and human life *see* human life and the doctrine of man
Origen's influence on 140
and service *see* service
and social justice *see* social justice
and solitude *see* solitude
spiritual roots and development 140–41, 189, 197
struggle for orthodoxy *see* orthodoxy, struggle for
and the Trinity *see* Trinity, doctrine of persons and relations within the Godhead
see also Basil of Caesarea (St Basil the Great); Gregory of Nazianzus; Gregory of Nyssa
Carthage 3, 167
Cassian, John viii, 168–9
Chadwick, Henry 8
chain of being 30, 31
Chalcedon, Council of (AD 451) 82, 202
Christology
of Apollinarius of Laodicea 75, 201
Arian controversy *see* Arian controversy
Christ and the Trinity *see* Trinity, doctrine of persons and relations within the Godhead
of Gregory of Nazianzus 201–2

Christology (*cont.*)
  of Gregory of Nyssa 202
  logos see *logos*
  monophysite 201
  Nestorian controversy 90, 193, 200–202
  and Nicaea see Nicaea, Council of (AD 325); Nicene Creed and orthodoxy
  of Paul of Samosata 48
Church
  in Alexandria 37, 38–9
  at Antioch 75
  Arian controversy see Arian controversy
  in Cappadocia vii, 13
  Chalcedon (AD 451) 82, 202
  discipleship see discipleship
  discipline 175, 177–8
  division in North Africa 7
  doctrinal struggle for orthodoxy see orthodoxy, struggle for
  Donatist 7
  Eastern 2, 7, 53, 54, 58, 174–80
  Edict of Milan (AD 313) 11
  episcopacy see episcopacy
  Eunomian 60–61
  and Hellenism see Hellenism; neo-Platonism; Platonism
  and human life see human life and the doctrine of man
  and Islam 7
  in Jerusalem 6
  and Judaism 8
  pacifism 6
  persecution 6–7, 35, 142, 167
  and Platonism see Platonism
  provincial Christian culture of the fourth century 19
  public penitents in Eastern Church 174–5
  and the Roman Empire 6–7, 167–8, 178–9
  service in the world see service
  and social justice see social justice
  spirituality see spirituality

  at start of the fourth century 5–12
  taxation 179
  and the Trinity see Trinity, doctrine of persons and relations within the Godhead
  Western 11, 28, 53, 54, 58
Church Councils 55
  Antioch (AD 339) 51
  Ariminum see Ariminum, Council of (AD 359, Western Council)
  Arles (AD 353) 54, 55
  Constantinople (AD 381) 5, 65, 68, 69, 77, 79–80, 169, 187, 188, 190
  Constantinople, Second (AD 553) 193
  Gangra 131
  Jerusalem (AD 49) 8
  Milan (AD 355) 54, 55
  Nicaea see Nicaea, Council of (AD 325)
  Rimini see Ariminum, Council of (AD 359, Western Council)
  and the rioting of peasant monks 143
  Seleukia (AD 359, Eastern Council) 55, 58
  Serdica (AD 346) 53
  Sirmium, First Council (AD 351) 53–4, 55
  Sirmium, Fourth Council (AD 358) 60
  Tyre (AD 335) 51
Cicero 3, 29
Cledonius 75, 138
  Gregory of Nazianzus's *Letters to Cledonius* 75, 201–2
Clement of Alexandria 10, 30, 31, 38, 39, 44
Cleomones 36
Cleopatra 37
Cloud of Unknowing 157
Constans 2, 53
Constantine I, the Great 1–2, 11, 50, 190
  conversion of 166, 167
  and Nicaea 45, 46, 49, 195
Constantine II 2

Constantinople 1–2, 5, 12, 49–50, 77
    Anastasia chapel 77, 78, 80, 82, 97, 101, 185–6, 187, 193, 194, 204
    Council of (AD 381) 5, 65, 68, 69, 77, 79–80, 169, 187, 188, 190
    Council, Second, of (AD 553) 193
    Creed (AD 381) 41, 59, 82, 83, 170
    Gregory of Nazianzus as Bishop and Metropolitan of 5, 23, 74, 76–9, 182, 185–7
    Hagia Sophia 139, 167
    Homoian Creed (AD 359) 58–9, 61, 172
Constantius 1, 2–3, 53, 54, 55, 58, 60, 61, 85, 178–9
    and Athanasius 54, 85–6
contemplation and the contemplative life viii, 22, 29, 96, 112, 142, 146, 147, 194–5, 199–200
    and action 22–3, 189, 194–5, 203–4
    and Augustine 194–5
    and Basil of Caesarea 61–2, 67, 96–7, 124, 146–7, 189 see also *Basiliad/Basileiados*
    contemplative leadership 196, 199–200
    and delight in God 194, 195
    and ecstasy 157–9, 200
    epinoia 66, 71
    and Gregory of Nazianzus 23, 135, 185
    and Gregory of Nyssa 71, 150, 156, 158, 160, 161, 162, 164, 188, 189, 194, 197, 198, 199–200
    monastic *see* monasticism
cosmogony, Platonic 29, 108–9
cosmology, Stoic 51
creation
    and the Arian controversy 44
    and Basil's *Hexaemeron* 109–19
    ex nihilo 29–30, 44
    God's pause before creation of man 116
    human life and the purpose of *see* human life and the doctrine of man
    of man in God's image 33, 116–17, 119, 120, 137, 151, 197
    and Origen 40
    Plato's cosmogony 29, 108–9
Cynics 23
Cyprian of Carthage 7
Cyril of Alexandria 39
    and the Nestorian controversy 90, 193, 200–201
Cyril of Jerusalem 56, 57

Damasus of Rome 76
Danielou, Jean 151
darkness, spiritual 155–7, 164–5, 189
Dated Creed 58
Decius, Emperor 6–7, 35
Dedication creed of Antioch 52, 60
Deferrari, Roy J. 171
Demetrius 34, 38
Demophilus of Constantinople 75, 76, 78
Demosthenes 181
desire 29, 122, 147
    eros 28, 160, 164, 195
    for God 95, 117, 154–5, 156–7, 160–61, 163–4, 194–5, 204
    sexual 9, 114, 146 see also *eros*
devil 9, 151–2, 165, 192
Dianius of Caesarea 61, 62, 171
Didymus the Blind 20
Diocletian 6
Dionysius of Alexandria 171
Dionysius of Milan 173–4
Dionysius of Rome 48
Dionysius I of Syracuse 26
discipleship 14, 107, 185, 203
    and human life *see* human life and the doctrine of man
    and renunciation viii, ix, 132–3, 134–5, 136–8 *see also* asceticism
doctrinal struggle for orthodoxy *see* orthodoxy, struggle for
Donatist Church 7
Donatus 7
Donne, John 154
Dragon, Gilbert 129

dualism, Platonic 27–8

Eastern Council, Seleukia (AD 359) 55, 58
ecstasy 157–9, 200
education
    Athanasius 51
    in Athens 21–2
    Basil of Caesarea 14, 15–16, 19, 21–2, 61
    classical/Hellenic 3, 14, 15–16, 19, 22, 197, 198
    Gregory of Nazianzus 15–16, 19–20, 22, 24–5
    Gregory of Nyssa 14, 15–16, 19, 25, 68
    imperial ban of Christians teaching in philosophic schools 198
Elijah 142, 146
Emmelia, St 140–41, 144
epectasis 152–5, 199, 200
Ephrem the Syrian 128
epinoia 66, 71
Epiphanius of Salamis 40, 43, 56
episcopacy
    in Alexandria 38–9
    Basil's episcopal ministry 170–80, 203–4
    city and country bishops 166–7
    and the conversion of Constantine 166, 167
    episcopal wars of Antioch 170
    Eunomian 61
    Gregory of Nazianzus's episcopal ministry 180–87
    Gregory of Nyssa's episcopal ministry 187–9
    monarchical 39
    the office and work of a bishop 166–89
    pastoral care *see* pastoral care
    relations between monks and bishops 168–9
    and the Roman Empire 167–8, 178–9, 196

    and the struggle for orthodoxy 170, 171–2 *see also* orthodoxy, struggle for
eros 28, 160, 164, 195
Essenes 8
Eudoxius
    as Bishop of Antioch 57, 59
    as Bishop of Constantinople 60, 63
    and Eunomius 60, 63
Eulalios 185
Eunapius: *Life* 21
Eunomius 59, 60, 63, 72, 85, 90, 190
    Apologetikos 63
    Apology for the Apology 63, 72
    and Basil of Caesarea 63–8, 84
    and Eudoxius 60, 63
    and Gregory of Nyssa 63, 68, 70, 72–3
    neo-Platonism 64, 65
    theology of the Godhead 64
Eupraxius 138
Eusebius of Caesarea 1, 38, 45, 46, 56, 63, 124, 136
    and Nicaea 46, 49
Eusebius of Nicomedia 1, 42, 45, 195
    letter from Arius 42, 44
    and Nicaea 46, 49
Eusebius of Samosata 173, 174, 180
Eustathius of Antioch 46, 49, 195
Eustathius of Sebaste 54, 62, 88, 89, 90, 91–3, 129, 143, 172, 174, 192
Evagrius Ponticus 138
evil
    and *apocatastasis* 192–3
    and Basil of Caesarea 113
    and Gnosticism 9
    and Gregory of Nyssa 108, 123, 151–2, 192–3
    and Origen 31, 192–3
    Plato's identification with non-being 192
    as violation of freedom 193
    see also devil

Fall of man
    Basil of Caesarea 111

Gregory of Nazianzus 137
Gregory of Nyssa 119-20, 151
Irenaeus 10
Origen 33
famine 125-7
Festus 6
forms, universal 27-8
freedom
   abused and lost in Fall 120, 137, 161
   from the body 9
   evil as violation of 193
   Gnostic notion of 9
   from the Law 8
   and man's being in the image of
      God 120, 137, 151
   from material attachments 23
   and Origen 33
   of virginity 150
Fritigern 4

Galates, Prince 181
Gamaliel 8
Gangra, Council of 131
George of Cappadocia 86
George of Laodicea 58
Gnosticism 9-10, 41
   and Irenaeus 10
   and Justin 9-10
   ousia 48
God the Trinity *see* Trinity, doctrine
   of persons and relations within the
   Godhead
Gordian III 30
Gorgonia of Nazianzus 14, 15, 24
Goths 4-5, 76, 173, 196
Greek philosophy 38
   Platonic *see* Platonism
Gregory of Cappadocia 51, 53
Gregory of Nazianzus 12, 73-83
   at Anastasia chapel,
      Constantinople 77, 78, 80, 82, 97,
      101, 185-6, 187, 193, 194, 204
   and Antioch's divisions 173
   and the Arian controversy 181
   asceticism and renunciation 74, 75,
      134-8, 145, 168

   as assistant-bishop of
      Nazianzus 181-2, 184
   Athanasius oration 50-51
   in Athens 20-22, 24
   Basil oration 21, 74, 125, 140, 181
   on the *Basiliad* 129-30, 134-5
   as Bishop and Metropolitan of
      Constantinople 5, 23, 74, 76-9,
      182, 185-7
   as Bishop of Sasima 13, 73-4, 169,
      180, 181, 182-3
   and Caesarius's will and estate 179
   care of the poor 199
   Christology 201-2
   contemplation 23, 135, 185
   correspondence with Basil 61
   education 15-16, 19-20, 22, 24-5
   episcopal ministry 180-87
   family background 14-15, 197
   Five Theological Orations 76, 80,
      97-8, 186, 193, 194
   and Gregory Thaumaturgus 13
   and the Holy Spirit 97-101, 183,
      184, 187, 193
   Letters to Cledonius 75, 201-2
   On Love of the Poor 75, 136-8
   and Maximus 77
   Orations, Forty-Five 22, 23-4, 68,
      77, 79, 80, 81-2, 97, 100, 135, 183,
      184-5, 186-7, 193
   Philocalia (with Basil) 35, 62
   on Pontus and Basil the Elder 14
   relations with Basil 13, 35, 61, 62,
      73-4, 134-5, 171, 180-81, 182-4
   and Roman officials 168
   in Seleukia 75
   and solitude 135
   and the threatened marriage under
      Julian between Hellenism and
      Christianity 198
   and the Trinity 68, 72-3, 75, 99, 183,
      185, 186, 187, 193
   Ullman on 82
   and Valens 181
   and virtue 23

Gregory of Nyssa 12, 68-9, 145
　Ad Ablabium 69-71
　Against the Followers of
　　Macedonius 101-3
　apocatastasis 192-3
　appointment to Nyssa 13
　as Bishop of Sebaste 69, 170
　Catechetical Orations 70
　Christology 202
　on Constantinople 77
　contemplation 71, 150, 156, 158,
　　160, 161, 162, 164, 188, 189, 194,
　　197, 198, 199-200
　Contra Eunomius 63, 68, 70, 72-3
　and darkness 155-7, 164-5
　On the Dead 151
　and ecstasy 157-9, 200
　education 14, 15-16, 19, 25, 68
　episcopal ministry 187-9
　and evil 108, 123, 151-2, 192-3
　exiled by Valens 169, 172, 188, 196
　family background 13-14, 15
　and Gregory Thaumaturgus 13,
　　140, 189
　and the Holy Spirit 96, 97, 101-3
　and human life 108, 119-23
　and the incarnation 152, 162, 165,
　　202
　Life of Macrina 13, 140
　Life of Moses 152-3, 155-6, 160-63,
　　165, 200
　and the Macedonians 70
　On the Making of Man 119-21
　and marriage 149-50
　and the neo-Arians 69-73
　On Not Three Gods 159
　and Platonism 68, 107, 121-3,
　　159-65, 192-3, 198
　and the progress of the soul 148-59
　reconciliation attempt between Basil
　　and Gregory of Nazianzus 183
　relations with his brother, Basil 68-9
　and resurrection 119, 122-3, 152,
　　165
　and sex 119-20, 123, 161
　and solitude 147
　'Song of Songs' commentary 153-5,
　　156-7, 163-5, 195, 200
　On the Soul and Resurrection 13,
　　108, 121-3, 197, 198
　spiritual roots and
　　development 140-41, 189, 197
　spirituality teaching as bridge
　　between Athanasius and
　　Augustine 193
　and Theodosius 76-7, 170
　and the Trinity 69-73, 96, 159
　and union with God 156-7, 164-5,
　　204
　On Virginity 143, 148-52
　and virtue 21, 120, 150, 151, 152,
　　161-2
Gregory Thaumaturgus 13, 139, 140,
　189, 197
　Address to Origen 35
Gregory the Elder 14-15, 73, 181-2,
　183, 184, 185
Gregory (uncle of Basil and Gregory) 69
Greuthungi 4

Hagia Sophia 139, 167
Harnack, Adolf von 83
Hausherr, Irénée 158
Hawking, Stephen 110
Hellenism
　education see education
　imperial ban of Christians teaching
　　in philosophic schools 198
　marriage of Gospel and the
　　Greeks 197-8
　Platonism and Hellenic ideas 19-35
　see also Platonism
　threatened marriage under Julian
　　between Christianity and 198
　see also Greek philosophy
Heraclitus 26
heresy 8-12
　Arian see Arian controversy
　Gnostic see Gnosticism
　Nestorian controversy 90, 193,
　　200-202
　Paul's warnings of 5

and the struggle for orthodoxy *see*
  orthodoxy, struggle for
heterousian party 59–60
  see also Aetius; Eunomius
Hilary of Poitiers 12, 54
Hillel 8
Himerius 21
Hippolytus 166
Holy Spirit 85–103
  and Athanasius 86–8
  and Basil of Caesarea 62, 67, 88–97, 170
  and Eunomius 60, 64
  and Eustathius of Sebaste 91–2
  and Gregory of Nazianzus 97–101, 183, 184, 187, 193
  and Gregory of Nyssa 96, 97, 101–3
  and Jesus 95
  and Marcellus of Ancyra 49, 90, 91
  and the Montanists 11
  and Origen 32–3, 41–2
Holy Trinity *see* Trinity, doctrine of persons and relations within the Godhead
homoian party and creed 57–9, 60, 61, 76, 172, 179, 181, 192, 195–6
homoiousios 56, 64, 67, 76, 84, 171, 192
homoousios 46, 48, 49, 52, 55–7, 65, 67, 84, 88, 90, 172, 184, 187, 191–2
Hosios of Cordoba 195
human life and the doctrine of man 107–23
  and Basil of Caesarea 108, 109–19
  creation of man in God's image 33, 116–17, 119, 120, 137, 151, 197
  discipleship *see* discipleship
  the Fall *see* Fall of man
  freedom *see* freedom
  and Gregory of Nyssa 108, 119–23
  knowledge *see* knowledge
  marriage *see* marriage
  sex *see* sex
  and social justice *see* social justice
  soul *see* soul
  virtue *see* virtue
humanism 16, 20

Huns 4
hypostasis
  and the Arian controversy 42, 44, 47, 48, 191
  and Athanasius 52
  and Basil of Caesarea 67, 96
  and Latin *persona* 11, 85
  and the Nicene Creed 47, 48, 172, 185, 191
  and Origen 11, 32, 41–2, 48, 85
  Plotinus and the order of being (*hypostases*) 31, 44
Hyppolytus 11
Hypsistarii 14

Iamblichus 43
idiomata 66
Ignatius of Antioch 6, 166
image of God 33, 116–17, 119, 120, 137, 151, 197
immortality of the soul 27, 28
incarnation
  and Apollinarius 90
  and Athanasius 51, 202
  and Gregory of Nyssa 152, 162, 165, 202
  and Origen 33–4
Irenaeus of Lyons 99
  and Gnosticism 10
  Against Heresies 10
Islam 7
Istanbul *see* Constantinople
Isychras 51

Jerome 35, 55, 142, 169
Jerusalem
  Church in 6
  Council of (AD 49) 8
  destruction of 126
Jesus Christ
  Christology *see* Christology
  and the Holy Spirit 95
  incarnation *see* incarnation
  Jewish rejection of 126
  and Mary Magdalene 202
  and the resurrection *see* resurrection

Jesus Christ (*cont.*)
  on simplicity 127
  teachings of 146
  Temptations of 142
  victory through death 151, 165
John of the Cross 157
John the Baptist 142, 146
John the Divine 157–8
John the Evangelist 9, 25, 56, 98
Judaism 8
  Diaspora in Alexandria 38
  Philo and the Jewish scriptures 38
  rejection of Jesus 126
Julian, Emperor 4, 21, 61, 88, 195–6, 198
Julian of Norwich: *Revelation of Divine Love* 157
Julian, tax official 168, 185
Julius, Pope 51
Justin Martyr 9–10, 20, 30, 38
  and the *logos* 9–10, 11–12
Justinian 167

Karbala 14
knowledge
  and darkness 155–6, 189
  divine 155
  gnosis 9 *see also* Gnosticism
  and Gregory of Nyssa 159, 160, 163, 165, 188
  man's knowledge of God 148, 188, 189, 200
  and Origen 33–4
  Plato's theory of knowledge and perception 26, 27–8
  replaced by love 158

Lampascus, council at 76
Leonides of Alexandria 31
Libanius 21, 61
Liberius, Pope 55
Licinius 2, 45
logos 25, 30, 64
  and Apollinarius 75, 90, 201
  and the Arian controversy 30
  and Justin 9–10, 11–12
  logos-anthropos school 200–201
  logos-sarx school 201
  and Origen 32, 33, 85
love
  agape 28, 164
  and Augustine 195
  eros 28, 160, 164, 195 *see also* desire
  replacing knowledge 158
  and union with God 156–7, 164–5, 204 *see also* desire: for God
  wound of 164
Lucian of Antioch 42, 59
Lupicinus 4

Macarius 50, 51
Macedonians (Spirit-fighters) 70, 88, 89, 93, 102
Macedonius of Constantinople 60, 93, 101
Macrina the Elder 13, 92, 139, 140, 144, 197
Macrina the Younger 13, 140–41, 145, 188, 197
  Gregory of Nyssa's *Life of Macrina* 13, 140
  and Gregory of Nyssa's *On the Soul and Resurrection* 121–3, 197
Magnentius 2, 8, 53
Majorinus 7
man, doctrine of *see* human life and the doctrine of man
Manichees 48
Marcellanism 192
Marcellus of Ancyra 40, 46, 49, 52, 53, 57, 65, 84, 88, 89–90, 91
  and Basil of Caesarea 84, 88, 91
Marcion 10
Marcionites 9
Mark, Apostle 37
marriage 3, 9, 24, 26, 131
  and Basil of Caesarea 114, 176–7
  and Gregory of Nyssa 149–50
  modern understandings of 191
Maximus, Magnus, Emperor 8
Maximus (former Governor of Cappadocia) 179

Maximus (philosopher and episcopal candidate at Constantinople) 23, 77, 79, 171, 176–7, 186
Meletios of Antioch 75, 77, 79, 92
　successor squabble 82
Melitian controversy 43
Melitius of Lycopolis 39
Mensurius of Carthage 7
Meredith, Anthony 195, 198
Milan 3, 168
　Council of (AD 355) 54, 55
　Edict of (AD 313) 11
Milvian Bridge, Battle of 2
modalism 48, 90, 172
　see also Sabellianism
Modestus 179, 181
Monarchian controversy 9
monasticism
　Basil's *Basiliad* in Caesarea ix, 125, 128–30, 134–5, 170, 199
　Basil's letter to a monk accused of adultery 177–8
　Basil's Rules 132–3
　development of the monastic ideal 130–31
　Egyptian 129
　monastic vows 142
　and origins of ascetic life in Cappadocia 142–5
　and Platonic dualism 28
　relations between monks and bishops 168–9
　and social justice 125, 129–30 see also *Basiliad/Basileiados*
monophysites 201
Montanists 9, 11
Moses 38, 110, 118, 146, 188–9, 200
　Gregory of Nyssa's *Life of Moses* 152–3, 155–6, 160–63, 165, 200
murder 113, 175
Mursa, Battle of 2

Naucratias 13, 144–5
Nazianzus 14, 20, 22, 80, 138, 168, 187

　Gregory as assistant-bishop of 181–2, 184
　taxation 185
Nectarius 83, 168, 176
neo-Platonism 23, 25, 26, 30–31, 38, 39, 192–3
　and Aetius 59
　and the Arian controversy 40–42, 44, 64
　and Eunomius 64, 65
Nero 6
Nestorian controversy 90, 193, 200–202
　logos-anthropos school 200–201
　logos-sarx school 201
Nicaea, Council of (AD 325) 11, 45–9, 56
　aftermath 49–54
　and the Arian controversy 43–50
　and Athanasius 46
　and Constantine 45, 46, 49, 195
　creed see Nicene Creed and orthodoxy
　and the Eusebians 46, 49
Nicene Creed and orthodoxy 41, 46–9, 53–4, 83, 171–2, 174, 190–92, 195, 203
　and the *anomian/heterousian* party 59–60 *see also* Aetius; Eunomius
　Athanasius as central force of Nicene orthodoxy 20, 52
　and Basil of Caesarea 63–8, 83–4, 124, 171–2, 173–4
　emergence from 350s of opposition groupings 56–8
　and First Council of Sirmium (AD 351) 55
　Gregory the Elder's defence of 14
　and the *homoian* party and creed 57–9, 60, 61, 172, 179, 181, 192, 195–6
　homoousios 46, 48, 49, 52, 55–7, 65, 67, 84, 88, 90, 172, 184, 187, 191–2
　hypostasis 47, 48, 172, 185, 191
　imperial opposition 178–9, 195–6

Nicene Creed and orthodoxy (*cont.*)
   ousia 47–8, 49, 55, 56, 191
   and theological labels of the nineteenth century 83
   see also orthodoxy, struggle for
Nicomedia 45
Nonna of Nazianzus 14–15, 185, 197
nous 30, 31
Nyssa 13, 181

Octavian (Augustus) 37
oikonomia 34, 38
Origen 31–5, 38, 65, 140
   and the Arian controversy 40, 44
   in Caesarea, Palestine 34
   Contra Celsum 35, 41
   and creation 40
   and evil 31, 192–3
   and the Fall 33
   and God's plan (*oikonomia*) 33
   Hexalpa 34
   and the Holy Spirit 32–3, 41–2
   hypostasis 11, 32, 41–2, 48, 85
   influence on Cappadocians 140
   'John' commentary 41–2
   and knowledge 33–4
   and the *logos* 32, 33, 85
   oikonomia 34, 38
   ousia 41
   Peri Archon 32, 35
   and Platonism 31–5, 38, 39, 40–2, 192–3, 198
   On Prayer 35
   'Song of Songs' commentary 34, 35
   theological influence of 34–5
   and the Trinity 32–3, 40–42
original sin *see* Fall of man
orthodoxy, struggle for viii–ix, 5, 8–12, 59–60, 190–202
   and Arianism *see* Arian controversy
   Basil of Caesarea vs Eunomius 63–8
   Christology *see* Christology
   and Church Councils *see* Church Councils
   as an episcopal duty 170, 171–2
   and Gnosticism *see* Gnosticism

   and the Holy Spirit *see* Holy Spirit
   hypostasis language see *hypostasis*
   and imperial power 178–9, 195–6
   Nicene orthodoxy *see* Nicaea, Council of (AD 325); Nicene Creed and orthodoxy
   ousia language see *ousia*
   and Platonism *see* Platonism
   summary of Cappadocians' contribution to 190–202
   and the Trinity *see* Trinity, doctrine of persons and relations within the Godhead
   see also Church Councils; heresy
Ossius of Cordoba 45, 46
ousia
   and the Arian controversy 42, 44, 47–8, 49, 55, 56, 65, 191
   and Basil of Caesarea 65, 66
   contrasted with *hypostasis* 41
   Gnostic use 48
   heterousian party 59–60 *see also* Aetius; Eunomius
   and Latin *substantia* 11, 85, 100
   and the Nicene Creed 47–8, 49, 55, 191
   and Origen 41
   see also *homoiousios*; *homoousios*

Pachomius 142
pacifism 6
Parmenides 26
parrhesia 158, 183, 184, 186, 200
pastoral care
   Basil of Caesarea 174–80
   episcopal ministry 166–89
   and social justice *see* social justice
Patripassianism 11
Paul, Apostle 5, 13, 25, 89, 96–7, 139
   and change 153
   execution 6
   in Rome 6
   story of Thecla and 143
Paul of Samosata 48
Paul of Thebes 142
penance 174–5

Pentapolis 42
persecution 6–7, 35, 142, 167
Persia 2, 4, 12, 30, 36, 53
persona see *hypostasis*
Peryer, Tom vii
Peter, Apostle 6, 13
Peter of Alexandria 39, 43, 79, 173, 186
Peter of Sebaste 13, 145
Pharisees 8
Philo 38, 39, 44, 157
philosophic life see asceticism; solitude
Philostorgius 42, 59
Philostratus, Flavius 24
Plato 16, 25–31
　Academy of Philosophy 26
　cave parable 29
　cosmogony 29, 108–9
　dualism 27–8
　Gregory of Nyssa's interest in 68
　and the immortality of the soul 27, 28
　influences 26
　Origen and the thought of 31–5, 38, 39, 40–42, 192–3, 198
　Parmenides 27
　and Philo 38
　Republic 27
　Symposium 27
　Theaetetus 161
　theory of knowledge and perception 26, 27–8
　theory of universal forms 27–8
　Timaeus 27, 29, 108, 109, 162–3
　and Utopia 26–7
Platonism
　and change 153
　concept of God 9–10
　creation 29
　and Gregory of Nyssa 68, 107, 121–3, 159–65, 192–3, 198
　and Hellenic ideas 19–35
　and Justin 9–10
　neo-Platonism see neo-Platonism
　and Origen 31–5, 38, 39, 40–2, 192–3, 198

Platonic Christian tradition 22, 23–4, 25–35, 39, 64, 198–9
Platonic dualism 27–8
Plotinus 21, 30–31, 44, 161, 163, 192, 193
　Enneads 30
Polycarp of Smyrna 6
Pompey 37
Pontus 14, 73, 146
　Annisa see Annisa, Pontus
Porphyry 30, 31
poverty/the poor
　charitable work 132, 179, 199, 204
　Gregory of Nazianzus's *On Love of the Poor* 75, 136–8
　and social justice see social justice
prayer viii, 147
　contemplative see contemplation and the contemplative life
Prohaeresius 21
Ptolemais 42
Ptolemies 36
Ptolemy XIII 37
Pythagoras 26
Pythagorians 29

Quadi 4
Qumran community 8

relics 173–4
renunciation viii, ix, 132–3, 134–5, 136–8
restoration of all things 192–3
resurrection
　and Gregory of Nazianzus 202
　and Gregory of Nyssa 119, 122–3, 152, 165
Rimini, Council of see Ariminum, Council of (AD 359, Western Council)
Roman Empire
　administration 3
　and Alexandria 36–7 see also Alexandria
　army 3, 4–5
　and the Church 6–7, 167–8, 178–9

INDEX

Roman Empire (*cont.*)
  civil war 3, 8
  decline and fall 2, 3–4
  education *see* education
  and the episcopacy 167–8, 178–9, 196
  fourth-century world of 1–5
  and the Goths 4–5, 76, 173, 196
  imperial power and Nicene orthodoxy 178–9, 195–6
  Senatorial families 3
Rome 3, 12
  Athanasius in 51–2, 56
  Origen in 34
  Paul in 6
  Plotinus in 30
  sack of (AD 410) 4
Rousseau, Philip 89, 182
Rufinus 34

Sabellianism 11, 48, 90, 92, 172
Sabellius 11
Sadducees 8
Sallust 3
Sanhedrin 6
Sarmatians 4
Sasima 13, 73–4, 169, 180, 181, 182, 183
Sebastianus 86
Secundus of Ptolemais 195
Seleukia (modern Silifke) 75, 77, 183, 185
Seleukia, Council of (AD 359, Eastern Council) 55, 58
  Creed from 60, 61
self-control 24
Septuagint 36
Serapion of Thmuis 86
  Athanasius's letters to 86, 88
Serdica, Council of (AD 346) 53
service
  charitable work 132, 179, 199, 204
    see also social justice
  episcopal 166–89
  pastoral *see* pastoral care
  and renunciation ix *see also* renunciation

social justice *see* social justice
Severus, Septimus 31
sex
  ascetic sacrifice of 142
  and Basil of Caesarea 175
  and Gregory of Nyssa 119–20, 123, 161
  and marriage 9
  misdemeanours 175
  and Origen 32
  sexual desire 9, 114, 146 see also *eros*
  virginity *see* virginity
Shakespeare, William 37
Simonetti, Manlio 40
Sirmium
  Arian Creed 55
  Dated Creed 58
  First Council of (AD 351) 53–4
  Fourth Council of (AD 358) 60
  second Creed 56
sober inebriation 157–9, 200
social justice
  Basil of Caesarea on 125–8
  and charitable work 132, 179, 199, 204
  Gregory of Nazianzus on 134–5
  Gregory of Nyssa on 134
  and monasticism 125, 129–30 see also *Basiliad/Basileiados*
Socrates 13, 26, 27, 131
solitude viii, 29, 61, 135, 136, 146, 147–8, 168
  and Basil of Caesarea 146–8
  and contemplation *see* contemplation
  and the contemplative life
  and Gregory of Nyssa 147
  and the search for virtue 146–8
Sophronios (Imperial official in Caesarea) 136, 179
Sophronius (priest) 92
soul
  apathia 158
  ascent of the soul viii, 31, 153–65, 200
  and darkness 155–7, 164–5, 189
  and ecstasy 157–9, 200

and *epectasis* 152–5, 199, 200
Gregory of Nyssa and the progress of the 148–59
Gregory of Nyssa's *On the Soul and Resurrection* 13, 108, 121–3, 197
immortality of the soul 27, 28
and Plotinus 30, 31
purging of the soul 34, 123, 192
and the resurrection *see* resurrection
world as vale of soul-making 111
Sozomen 129, 131
Spirit
Holy *see* Holy Spirit
as *nous* (Plotinus) 30, 31
Spirit-fighters (Macedonians) 70, 88, 89, 93, 102
spirituality
apophatic *see* apophatic theology/ spirituality
ascetic *see* asceticism; monasticism
contemplative *see* contemplation and the contemplative life
and darkness 155–7, 164–5, 189
and ecstasy 157–9, 200
and *epectasis* 152–5, 199, 200
Gregory of Nyssa and spiritual progress 148–59
and human life *see* human life and the doctrine of man
and the soul *see* soul
spiritual roots and development of the Cappadocians 140–41, 189, 197
theosis 95, 99, 137, 197
Stephen, Bishop of Rome 7
Stoicism 23, 51, 66
Studer, Basil 40
subordinationism 40, 42, 56, 58, 59
substantia see *ousia*
Symeon the Stylite 143
Syrianus 54

Tatiana 35
taxation 179, 185
Telesphorus of Rome 6
Terence 3

Tertullian 6, 11, 85, 198
Tervingi 4
Thecla, sister of Basil and Gregory 143
Thecla and St Paul, story of 143
Theoctistus 34
Theodora 132
Theodosia 78
Theodosius, Emperor 2–4, 5, 59, 76, 78, 83, 97, 170, 173, 187, 196
Theodosius, notary 138
Theodotus of Nicopolis 92
Theonas of Marmarcia 195
Theosebeia 68
theosis 95, 99, 137, 197
Theotokos 11, 201
Thomas Aquinas 28, 199
Thrace 5, 58, 174
Tiberius, Emperor 12
Trajan 179
Trier 3, 51
Trinity, doctrine of persons and relations within the Godhead viii–ix, 56–84, 190, 191, 203
and the *anomian/heterousian* party 59–60 *see also* Aetius; Eunomius
Arian controversy *see* Arian controversy
and Athanasius 52–3, 56, 57, 86–8, 96, 190
and Basil of Caesarea 63–8, 93–4, 171–2, 191–2
and Christology *see* Christology
and the Constantinople Creed 41, 59, 82, 83
emergence from 350s of opposition groupings to Nicene Creed 56–8
energia 66
and Eunomius *see* Eunomius
Father and Son controversy *see* Arian controversy; Nicaea, Council of (AD 325); Nicene Creed and orthodoxy
and Gregory of Nazianzus 68, 72–3, 75, 99, 183, 185, 186, 187, 193
and Gregory of Nyssa 69–73, 96, 159

Trinity (*cont.*)
  Holy Spirit *see* Holy Spirit
  and the *homoian* party and
    creed 57–9, 60, 61, 76, 172, 179,
    181, 192, 195–6
  homoiousios language 56, 64, 67, 76,
    84, 171, 192
  homoousios language 46, 48, 49, 52,
    55–7, 65, 67, 84, 88, 90, 172, 184,
    187, 191–2
  hypostasis language *see hypostasis*
  idiomata 66
  and the incarnation *see* incarnation
  logos see logos
  and Marcellus of Ancyra 40, 49, 57,
    65, 84, 89–90, 91
  modalism 48, 90, 172 *see also*
    Sabellianism
  and Nicaea 43–50 *see also* Nicene
    Creed and orthodoxy
  and Origen 32–3, 40–42
  ousia language *see ousia*
  Patripassianism 11
  Sabellianism 11, 48, 90, 92, 172
  and Sirmium *see* Sirmium
  subordinationism 40, 42, 56, 58, 59
  and *Theotokos* 11, 201
  and the unknowable *see* apophatic
    theology/spirituality
Tropici 86
Tyana 12
Tyre, Council of (AD 335) 51

Ullman, Carl 82, 185
universal forms, theory of 27–8
Ursacius of Singidunum 58
Utopia 26–7

Valens, Emperor 4, 5, 12–13, 68, 74, 76,
  130, 172, 173, 174, 181, 196
  exiling of Gregory of Nyssa 169, 172,
    188, 196
Valens of Mursa 58
Valentinian, Emperor 76
Valerian, Emperor 7
Vandals 4

Virgil 3
virginity viii, 143
  Basil's counsel to a fallen virgin 178
  Gregory of Nyssa's *On Virginity* 143,
    148–52
virtue 14, 15
  and Basil of Caesarea 21, 22, 127,
    130, 132, 134, 147
  evil's opposition to 113
  and Gregory of Nazianzus 23
  and Gregory of Nyssa 21, 120, 150,
    151, 152, 161–2
  the philosophic life and the search
    for 146–8
  and Plato 27, 29

Western Council *see* Ariminum, Council
  of (AD 359, Western Council)
Williams, Rowan 43

Lightning Source UK Ltd.
Milton Keynes UK
UKHW021626200721
387470UK00010B/1985